THE SEA ~~AHEAD~~

Shally Hunt's first book, *The Sea on Our Left*, was a bestselling memoir about her 4,300-mile walk around the coast of mainland Britain. She went on to write *The Medway: Sketches Along the River*. The author lives in Kent with her husband Richard.

The Sea on Our Left:

'Although many dream of it, few achieve it…
An intrepid adventure'
Evening Standard

'Living like a tortoise, carrying the whole world on your back, can reduce to a tortoise's pace, as Shally and Richard found…They have worn through three pairs of boots each, fought blisters and stomach cramps, fended off Highland midges, heaved their rucksacks up mountains – and come close to destroying their marriage'
Sunday Express

'This book leaves you wondering why you haven't got the nerve to do it' *Adventure Travel*

'A remarkable trip of endless diversity and surprises… A unique travelogue'
Earth Matters

Cape Wrath — Nice

cape Wrath - lighthouse

THE SEA AHEAD

Shally Hunt

summersdale

THE SEA AHEAD

Copyright © Shally Hunt 2005

Maps by John Hill Dip. Arch. A.R.I.B.A.

Drawings by Joanna Vincent

The right of Shally Hunt to be identified as the author of this work has been asserted in accordance with sections 77 and 78 of the Copyright, Designs and Patents Act 1988.

Condition of Sale
This book is sold subject to the condition that it shall not, by way of trade or otherwise, be lent, resold, hired out or otherwise circulated in any form or binding or cover other than that in which it is published and without a similar condition including this condition being imposed on the subsequent purchaser.

Summersdale Publishers Ltd
46 West Street
Chichester
West Sussex
PO19 1RP
UK

www.summersdale.com

'Reconciliation' copyright Siegfried Sassoon by kind permission of George Sassoon

Disclaimer
Every effort has been made to obtain the necessary permissions with reference to copyright material, both illustrative and quoted; should there be any omissions in this respect we apologize and shall be pleased to make the appropriate acknowledgements in any future edition.

Printed and bound in Great Britain

ISBN 1 84024 434 8

CONTENTS

Acknowledgements

Richard and I would like to thank all the friends who gave us hospitality on the walk, took us to and from start and finish points, and gave us sponsorship and encouragement.

The author would like to thank Merran Wrigley of Sony Ericsson for the loan of their P800 mobile phone and associated calls; Bob Warren for his help with the draft of this book (thanks to him I now know how to spell dessert and lightning); John Hill A.R.I.B.A. for all his beautiful maps and Jo Vincent, our daughter, for her line drawings (no easy task with two small children). Alastair and Stewart from Summersdale Publishers were kind enough to see us off in Dover. Their parting gift was an outsize bar of chocolate that launched us across the North Downs.

Most of all Shally would like to thank her husband Richard, not only for his excellent route planning and (nearly) unerring sense of direction, but also for his considerable help with the manuscript of *The Sea Ahead*. Without him there would have been no walk and no book.

To the Countryside Agency who promote and fund the National Trails in the UK and the French Ramblers' Association (FFRP) who oversee the waymarking and maintenance of their long distance paths (Grandes Randonnées).

Prologue

Intermittent showers turned to heavy rain. We fought our way past umbrellas, cars, traffic lights, policemen, McDonald's, Laura Ashley, C&A. We tripped over tiny bedraggled dogs, bumped into lamp posts and elbowed a stream of unsuspecting pedestrians.

Just keep going. It's down there somewhere.

Cars splashed waves of dirty water over our boots as we stepped timorously onto pedestrian crossings. French cars don't stop. I panicked, racing across the broad white lines.

Palm trees. Must be nearly there. Where is it? Just keep him in sight.

Richard had stopped outside a Credit Lyonnais and was fumbling for wallet and cards. I screeched to a halt beside him and my fifteen-kilo rucksack dislodged a woman's handbag from her shoulder. She took revenge with her umbrella. Meanwhile, the hole in the wall gobbled up Richard's plastic and promptly spat it out. No euros for *les anglais*. We continued our southward dash through wet streets until Richard stopped again and waited for me to catch up.

'Look,' he said calmly, pointing over the busy road to a palm-studded pavement. 'That is the Promenade des Anglais and there is the Mediterranean.' I peered through tearful glasses. And there it was: a grey sea co-ordinating perfectly with clouds and stony beach.

I stared in disbelief and stammered, 'I'd forgotten it wasn't sand.'

A pair of blue slatted chairs was squatting a few metres from the murky sea. Uncertain what to do next, we perched on the wet seats and watched timid waves washing the grey pebble beach.

For weeks now I had conjured up this special moment of arrival. The sparkling blue sea would be foaming gently onto golden sand. I would throw off my clothes, or most of them anyway, and run into the water, screaming with elation. Like the youthful French, I would make a fist in the air and shout, 'YES!' Champagne bubbles up my nose and hugs from children and grandchildren…

Little pools of water on the chair seats were making their presence felt. We stood up and dipped our boots in the sea. A ring of red mud swirled round them. We looked at our watches. Nearly four o'clock. Time to be at the Negresco Hotel to meet our family. Back on the promenade the white awnings, erected to give protection from the sun to the great and the good, gave us temporary respite from the rain. We crossed the road, narrowly missing being hit by a car, and found ourselves looking up at a flight of curved white steps leading to polished glass swing doors. Chauffeur-driven cars were two deep in the street while an army of doormen, dressed in knee breeches, brass-buttoned tail coats and buckled shoes, deftly lifted Gucci and Samsonite from gaping car boots. Women in little black suits with silk scarves, men in crisp shirts and shiny shoes, were ushered up the steps under ample umbrellas. Through the glass doors lay a world of deep pile carpets, chandeliers, and three-piece suites so deep it is an art form to get out of them. I caught a whiff of expensive perfume.

Only this morning I had fantasized about speaking to a friendly doorman, telling him what we had done, asking him if we might change in a hotel cloakroom and have tea there with our family. Now I noticed one of the brass buttons eyeing us as a bouncer might eye a troublemaker about to enter his night club.

'I don't think we can do this,' I heard myself mutter to Richard. 'I'll just ask if we can check if the family have arrived.' Acutely aware of my dishevelled appearance and muddy boots, I walked hesitantly up the white marble steps to the nearest doorman and put my question to him in the best French I could muster. There was a long pause while he eyed first me, and then Richard.

'Only one of you,' he said at length. 'And without the *sac à dos*.'

I was thankful to see Richard slip off his rucksack and march boldly through the glass doors to a chic lady at the reception desk. He was back in seconds.

'No,' he said to my enquiring face. 'They haven't checked in.'

We bolted gratefully down the steps and huddled under an awning round the side. Moments later a doorman appeared with a mop and began wiping water and smudges of red mud from the immaculate steps.

Introduction

When they retire, most people want to make use of their newly acquired freedom by doing something different, something they had always wanted but been unable to do because of the constraints on their time. Travelling, walking, enjoying a hobby, learning new skills, or seeing more of their grandchildren. Richard and I are no exception. We both enjoy walking so much that in 1995 we took a year out of our lives to walk 4,300 miles (6,880 kilometres) round the coast of mainland Britain. We did this simply because we wanted to and worried that, had we waited for retirement in another seven years, failing health or creaky joints might have prevented us from accomplishing such a demanding venture.

Ten months and three pairs of boots later, we arrived back on schedule at our start point in Eastbourne. We were a little older, a little wiser and a lot leaner than when we left. We had discovered the full drama of our varied coastline and had been shown great kindness and hospitality. As a couple we had been dependent on each other twenty-four hours a day for ten months, and this had imposed some strains on our relationship. We had been averaging sixteen miles a day, carrying everything with us including a tent for the summer months. In spite of this, there wasn't one day when we didn't wake up eager to continue the walk. We both realized it was a privilege to be away from the bustle of our daily lives, enjoying fresh air, space and an ever-changing landscape. The great irony was that having succeeded we found the hardest problem was stopping. Perhaps that was why, seven years later, we were planning to walk out of retirement and indulge in another pedestrian exercise.

In 1999 Richard saw an article in the paper mapping out an assortment of European footpaths, all numbered and prefixed with the letter E like the enhancers in unhealthy foods. This sparked the idea of taking the E2, a long distance European footpath through the UK from Stranraer in south-west Scotland to Dover in Kent, which once across the Channel becomes the GR5 all the way to Nice. Only time would tell how healthy or unhealthy it would prove to be. When Richard was planning the route, he decided not to go to Stranraer, but to walk from the Scottish Borders to Edinburgh and Glasgow and on up to Cape Wrath at the north-western tip of Scotland. This, he felt, would be more of a challenge, and take us to our favourite Scottish haunts. He decided to start from Dover and walk south to north, so we would have the advantage of summer in the hostile environment of the Cape Wrath Trail. The plan was to reach Cape Wrath by 8 June and return home by train from Durness on the ninth, then take a three-day break before setting off on the European section. This way we hoped to reach Nice before snow settled on the passes in the High Alps. We had just seven months to complete the 2,300 miles (3,680 kilometres).

Time is a strange phenomenon. As I walked to work the final weeks before my retirement at the end of October 2002, I happily listed everything I wanted to achieve in the four and a half months before the start of our walk on 15 March 2003. In my head unstructured time stretched to the horizon like a mirage. My action list grew daily: I would finish my novel, research our E2 route, listen to a CD of birdsongs, brush up my French, spring clean the house and organize a desk groaning with redundant paperwork. Then there was the small matter of letting the house, arranging for a full-time carer for great-granny, training ourselves for the walk, and looking after my granddaughter two days a week. When I wasn't doing any of those things I'd use my newly acquired Senior Rail Card to pop up to London to enjoy museums and galleries or visit friends.

We had also decided to make it a sponsored walk and had again chosen to raise money for our local hospice. Fund-raising is a time-consuming occupation, and we could only invite our long-suffering friends, colleagues and patients to sponsor us and hope that interest in our walk would generate further funds once we had started.

I have heard many people say that, once retired, they didn't know how they had had time to work. I wasn't convinced, until a few weeks into my own retirement I found all that wonderful unstructured time shrinking like a woolly jersey in a hot wash.

Just after New Year, my manager was on the phone asking me if I could spare a few hours to help out on the Physiotherapy Bank. She needed cover for an orthopaedic ward and I was asked to do a job-share with two other retired colleagues. I said I would think about it. Richard and I were just working out the cost of our seven-month wanderings and I weakly decided that a little extra cash might be useful. After all, I reasoned, it would only be for two days a week. Well yes, there was young Molly to look after a further two days a week when my daughter was at work, but that still left Fridays and yes, French conversation class took most of the morning, but I convinced myself I'd manage.

I had to prioritize. The luxury of writing was abandoned along with trips to London, researching our route and learning to recognize bird songs. Not having time to research our route was a bonus; if I had realized the daily vertical distance of this marathon I would certainly have funked it. Richard and I made vain attempts to rule off weekends so we could go for long walks, but they seemed to fill up with family commitments. I packed a large roll bag with all our camping things, plus spares of almost everything else we might need, and Richard gave them to a fellow Rotarian whose son lived near our route on the Pennine Way. He took them up to his son's house and the handover date of 13 April was arranged. My training for the walk consisted of marching up and down the hills of Tunbridge Wells, carrying shopping back from the supermarket and pushing a two-and-a-half-stone toddler in a buggy.

Retirement brings with it major financial, physical and psychological changes; perhaps deferring this seminal moment was part of the attraction of another long walk. For the past year we had watched the stock market tumble dragging pension funds with it. We shuffled sheets of paper, cancelled standing orders and braced ourselves to become pensioners. After thirty-seven years as a dentist in the same practice, Richard planned to work right up to his big 60 only a week before we set off; he had, however, spent many months planning our route, working out our itinerary, and booking accommodation where possible. Even so, they were hectic final weeks of birthday parties, retirement parties, getting our gear together and leaving our house ready for tenants.

Then there was the vexed question of my feet. Our last walk hadn't impressed them, so I told them there would be no problem as this was only half the distance. They sulked so I consoled them with a specially moulded insole, lavished moisturizing cream on them, and told them not to whinge.

Then there were only sixteen days to go. Bush and Blair were poised to attack Iraq in a couple of weeks' time with or without UN backing. Protests from 'the people of this country' went unheeded. It seemed like a good moment to escape.

PART ONE

United Kingdom

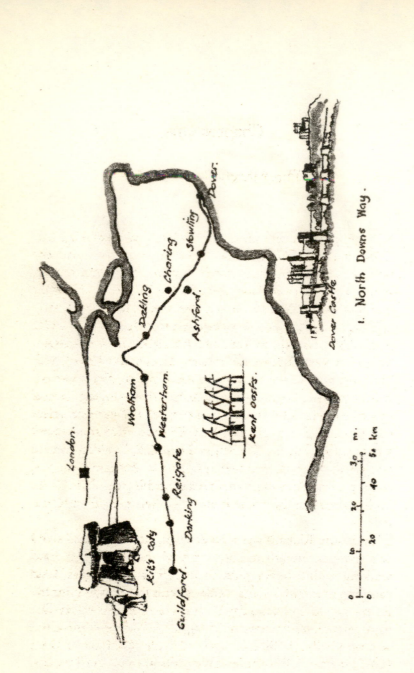

1. North Downs Way.

Dover Castle.

London.

Kit's Coty

Guildford.

Dorking.

Reigate.

Westerham.

Wrotham.

Detling.

Charing.

Stowting.

Ashford.

Dover.

Kent oasts.

m.
km.

0   10   20   30
0   20   40   50

Chapter One

The North Downs Way

Something about the fifteenth of March was worrying me. Long after we had decided on that date to start our walk the unreasonable reason came to me: of course, the ides of March. A niggling voice from the irrational side of my brain whispered that it might be an inauspicious day to start such a venture.

This was, after all, no ordinary walk. Richard's careful planning would take in some of the toughest trails in Britain, long-distance paths like the Pennine Way, and the Cape Wrath Trail. Every time we mentioned the Pennine Way someone would tell us a horror story. Richard's fives-playing friends described in detail how they spent a week pulling each other out of peat hags. Its very length of 265 miles (424 kilometres) was daunting. Names like Kinder Downfall, Cauldron Snout and Great Shunner Fell were enough to give me a pang of anxiety. David Paterson, in his book describing the Cape Wrath Trail, writes that this route is equal to almost any Himalayan trek.

I was sure Richard was man enough, but not certain that I was woman enough to cope with all the challenges: hard walking with a heavy pack in uncertain conditions, wild camping in remoter spots, walking with the man in your life for twenty-four hours a day for one hundred and eighty-five days when you have passed the big 60. As for our continental section on the 1,700 kilometre Grande Randonnée Cinq (GR5), neither of us could really think about it until we had completed the UK leg. We just knew it was a high-level path which got higher as we walked south from the Ardennes, through the Vosges and Jura mountains to the High Alps where we would be crossing some passes that were nearly three times the height of Snowdon.

I cleared my throat nervously, addressing the back of Richard's head. 'How about we leave Dover on March the sixteenth?' There was a long pause. This is usual. His rational brain was contemplating yet another map, and my explanation for moving the date forward didn't impress.

'Don't be ridiculous,' he said with scorn that would have sent Julius Caesar packing. 'All things being equal we leave on Saturday March the fifteenth and that's that.'

All things were equal and we found ourselves in Dover's Market Square on a bright spring morning with family, loyal friends, and a TV crew who had an obsession with our lower legs, filming them from all angles. Their enthusiasm for the back end of our boots was so great they were even prepared to lie on the cold pavement and film as we walked over the cameraman. Then the usual questions were asked: why do this? Will it impose a strain on your marriage? How much money do you hope to raise? How do you feel now?

At last we were able to say goodbye to friends and family and turn our backs on the little crowd and take our celebrity boots up an unending flight of steps to Western Heights. It was hard to realize that all the months of planning and anticipation were over and this was the real thing. Richard then told me he had picked up what he thought was hairspray that morning and applied it vigorously to his head. Later, when packing his rucksack, he noticed that it was boot polish. With his head waterproofed, he realized that hairspray belonged to the old life and would not be needed for the next six months.

From Western Heights, one of the garrison forts above Dover built to deter Napoleon and his army, we had a good view of the town with its ancient castle. The scale of the impressive fortifications and defensive ditches known as the Drop Redoubt or 'Devil's Drop of Mortar' showed that the English government at that time took the Napoleonic threat very seriously. Defence was a recurring theme on the walk, and we saw forts dating from the Iron Age to the Second World War, starting at Dover and finishing in the Southern Alps; nothing changes except today the technology is more sophisticated and the defence systems are less visible.

Man has used the network of ancient routes on the Downs as a trading link with Europe for many thousands of years. For the next few days we would be following footsteps that went back into pre-history: Neolithic man's, pack animals', peasants', Romans', pilgrims', traders' or just plain walkers' like our own. We would leave our twenty-first-century footprints on Roman roads, drovers' paths, mule tracks, and the occasional twentieth-century tarmac, either on ridge tops or sheltered by trees under the chalk escarpment. From time to time we would emerge from the peaceful 'old' world and pop up into the noisy present with its roaring motorways and vibrating railways.

Far below, toy boats on a blue background were moving in and out of Dover harbour.

'If we make it to Cape Wrath, we should be on one of those ferries the second week in June,' Richard commented with no stress on the if.

'Mmm,' I replied, hardly able to imagine that we would ever reach Cape Wrath. 'And that's the next time we meet the sea.'

The first four miles (six kilometres) to Folkstone gave us a sense of déjà vu; the sea was now on our left and we had walked the same coast path in October 1995 a few days before finishing our round Britain walk. From Shakespeare Cliff we could look down on brick ventilation shafts for the old Victorian railway and the glass and steel ones of the new Channel Tunnel. Freight lorries rattled along the M20 to and from the port, car ferries plied their way in and out of the harbour. If we screwed up our eyes we could just make out the coast of France. It would seem this part of Kent is the umbilical cord between Britain and Europe.

High above Folkestone we turned north-west although there were no waymarks or signs to tell us not to plod on to Land's End before changing course to find the elusive E2. However, later that day we did find a very smart signpost which read: *National Trail – Grande Randonnée – European Path North Downs Way*. A painted representation of the European flag, a gold circle of stars on a blue background, gave it credence. The next time we found a similar signpost was approaching Kirk Yetholm at the northern end of the Pennine Way.

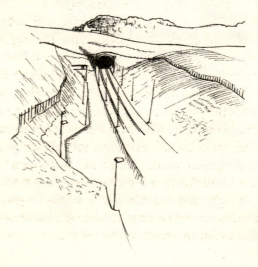

We ate our sandwiches on a small round hill with traffic from the M20 disappearing into it beneath our feet. After lunch we looked down on the marshalling yards and loading ramps of the Channel Tunnel terminal; hectares of steel spaghetti, lights, transformers and metal trucks with their cargo of vehicles snaking into the tunnel itself. The roar was constant, with a loud jolting sound as cars drove over the ramps into the carriages. The screeching rang in our ears long after we turned our backs to it. As we climbed away from the high-tech hubbub our spirits rose. We were low-tech pilgrims with our backs to Canterbury in search of adventure and we were on our way. The sun was low in the sky as we passed the radio mast at Etchinghill before descending to our rendezvous point at the Tiger Inn at Stowting ahead of schedule. By now the sun had disappeared and the temperature had plummeted. To make matters worse there was no room in the inn. The lights were on, showing a cosy bar and comfortable chairs, but the door was firmly locked. Our tired over-heated bodies quickly cooled, a sensation reminiscent of pulling on a wet swimsuit. Darkness fell. In spite of several other hopeful customers, the inn door remained locked.

Geoff and Pat, a dentist friend and his wife, who live near Canterbury, had offered to put us up for two nights. We had also arranged to meet Alan (an old friend and Richard's best man), at the Tiger Inn. When we had all assembled outside the pub, Geoff and Pat drove us back to their warm and comfortable house, where we thawed out in front of the Aga with the help of a little whisky. It was a chance to meet Alan's second wife Julia for the first time and his ten year-old son Max. We discussed seeing them again in Switzerland where Alan had a small flat near Lake Geneva. As it turned out the GR5 went right through his village of St-Cergue so a plan was hatched to spend two nights in their apartment and they would fly out for the weekend to meet us.

In our comfortable bedroom there were two cards, one with the Irish blessing: *May the road rise up to meet you, may the wind be always at your back...* The other card showed one solitary figure on a lonely road and the quote: *Life shrinks or expands in proportion to one's courage.* We knew the wind wouldn't always be on our backs and that courage would undoubtedly be needed.

Not, however, for the next two weeks, when we would be firmly in the comfort zone staying with family and friends. The walk was an opportunity to catch up with people whom, in the merry-go-round of our daily lives, we rarely saw any more. Geoff and Pat both sang in Canterbury Choral Society and we had attended several of their concerts and had supper with them afterwards. They were constantly busy with work, village and church activities, children and grandchildren, yet their home was always open house to anyone in need. Pat explained away their hospitality modestly. 'It comes of being a vicar's daughter. While I was growing up our house was always full of people and nobody was turned away.' These good friends collected us, dropped us off, and made us packed lunches. It was as though we were living in two worlds, the one of walking by ourselves, carrying packs and just absorbing the landscape, and the other of socializing with kindred spirits. Our evening menu ran something like this: bubble bath therapy, tea and cake, drinks before a roaring fire, a delicious satisfying meal and a comfortable bed.

The next few days were sunny and warm with temperatures reaching the unseasonable highs of 18–20 degrees centigrade. We weren't complaining. The Downs were a delicious mixture of steep green slopes and coffee cream ploughed fields interspersed with copses of trees. Newborn lambs lay near their watchful mothers, nooks and crannies were bright with primroses, and the white blackthorn blossom stood out against a blue sky. The character of this rolling chalk countryside has been created over thousands of years by the grazing of livestock, and it has provided a home for many important and attractive species of plants and animals. Much of this traditional habitat has disappeared as the Downs have been ploughed up for arable farming, but the hundred hectares of the Wye Nature Reserve have been preserved as original downland and are home for many typically English wild flowers. We certainly saw plenty of violets and cowslips as well as snowdrops, wood anemones and bluebell woods. Above us skylarks trilled and kestrels and buzzards freewheeled on the thermals.

Away from the noisy transport routes and the industry of the Medway valley, everything about the Downs is the sort of Englishness that I imagine people want to fight for. Villages like Wye and Charing, Boughton Lees and Wrotham, with their Georgian high steets, old pubs, stone churches, and village greens; churchyards filled with daffodils and the scent of new-mown grass, and a patchwork of fields rolling into the hazy distance among the beech woods. Sitting outside a pub in temperatures more like July than March and savouring a pint of hard-earned beer was one of the pleasures of those early days of the walk. If we hadn't strenuously resisted the temptation to chase one pint with another I think we would never have left Kent, let alone reached Cape Wrath.

In Hollingbourne, we found a hostelry called the Dirty Habit, a must for sweaty walkers. We ordered our pints and picked our way carefully over scaffolding and bricks to find a table on the patio in the sun, where, unabashed, we ate our sarnies. This particular habit is discouraged by the French in bars likely to be used by hikers; they put a large notice on the door stating *Rien hors de sac à dos*, a succinct way of saying don't eat your own food on the premises. We had no scruples about it here as we had paid so much for the drinks we felt the laundry bill must be included.

We were now on the route of what is called the Pilgrims' Way. It is a moot point whether pilgrims going from London to Canterbury ever used it; more likely they used the A2 (once the Roman road from London; an extension of Watling Street, which ran to London from the north-west). It is now thought that the name Pilgrims' Way may have been coined by an Ordnance Survey officer in the 1860s. Pilgrims from Winchester would almost certainly have used these ancient routes over the Downs. Perhaps it should have been called the Drovers' Way, less exotic but more accurate. In any case it was fun to imagine ourselves as latter-day secular pilgrims. With our backs to Canterbury and our sights on Cape Wrath we were more grimpils than pilgrims, walking through Middle Earth in search of adventure.

We lived with a sense of unreality for the entire walk. Staying with our children in Tunbridge Wells for three of our eight nights on the North Downs Way heightened our initial disorientation. Our daughters collected us at the end of each day's walk and drove us back to stay with them in Tunbridge Wells; the next morning it was an eighteen to twenty mile (thirty kilometre) drive back to our finishing point. Somehow they managed to fit this in between work and child care. Apart from seeing the family, this arrangement meant we could be free of our packs for two blissful days. During that short stay in Tunbridge Wells, patients, acquaintances and shop assistants accosted us.

'We saw you on TV,' they grinned, obviously impressed. 'How are you doing?' If this is fame, I thought, you can keep it. I contemplated wearing a large hat and sunglasses.

On our third day Steve from Radio Kent met us at 8.30 a.m. by the Cock pub in Detling. There was an aerial that reached to the sky on the roof of his maroon van; a large round clock with a jumble of boxes, wires and dials took up most of the back seat. If the van hadn't had Radio Kent all over it, I think we would have rung for the police. His interview gave us another chance to make a plea for sponsors for our hospice charity before we moved off for our twenty-one-mile (thirty three kilometre) day. When our itinerary showed any distance over sixteen miles (twenty-five kilometres), I would experience a moment's panic, for at this stage we were not in the peak of fitness. However, thanks to our children's help, we had no more than a day sack on our backs, so the distance proved surprisingly easy. That evening I still had enough energy to help my daughter Katie get the supper; a confidence-booster for future long days of foot slogging.

When we finally bid the family goodbye on 20 March, there were big hugs and damp eyes, for it would be many miles and a few adventures before we met again in June.

The good weather gave us rewarding views after each climb back onto the ridges; although the height of the Downs is nowhere more than 655 feet (200 metres) the well-signed path rollercoasters you gently along. After a ridge walk with views over river valleys and rolling countryside to the distant sea, the path would take us down into the valleys along almost subterranean tracks, often in the trees. It was on these ancient routes that we felt furthest removed from the modern world, and our thoughts turned to the knights, squires and priests of Chaucer's *Canterbury Tales*. We would emerge blinking, to find ourselves on the metalled roads of a village, released from the underworld of our imaginings.

Wooden steps on some of the steeper slopes meant hard work for thigh muscles. Why is it so difficult to make steps to suit the average walker's stride? Some are giant-sized and some pigmy-sized. It is almost always impossible to go up one foot after the other so it's 'dot and carry one' with the dominant leg doing all the work: a sure way to diagnose any incipient knee problems.

From Hollingbourne we could see across to Leeds Castle standing serenely beside its lake and beyond it the Greensand Ridge with a glimpse over the Weald of Kent. A minor problem on this stretch was negotiating kissing gates. Perfect for lads and lassies to have a gate-width fond farewell, but when it came to squeezing through with a big pack there was a tendency to get stuck, rather like Pooh in Rabbit's house. The only way forward was to clamber onto a rail and balance precariously while opening the gate. If you could manage to keep the gate open long enough to drop down the far side, you could continue your walk. If not, you had to remove your rucksack which was not a desirable exercise.

Descending through woods ankle deep in blue bells and litter we approached the Medway crossing. Fly tipping is endemic in this industrial area, and we passed rusty washing machines, burnt out cars, soggy mattresses and inverted prams. At Burham Down we discovered Kit's Coty, a Neolithic burial chamber with three Stonehenge-type rocks supporting an equally large headstone: a sort of prehistoric bus shelter. It has been a tourist attraction for several hundred years and is heavily decorated with nineteenth- and twentieth-century graffiti. An eighteenth-century artist called Samuel Ireland described it as a 'rude and inexplicable monument of antiquity'. Dickens enjoyed picnics up there with friends, requesting them to take their litter home. In those days the view of the Medway Valley would have been more hop fields and orchards and less of the industrial incontinence from Snodland, the Aylesford paper recycling plant, and the cement works at Cuxton.

Dickens would certainly not have recognized the Medway crossing which is now an elegant new motorway and high-speed rail bridge a mile or so upstream from Rochester. From Holly Hill, on the south side of the River Medway, we had an aerial view of the three-in-one concrete bridge which was crawling with heavy plant and machinery. As we walked towards it, we were amused to see a terraced flight of steps going up the embankment onto the new road reminiscent of the steps to an Aztec temple. However, on reaching the Medway Bridge we were told that anyone intending to use two feet would have to walk to Rochester Bridge and cross there, a four-mile (six kilometre) detour. We looked so horrified that Bob the builder suggested we call the minibus. Thanks to the wonders of modern technology, the man-with-a-van soon arrived, drove us round and deposited us on the other side of the Medway.

Apart from saying farewell to the family, Thursday, 20 March was a date to remember, as the much-vaunted war with Iraq began and coalition forces started their bombing campaign. We savoured our good fortune walking through woods and fields, past prosperous farms and substantial brick-and-timber houses sparing a thought for war-torn Iraq. That day we left Kent for Surrey, as we looped round south-west London towards the Thames Valley Path.

Richard stopped at an unlikely-looking post in a field. 'This,' he said, reading from an information board, 'is the point where the North Downs Way and the Vanguard Way cross the Greenwich Meridian Line.' He dug deep into his pockets, produced a global positioning satellite gizmo given him, at his request, as a farewell present by his dental colleagues. Having studied it carefully he muttered with a chuckle, '0.00085.'

All Greek to me, but to the cognoscenti those figures would mean a slightly inaccurate longitude reading. Later on the walk he tested it again, and this time the latitude reading was a quarter of a mile out. Richard shook his head in disbelief. 'No good if we break a leg in the Scottish wilderness.' He grinned ruefully as he stowed the GPS back in his rucksack. 'I think Nick and the others want us to get lost,' he joked. 'We'll have to send it home. It's heavy, uses lots of battery and can't give an accurate reading.'

In that extraordinary spring, temperatures crept up to record levels. Wearing shorts at this stage would, we thought, be tempting providence so we rolled up our trousers, 1950s style. One afternoon we were sunning our pale legs on a convenient bench, when two riders cantered up the path and were forced to rein in their steeds in order not to knock us off our perch. Both horses and riders glared at us, and one man shouted to his companion, 'Don't know why they put seats on a bridleway, d'you, Charles?' Snorting, he dug his heels savagely into the horse's flank. There was a loud report under the whisking tail, hooves hit the air and we were showered with dead leaves.

The M25, a fast-flowing river of vehicles, was a constant travelling companion. We had often been in one of those cars looking up at the North Downs Way, aware that we would be walking along it in 2003. Crossing a footbridge over this roaring motorway, we were momentarily hypnotized by a constant stream of cars and lorries pounding frenetically along the tarmac in a haze of exhaust fumes, overtaking and being overtaken as if in some demonic dance.

We were soon walking through the calm of beech and yew woods emerging from time to time to look over the Surrey hills. I had paused when we could see Limpsfield, for this was where my mother grew up. She never lost her love of these wooded hills and I felt she would have been proud of our current endeavour. She is laid to rest in a family grave under one of the oldest and largest yew trees in the country, in Tandridge churchyard, and for a while she followed me.

Reigate Hill was smart. So smart that some of the wheelie bins outside the mock Tudor homes were wallpapered. Richard too was in memory lane mode.

'When I was at King's I walked from London to Brighton,' he said with a hint of pride. 'It was run by Guinness and I still have the tie to prove I made the fifty-six miles.' He hesitated a moment and then continued. 'Well, I made it at the second attempt. First time round I stopped, cooled off and promptly pulled a hamstring. The second time I walked with a fellow student and we didn't stop at all.'

It took a while for this to register. 'Wow!' was all I could manage before adding, 'Just don't expect me to walk fifty-six miles without stopping.' Walking I thought, was obviously in the Hunt genes.

We crossed a suburban road and then he went on, 'They stopped the walk shortly afterwards. It was at night and too many students got run over.'

The fort on Reigate Hill was worth more than a glance. It was built in the 1890s as one of thirteen installations that formed a chain of defence stretching seventy miles along the North Downs escarpment. The English were in a state of xenophobia at that time and these forts or mobilization centres were designed to house guns, axes and saws.

It was thought that local volunteers could disperse along

the lines of motte and bailey type defences strung along the Downs and so protect a large area in an amateur last ditch of defence. They were never manned and closed in 1906 when confidence in the Royal Navy had been regained. We discovered some impressive mounds and ditches under the trees that had grown over them and decided that, in appearance, they were little changed since the forts of the Iron Age. Today attacks take place from the air or from civilian cars with a bomb on board.

The Downs are thought to contain half the world's remaining chalk grassland, and around 10 per cent is in Kent and Surrey. Walking past the Brockham lime works we read that the area with its lime kiln, mine shaft and narrow gauge railway was once a busy quarry supplying chalk to two batteries of kilns which was then burnt to produce quick lime. The site was at its peak at the turn of the century and closed in 1930. Today the bare chalk is being covered by grass and herbs and the decaying buildings are undergoing renovation.

'It's ironic,' I mused, 'that these unsightly industries are being resurrected for tourists. Who knows, one day they may dig up a section of motorway, and restore it for the general public to show them that people in the twenty-first century actually sat in cars for hours in traffic jams!'

We stayed in Dorking with Ann, a family friend of Richard's. She was an energetic lady in her mid-sixties just back from walking the Milford Sound trail in New Zealand. Our bedroom window looked over the gentle slopes of Denbies Vineyard to Ranmore Common on the North Downs Way, a peaceful scene in the evening light. After supper we watched the bombing in Iraq unable to register the full horror of war from the comfort of our armchairs and heard that two coalition helicopters had collided, killing eight British and four US soldiers.

The following day, Richard had moments of nostalgia.

When he was a boy, he used to walk on the Surrey hills with his father; the wooded summit of Box Hill was a particular favourite.

As we stood at the top he suggested I had a good sniff. I had started the walk with a cold but thought it was improving. He then asked me what I could smell.

'Mmm. Something sweet and sour. It's the box, isn't it?' I replied thoughtfully. Richard picked a few sprigs from the bushes all around us and handed them to me.

'This hill on a Bank Holiday was something else,' he said dreamily. 'All the world and his wife swarmed up here, taking the Green Line bus or a train from the suburbs of south London and then clambering up the hill. Not many people owned cars in the fifties.' He paused, surveying the empty grassy slope and rather hazy view over fields to the south coast. 'You could hardly put a pin between the bodies,' he continued. 'Mums armed with picnic baskets, dads with knotted handkerchiefs on sweaty heads, children screaming, dogs barking; a day out like a hole in the head.'

'In the time-honoured tradition of Jane Austen's *Emma*,' I replied, sniffing my box cutting delicately.' Only their picnic would have been a little more elegant and a lot quieter.

Today the National Trust does a good job keeping the scrub at bay, preventing soil erosion by rain, and maintaining the oak and birch woodland. People still come and visit the hill, but I suspect a good few more take themselves off in a no-frills airline to the more reliable sunshine of Spain on a Bank Holiday.

I was surprised at the steepness of our descent to the River Mole which flows between banks of mature trees and has a line of eighteen stepping stones for the walker to use. We stopped briefly for a snack in a café near the Burford Bridge Hotel, the latter hostelry being perfect for the likes of Keats and Lord Nelson, but too smart for us. It was in the modest café that we overheard a young man telling his mates that he had received his call up papers in the post that morning. Suddenly the war seemed real.

As we climbed up to the little church of St Martha on the Hill the soil was a rich golden colour with heathers on either side of the path. We had swapped the chalk downland for sandstone and nearly completed the first part of our walk. We found this golden sand again down on the River Wey by the old ford which gave Guildford (gold ford) its name. St Martha's Hill is 525 feet (160 metres) above sea level and, on a clear day, eight counties can be seen. The church, which dates back to the twelfth century, was and still is used by pilgrims. Like so many churches nowadays, it was closed.

Soon we were on the outskirts of Guildford and could see the River Wey with its weeping willows and long boats. This first section had taken eight days and we had covered 112 attractive but noisy miles (180 kilometres). That night my cousin Anna and her husband Peter took us to a performance of The St Matthew Passion in Guildford Cathedral. Inside this soaring neo-gothic space not only did the music stir our souls but the counter tenor's uncanny voice gave us shivers of delight. We had completed the first warm-up leg of our walk in perfect weather, been reunited with old friends, and felt ready to tackle anything. Only the clouds of war hung over us. It was a time to pause and reflect.

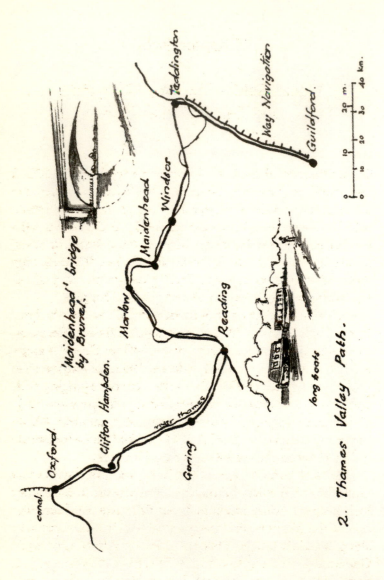

'Maidenhead' bridge by Brunel.

long boats

conal.

Oxford.

Clifton Hampden.

river Thames

Goring

Reading

Marlow

Maidenhead

Windsor

Teddington

Way Navigation

Guildford.

0   10   20 m.

0   10   20   30   40 km.

2. Thames Valley Path.

Chapter Two

Liquid Gold – The Wey Navigation and Thames Valley Path

Forget the car. Walk along the canal towpath in Guildford and you'll be pleasantly surprised. No tarmac, no cars, no shops; just a riverside walk past a theatre, pubs and a waterside café. We found the golden sand of the old ford, and crossed a footbridge over the River Wey where colourful narrow boats, kayaks and motor boats were out on the water. Walkers, dogs and cyclists filled the towpath. Fresh green willows wept from the banks, and ducks splashed and quacked happily.

Richard and I felt a buzz of excitement. We had reached our first waterway and would now be on canals and rivers almost up to Birmingham. We left the bustle of traffic and retail therapy addicts above us as we walked under the 1986 footbridge and on to the refurbished warehouses which were once bulging with corn, flour, coal, bark for tanning and rags for paper-making, their bright orange brick reflected in the still canal water. A little further on we saw the great bulk of Guildford Cathedral astride its hill, between-the-wars-Gaumont with tower.

Our next surprise was Stoke Lock, the first lock below Guildford on the Wey Navigation. The seventeenth-century lock-keeper's house has been beautifully preserved and was one of the oldest of the many we were to pass on our way along Britain's canals. This navigable waterway runs from Godalming via Guildford to the Thames at Weybridge. It is now owned by the National Trust which describes it as 'a tranquil waterway through the heart of Surrey'; a well-watered one at that, with no less than seventeen pubs.

A gentleman called Sir Richard Western began planning the Wey Navigation in the early seventeenth-century when waterway engineering was a new science. Being an entrepreneurial young man in his twenties, he saw the potential of contemporary engineering and seized the opportunity to open up the River Wey to barges. The project was shelved during the Civil War and recommenced at the end of fighting. The young Sir Richard, a Royalist, then teamed up with James Pitson, a Roundhead, who in 1651 obtained an Act of Parliament to permit the building of the Wey Navigation, which opened in 1653. Like the Channel Tunnel today, the enterprise cost so much more than the shareholders had subscribed that the Navigation's finances were in debt from the start.

The Godalming extension was opened in 1764 giving access to a whole network of waterways. The Arun canal, built in 1816, joins the Godalming Navigation at Stonebridge and enabled sailing boats to transfer their cargoes at Chichester to freight-sized barges capable of carrying eighty tons. The barges would have been horse-drawn and the animals rested overnight in shelters along the towpath. Tugs gradually replaced them but horses were still pulling barges as recently as 1950.

We noticed the indentations left by barge ropes on wooden rolling blocks placed at bends in the waterway, to prevent the barges going into the bank. It was difficult to imagine the shouting and thumping, the sweating and swearing, and the smell of coal and sawdust on this waterway in its heyday; hard to picture barges filled with cargoes of corn, timber, coal or gunpowder, and great carthorses churning up the towpath as they negotiated the twelve locks.

Our towpath was dry and firm, and the meadows golden with celandines. The only water traffic was narrow boats with names like *Rosy and Jim* and *Cardigan Ted* and the occasional silent kayak. A few retired working barges lay along the bank. Canada geese honked noisily watched by supercilious swans. The only other noise was the muted roar of traffic from the M25 and the hum of conversation as we approached yet another pub.

The owners of some of the narrow boats were busy with the paint pot, ensuring that every stylized flower was bright and glossy ready for the season. A few of the boats moored on the bank were permanent homes, with smoking chimneys and washing lines on the deck. Some had roof gardens on top and a sitting area on the bank, while others used this space as storage for children's swings, plastic chairs and toy prams.

We found ourselves enjoying this first taste of canal and riverside walking. Not only was it flat and easy going underfoot, but also there were frequent changes in the landscape: the bustle of motor boats and narrow boats as they negotiated the locks, our own concentration as we crossed the busy road bridges, and the Wey itself, sometimes enclosed with hedges and trees and sometimes opening up into water meadows. A peep through the trees across the canal to the stone tower and roof of Send church made a picture postcard view. A heron stood hunched among the reeds like a geriatric cleric with a hangover.

On the canal bank, in the grounds of Pyrford Place, a charming domed summerhouse caught our eye. The equally charming story goes that John Donne, poet, preacher and one-time dean of St Paul's, flirted in this summerhouse with none other than Elizabeth I. Sadly, the story has been dismissed as the summerhouse was not built until the end of the seventeenth-century, long after Elizabeth's death. However, Good Queen Bess did visit Pyrford Place because she had leased it to her Latin Secretary, Sir John Wooley who was married to one of the Queen's ladies-in-waiting, Elizabeth More of Loseley near Guildford.

There were a number of cyclists enjoying a ride along the narrow towpath. Notices asked them to give way to pedestrians, but in reality it was the other way round. We had no idea they were coming until there was a shout of 'Look out', ''Scuse me' or just 'Shit'. We needed good reflexes to avoid being mown down. Cycle bells are obviously not considered cool, as only those over sixty seemed to have them. There might be a niche in the market for pedestrian wing mirrors, we thought, as Richard stepped towards the water to enable another one to pass. Unable to change course, this cyclist somehow negotiated the few centimetres of bank between Richard and the water without getting wet.

It was well past lunchtime and we were longing to sample one of the seventeen pubs. The Anchor hove into sight at Pyrford Lock but the whole of south-west London had got there first. Such was the press of cars, men, women, children, squawking babies, dogs, bikes, and personal stereos and mobile phones, that we couldn't spare the time to queue and then find that the pub had run out of beer. We finally stopped in a thicket by the narrow towpath and, after sandwiches and water, snoozed on a low branch of a tree like a couple of big cats.

As we approached Parvis Wharf, green fields gave way to the canal-side residences of Byfleet: rows of houses with shiny windows, manicured lawns and choreographed daffodils. It was these gardens that sheltered us from suburbia, a green band round the wide skirts of greater London. Now the roar of the traffic had reached Niagara Falls proportions and soon we were under the massive concrete pillars of the M25 where the roar ceased, as if someone had turned off a switch, and a group of youngsters was creating a provincial Tate Modern on the dull grey concrete with colourful graffiti.

Here we appeared to be on a jogger's motorway, once again standing aside to let the panting, sweaty bodies pass. With the London Marathon only weeks away, hopeful joggers were busy getting into peak condition. We didn't envy them. Twenty-six miles is quite enough to walk let alone run.

The last of the effortless fifteen miles soon disappeared and we were on the Thames Lock at the northern end of the Wey Navigation. I once shared a flat with an American girl who was engaged to a city businessman. While I was slumming it in a basement flat in Notting Hill she and her man moved in with the glitterati to St George's Hill, Weybridge. I was hoping our path would take us to this illustrious spot, but all we could see of the town was the church spire rising above the wooded riverbank.

Blackmoor's Grove, Teddington was where R. G. Blackmoor wrote his classic novel *Lorna Doone*. Blackmoor died in 1900, and the land was purchased for development and became a street of charming Victorian terraced houses called Thelma Avenue. This was where Cathy, a nursing friend we hadn't seen for thirty years, was hosting us for the night. She had only recently moved into the area, and, with the help of her orienteering skills and both our mobile phones, she was finally able to locate us on a patch of grass in the middle of the road near Chertsey Bridge. Cathy had shared a flat in

London with Anna, my Guildford cousin, for many years when they were both at St Thomas's Hospital. Richard and I were just married and living in Tunbridge Wells and their flat made a great place for us to stay after a night on the town. We left our fourteen-month old daughter Katie with them the very weekend she chose to take her first solo walk. Cathy embraced us by a signpost and we decided that our friends always go on looking the same; it is only their children who change. She drove us back to her recently acquired retirement house, and after catching up the thirty years we discovered that her uncle just happened to be Stanley Spencer's younger brother Gilbert, and her little house was full of wonderful paintings. We went to bed clutching *Memoirs of a Painter*, her uncle's book about his brother Stanley.

RING FOR FERRY was clearly written on a notice at Thames Lock, Weybridge. A ship's bell was chained to the post and we clanged the clapper as loudly as we could. It seemed a very small sound to carry across such a width of water. We waited. Nothing. We clanged the bell again. Still no sign of life on the Shepperton bank. On closer inspection of the notice, the small print gave us a phone number, and we reluctantly dialled for a lift. Very soon one of the few remaining ferries on the Thames appeared and took us swiftly across to the north bank. The mobile phone, it seemed, was an essential piece of equipment for crossing rivers.

Once across, we were on the Thames Path, which was declared a National Trail in 1989. It takes the walker along 180 miles (290 kilometres) of riverside from its source in the Cotswolds to the Thames Barrier at Greenwich, passing through water meadows, suburban walkways, and the great metropolis.

The River Wey was a tadpole compared to this wide belt of slow-moving water. Party-sized double-decker motor cruisers hogged the river, and houseboats were often used as de-luxe summer residences along the bank. Daffodils, grape hyacinths and primulae lined the path that took us past elegant riverside homes, one with a giant alabaster chess set beside the Jag in the garden. Across the water substantial brick houses with conservatories, boathouses and moorings stood on the islands. Willows wept inconsolably beside pristine lawns.

'I'll bet they're prone to flooding,' Richard mumbled.

'And you'd have to like messing about in boats. I wouldn't fancy unloading a week's shopping from a mooring,' I said, wondering whether on-line shopping would include waterside deliveries. My reverie was interrupted by strange squawking cries coming from the trees above our heads.

'Parakeets,' said Richard, squinting up into the branches. At that moment there were flashes of brilliant green and a pair of parakeets flew down onto the grass at our feet. We thought they must have escaped from captivity, but we saw dozens as we walked along and realized they must be breeding successfully in the jungle of greater London.

A passenger launch under wraps intrigued us. *The Silver Queen* was built in 1926 and used in the evacuation of Dunkirk. Because of her small size, she was towed across in a great flotilla and much to everyone's surprise and delight returned unscathed. As a reward for services rendered, she was given a regular daily run from St Peter Port in Guernsey to St Helier in Jersey. This service continued until 1996 when the owner retired. She was then laid up and began to deteriorate. Now she was about to be restored. It was strange how many boats we saw along this opulent part of the river lying half-submerged like rotting carcasses.

We walked towards Staines Bridge accompanied by the chug-chug of a gin-palace motor launch and a narrow boat with owner in striped blue-and-white T-shirt and navy beret. With ample stomach and mini-moustache, he looked as though he must have just crossed the English Channel. We found to our surprise that we kept abreast of him which meant that we were walking at nearly four miles an hour, probably because I was looking for a loo at the time. You can't just dive behind a bush on a broad metalled path into the garden of some highly desirable residence however much you might desire to do so. Staines was being given a face-lift, with outsize waterside apartment blocks and many prestigious new buildings. Improvements to the riverside path meant seeing more of Staines than we had intended.

We were surprised to find ourselves in an attractive market square resplendent with an 1880 town hall in yellow brick and white stone. A donated waterside seat engraved with the words 'Cli and John welcome you' proved a useful place for elevenses.

Just before we went under the M25 again Richard spotted a white iron post by the towpath. This, he informed me, was a coal post to warn merchants that under an act of 1831 they were now due to pay a levy on coal. Nor was that all.

'D'you see that stone almost hidden in trees on the far bank?' he added. I put on my specs and managed to locate it. 'That's a replica of the London Stone to mark the upstream limit of the City of London's jursidiction over the river.' At this point his head disappeared into the *Thames Path National Trail Guide*. 'This,' he read gleefully, 'lasted from 1285 to 1857, when the first Thames Conservators took over.'

It was a real joy to have an observant and well-read travelling companion. Whether it was flora or fauna, birds or buildings, Richard would spot them and usually know what they were. I only noticed the price asked by an 'estate agent' for motor boats; you could start modestly at £2,000 or go the whole hog at fifty grand for a forty-three-foot combi-cruiser. The bricks and mortar variety would work out at rather more.

Apart from the roar of planes taking off from Heathrow,

Runnymede was tranquil. In olde English, runny means meeting place and mede a meadow. It was chosen for its historic assignation as it lies equidistant between Windsor, where the King lived, and Staines where the bishops and barons lived. Now trees rather than houses lined the river banks and hid the twelfth-century nunnery of Ankerwycke on Magna Carta Island. No one is sure where King John put his cross on the famous charter in 1215, which recognized the rights and privileges of barons, knights and freemen. I do remember being a very surprised eight-year-old when informed that King John couldn't read or write.

Across the green sward, we admired the famous Lutyens gatehouses, curved brick buildings of Empire proportions which give suitable gravitas to this 'birthplace of democracy'. Lady Fairhaven commissioned them in 1931 when she donated Runnymede to the National Trust.

Her Royal Highness Queen Victoria did not wish her royal Windsor Great Park to be soiled by the boots of her non-royal subjects. It is, after all, a Crown Estate. We walked across Albert Bridge to the other bank and an unpleasant mile on the roads of greater Datchet before rejoining the towpath at Victoria Bridge. These two identical bridges were built in the 1850s to create a private riverside park for the Queen. Looking at these solid iron twins, resplendent with coats of arms, we felt a momentary surge of republicanism.

The old bridge had been half iron and half wood. The reason for this was that the boundary of Berkshire and Buckinghamshire ran through the centre of the span; in the 1830s, when the bridge was in dire need of repair, Berks rebuilt their half robustly in iron while the impecunious Bucks merely used wood.

I spent my early childhood in a suburb of Windsor. Fragments of memory returned: the dreadful wailing of the air raid alert during the war which my brother John nicknamed the 'all queer'; the smell of new-baked bread when we collected it from the local baker (once John and I were allowed to collect the bread on our own and I remember watching with horror as he devoured the crusts at both ends); being shoulder-lifted up to see the King and Queen at a ceremony of the Knights of the Garter; staring with amazement at Queen Mary's lavish doll's house.

The Royal Standard was flying from the familiar round tower of Windsor castle. 'I hope she's expecting us,' I said, gazing at the strong grey walls. I'd forgotten what a fortress it was.

The Eton chapel clock struck four as we passed the disused Windsor and Eton Riverside station, built in 1849 complete with Royal Waiting Room. After a steep pull up the hill into the town we found ourselves outside the Central Station, built in 1850 for the GWR (the Great Western, otherwise known as God's Wonderful Railway). It was from here that my father, bowler-hatted and pinstriped, commuted to London on a steam train for eight grey post-war years. I could imagine him sitting on the train behind his copy of *The Times*, deftly smoothing the personal columns which adorned the front page, before folding it neatly to alight onto the steam-filled platform at Victoria Station and make his way with a stream of clones to his office.

Shops in this gold-plated town were bulging with royal souvenirs from guards with busby hats to teddy bears in tartans, and the Jubilee precinct gleamed red and gold. We had hoped to stay in the Windsor youth hostel, but it had been sold to raise funds after the outbreak of foot and mouth disease in 2001, and we were forced to spend a 'gold-plated' night in a B&B.

The next morning we crossed the Thames on the oldest iron bridge still in use, designed by the engineering god Brunel.

We had arranged to meet Fred, an old friend who had been one of the lads with Richard in Round Table (a community service club for the under-40s) and walk along the Thames Valley Path with him for the day. In 1988 he and his son Chris invited Richard to join them on the Tour of Mont Blanc, and Fred was planning to walk with us again in the Alps at the end of August. Although we didn't see a lot of Fred and his vivacious wife Margaret, it had become a tradition that, on Shrove Tuesday, we tossed pancakes and jokes in equal measure in their kitchen. Their Jack Russells looked on, hoping someone's pancake would miss the pan. Sadly Margaret died of cancer in November 2001, which was one of the reasons we had chosen once again to walk for our local hospice.

That perfect spring morning, we spotted Fred with his two Jack Russells near the playing fields of Eton. Henry VII's fifteenth-century college and its magnificent chapel stood elegantly on one side of the swan-filled Thames, with the old town dominated by the great castle on the other; royalty was back in favour. On a large chunk of sandstone by the river we discovered the following notice:

BATHING REGULATIONS FOR ATHENS 1921
5TH FORM MANSE IN 1ST HUNDRED & UPPER
& ALL MIDDLE DIVISIONS MAY BATHE HERE.
NO BATHING AFTER 09.30 ON SUNDAY.
ALL BOYS WHO ARE UNDRESSED MUST GET IN
THE WATER OR BEHIND SCREEN WHEN BOATS
WITH LADIES COME IN SIGHT.

We had a good fifteen miles (twenty-four kilometres) to walk to Marlow and one of Fred's two Jack Russells was an elder statesman with a potbelly and Chippendale legs. His aristocratic legs were the problem. The ball and claw joint at the doggy equivalent of the wrist had given way, and sagged badly, accentuating the Chippendale effect. His companion was a cheeky slip of a girl who exuberantly quadrupled our mileage. Joe trailed nobly on until lunchtime but then, missing his afternoon nap, lay down on the towpath and would not budge. We took it in turn to carry this warm and weighty bundle, somewhat reminiscent of a grandchild, until we finally reached Marlow. I decided that carrying a rucksack was a lot easier than dog portage.

Brunel's Great Western Railway bridge at Maidenhead was worth scrutiny. It was built in 1838 to carry his broad gauge line to the West Country. In order to span both the towpath and the navigation channels the brick arches are the widest and flattest in the world, thirty-nine metres (127 feet) across, with a rise of just over seven metres (twenty-three feet). There seemed to be no challenges too great for this engineering genius. The bridge has been immortalized in Turner's famous study, *Rain, Steam and Speed*. In spite of predictions from nineteenth-century experts that the bridge would collapse twenty-first-century trains still speed over it today.

A little further up the river we came across a little ditty inscribed on a plaque:

> Old Father Thames goes gliding by
> As ripples run he winks his eye
> At Cotswold cows and Oxford dons
> Nodding to Windsor's royal swans
> He bears our nation's liquid crown
> By lock and weir to London Town.
> They all that know and love his banks
> Rest here awhile to offer thanks.

We did, watching a motor cruiser called *Pink Champagne* chugging along as we made our way towards Boulter's Lock, a great place for picnics in the days of punts and parasols.

Thirsty though we were, we eschewed refreshment at the Boulter's Lock Hotel when we saw a sports Jag and a Rolls outside the smart exterior.

The unusually warm weather had prompted the leaves on the trees to make an early appearance. Horse chestnut buds were unfurling and beech buds swelling in the hanging woods of the Cliveden estate. Cookham churchyard, where we paused to look at Stanley Spencer's modest grave, was a mass of daffodils and primroses. Then we were weaving our way round the black and white houses of the old Close before regaining the riverbank. In just one typical Thames Path day, we had walked through water meadows and woods, past locks, across weirs, under bridges and through villages.

On reaching Marlow, we refreshed the parts that most beers can reach, and Fred phoned for a taxi.

'I've got two dogs with me,' he told the taxi man as an afterthought. There was a long pause.

'Sorry, guv. Carn 'ave them in me brand new Merc. Try someone else.'

There was, it seemed, a dearth of taxi drivers in Marlow. After further refreshment Fred rang the same man again.

'Look, they're only tiny dogs and I can't get hold of another taxi. D'you know anyone I could try?'

There was another long pause. 'OK, guv. I'll come in the people carrier and bring a dustpan and brush.'

At last we were rid of the roar of planes and cars. Now only the squabbling of Canada geese, the splash of a weir, and the occasional chug-chug of a motor boat broke the peace of the slow-moving river. A kingfisher flashed electric blue, dabchicks busied themselves near the banks, and great crested grebes looked down their beaks at the world in general.

The stretch of the Thames from Marlow to Reading is probably the best known and the best loved. Marlow, Cookham and Henley conjure up regattas. When Richard and I first knew each other, we used to spend summer weekends at Cookham Dean with a friend who owned an elegant nineteenth-century skiff. The Victorians were passionate about rowing and the tradition lives on. The weekend of the Henley Regatta, we took a picnic with us and sculled up the river to watch the event. Moving gently through the water from our mooring, we thought about the legacy the Victorians had left. This was the Thames of Jerome K. Jerome's *Three Men in a Boat* and the inspiration for Charles Dodgson's stories that were published as *Alice's Adventures in Wonderland*. It was along here that Kenneth Grahame had created his characters for *The Wind in the Willows*. We saw Ratty busy amongst the reeds on the bank, and plenty of Toad Halls. Mole was probably whitewashing his little home. It was the perfect day, hot sun and cloudless skies. We had a shady picnic near the start of the races at Temple Island and then rowed upriver to jostle with lots of other small craft near the finish at Henley Bridge. A ribbon of white marquees lined the far bank where official spectators in official dress sipped champagne and sweated under exotic hats. Later came the fireworks, banging, fizzing showers of colour mirrored in the river, and later still the silence, broken only by the skimming and dipping of oars as we sculled downstream in the moonlight.

Now, thirty-seven years later, we were walking along the regatta reach and remembering. At that moment, a rowing eight practising for the boat race shot past, there was a loud slap on water, a fleeting skid, and the crew slumped, panting over their oars. Behind them, on Temple Island, the naked lady in her cupola looked coldly down on the sweating bodies.

The first Oxford versus Cambridge Boat Race was held between Hamilton Lock and Henley Bridge in 1829. It moved to London in 1839. Not to miss out on the obvious advantages of having the race, Henley town hall established the Regatta ten years later.

At Temple Lock the riverbanks gleamed with double-decker motor cruisers. Their pointed fibreglass bows, glass-eyed spray-shields, and bristling antennae, gave them a predatory appearance. Mr Toad would have enjoyed a ride in one of these. At the weir there was a notice to say that the salmon ladder had been sponsored by Nuclear Electric plc and opened in June 1995. Much effort and cash has been employed to provide salmon ladders and clean up outfalls of industrial waste in an attempt to purify England's premier river. Success has been partial. Only a few salmon have been able to breed, and the water still looks murky. Nuclear Electric, and the other companies working on the project, have their own agendas, but money spent on cleaning up the equivalent of the nation's bathroom can't be bad.

Standing on Henley's attractive stone bridge and clicking the over-photographed view of the river and Temple Island, I was informed by a sign on one side that it heralded the Royal County of Berkshire, while Oxfordshire was on the other side. That morning we had been in Marlow, Buckinghamshire. I am always confused when it comes to direction and felt that if I had three legs that were long enough, I could stand in three counties at once. Then a moment of panic: Richard's red pack had disappeared. Was he in Berkshire or Oxfordshire?

When I caught up with him he was watching a pair of great crested grebes bobbing their long necks up and down in a strange mating ritual. It was the time of year. All the waterfowl on the river were busy pairing, mating and nesting, as vociferous as humans.

The eleven brick arches of Sonning Bridge glowed in the late afternoon sunlight. This charming hump-backed bridge had an identity crisis, for it, too, spans the county boundary between Oxon and Berks. This might explain why all the arches are different sizes. We had no time to explore this historic Thames village as we had three more miles to Reading and a friend to meet. Richard, who hates being late for an appointment, had lengthened his stride and it took all my concentration to keep up with him.

Soon we were in King's Meadow and thrown back into the twenty-first-century. Gasometers and skyscrapers filled the horizon. On past a huge business park and a giant shopping centre called the Oracle and the Horseshoe Bridge where the River Kennet meets the Thames. Until recently slatted for packhorses, this has now been redecked for walking boots. Pedestrians have a choice here, either turning left along the restored towpath of the Kennet and Avon Canal to Bath and Bristol, or heading straight on to Oxford. This spot is known as the Kennet Mouth. The canal route was created in 1810 when the rivers Kennet and Avon Navigations were linked. Contrary to popular belief, Reading itself is on the River Kennet, not the Thames. We plodded on under the road/rail bridge towards the concrete, glass and brick of downtown Reading.

We were being met and given hospitality by a friend of our daughter's called Lizzie. Her sister Judith was engaged to a Royal Engineer who was on active service in Iraq. They were due to be married in June, and if the war continued until then he would only have four days' leave. A letter had just arrived from him in which he bemoaned the lack of resources to do the job to his satisfaction. Walking peacefully along the gentle river, we had forgotten about the war, which was not going well for the coalition forces.

Reading dates back to Saxon times, and when the cloth industry declined in the seventeenth-century the town produced malt for beer instead, and still does; the Courage factory advertises itself to all thirsty drivers on the M4. We weren't sorry to leave the busy town and head out towards the charming villages of Mapledurham and Whitchurch and the Chiltern hills.

At Mapledurham Lock we began to feel we had left the noise and bustle of the south-east behind. This lock has the only working water mill on the Thames; the few old houses, church and sixteenth-century manor house hide behind a screen of trees across the river. Either Mapledurham House or the mellow brick Tudor mansion of Hardwick House might have been the model for the Toad Hall of Kenneth Grahame's *The Wind in the Willows*. We could easily imagine Ratty and Mole's skiff, complete with picnic basket, sculling along this stretch of the Thames. The Swan Inn beside Pangbourne Weir was another legendary spot, where Jerome K. Jeromes's 'Three Men' abandoned their boat and headed for home. His enduring book was published in 1888, just as the growing population of London realized that the playground of the Thames was only a cheap rail fare away. Boating became a craze, and in 1889 the number of boats on the river grew from 8,000 to 12,000.

The Thames would be unrecognizable without its population of mute swans; for many centuries they were domesticated for the table and each swan would be marked by a nick on its webbed feet or beak to denote ownership. Any unmarked birds became Crown property, and the swan was known as the 'royal bird'. Although swan doesn't appear on many menus today, the tradition of swan-upping (rounding them up) is still practised by the Worshipful Companies of Vintners and Dyers on the River Thames in London. Swan feathers made excellent quills for writing, and their leathery webbed feet and wing bones were once used for making whistles. Swans are the prima donnas of the river: floating serenely on the water, fluffing their wings like white crinolines, landing like Concorde and hissing like a train when alarmed; their royal association seems richly deserved.

Whitchurch, another unspoiled Thames village, had an old church, a lock, two pubs and a hundred-year-old latticed toll bridge. We noted the cost of the crossing in the days before the car:

Every person on foot half a penny.

Every horse, mare, gelding or mule, laden or unladen and not drawing, twopence.

Every carriage with two or more wheels twopence and for each and every wheel twopence.

Today cars were charged forty pence and pedestrians, laden or unladen, went free.

Soon after leaving Whitchurch the path deviates from the river. We found ourselves climbing up and down on a hedged trackway and along the edges of the wooded slopes of Goring Gap. Until we rejoined the Thames again we might have been back on the North Downs Way. We had the woods and hills and river all to ourselves until we reached Goring, our destination for the night. It was only three o'clock in the afternoon.

When we planned the walk we decided not to build in rest days. We had to press on every day to reach the Alps before the snow did and it was essential to keep moving. Instead, we arranged to have a few half-days when we could finish early and rest up. This was only our second short day and we both felt ready for some uninterrupted rest with no social obligations. Richard looked at his watch as we walked up the drive.

'A bit early to arrive at a B&B, isn't it?'

'Tough,' I replied, ringing the bell. 'We have arrived.'

Between loud barking, we could hear the drone of a vacuum cleaner.

Jenny answered the door holding a vacuum in one hand and restraining a golden labrador with the other. We explained what we were doing and apologized for arriving early.

Unperturbed, she broke into a half-smile. 'You'd better come in,' she said. 'Your room is ready, though I'm still doing the stairs.' With the door shut behind us she released the dog and vacuum and showed us to a large airy room with a plump duvet on a very inviting-looking bed. 'Come down when you've had your bath and I'll give you a front door key. We'll be out tonight.'

Very trusting, I thought, running a bath and savouring this special moment of the day when all we had to do was relax. After a cup of tea, something we were to miss desperately in France, we both fell into bed exhausted and slept for several hours. Neither of us said anything, but we wondered how we would manage when the going really got tough. Walking along riverbanks and towpaths was hardly challenging.

It transpired that our landlady was born and bred in Achiltibuie. This hamlet was a short boat trip away from the Summer Isles in Sutherland on the north-west coast of Scotland. Richard had visited Achiltibuie on a family holiday in the mid 1950s and taken a boat over to the island of Tanera Mor, then just used for summer grazing. Fraser Darling, a pioneer of the ecological movement in Scotland, had subsistence-farmed on Tanera with his family between the wars; a brave thing to do at a time when the word ecology was not in most people's vocabulary. Richard had taken me to visit Achiltibuie and we had walked through it on our coastal walk in 1995. We love it for its naked beauty, unforgiving mountains and pale sand that bears no footprints. The Summer Isles lie just offshore like a group of basking whales.

Munching bacon, eggs and sausages we were given a fascinating update on the island's history in Jenny's ironed-out Scottish accent.

'And ma cousin owned Tanera Mor in the 1960s. It's grand up there but a harsh spot to live. Now it belongs to an American sect called the Children of God.' Jenny raised her eyes to the ceiling.

'Did your cousin know Fraser Darling?' we asked in unison.

'Yes indeed. He was a kind man and everyone loved him.' She put a large cafetière of coffee and a rack of toast on the table before continuing thoughtfully. 'Kinda tough for his wife though. Three and a half years subsisting on Tanera and you've got to be made of something special.'

'The Scots are,' I mumbled through toast and marmalade. Richard had a secret yen to retire to Achiltibuie and I had told him that if this was a serious proposition, he would be on his own.

The first few miles of the day Richard and I were usually happy to chat. After that we walked quietly, Richard reading maps and landscape, while I dreamed away about something or nothing. We had left our comfortable B&B later than intended after a leisurely breakfast, and set off briskly past the tile-hung cottages and old stone church of Goring-on-Thames. Pausing on the bridge to take a photo I addressed Richard's back. 'How incredible to have found a landlady here of all places who could tell us how to pronounce Tanera properly.' (The accent, we were told, is on the first syllable not the last.) The back had turned round and I couldn't help adding the Aunt Sally, 'D'you envy her cousin?' There was a puase before Richard replied slowly. 'Of course I envy her cousin. I'd give my right arm to live up there. But as you know, it wouldn't work for you.' Richard is practically and intellectually much more self-sufficient than I am and would be happy to tuck himself away on the coast of north-west

Scotland or west Cornwall. I couldn't even contemplate putting all those miles between me and my friends and family however wild and magical the landscape. Decisions about a definitive retirement house are on hold.

The early mist cleared and gave us another perfect spring day. An island in the river was golden with daffodils and the woods a hazy green as buds slowly opened in the warm sun. Pollarded willows lined the river and the straw-coloured reeds contrasted with the green water meadows. It was good to see the spring unfolding along the riverbank; just the sort of day when Mole would have said 'hang whitewash' and gone out on the river with Ratty. Blackthorn blossom gave a white veil to the hedgerows and the waterfowl were in romantic mood.

Wallingford's packed history dates back to prehistoric times, for it was one of the few spots where men could ford the Thames at any season. The Saxons discovered Wallingford, the Romans settled it and William the Conqueror fortified it. We passed the scant remains of the Norman castle, one of Cromwell's casualties, on a grassy mound. It was market day in the town centre; the stalls, laden with spring cabbages, apples, oranges, cheeses and bunches of flowers, spread a patchwork of colour across the Georgian square. We wove our cumbersome way past old ladies trailing shopping trolleys, young mums pushing baby buggies, and the middle-aged with large baskets and small dogs.

We had time to dawdle a little in Shillingford, admiring the mellow brick houses with their splashes of mauve aubrietia and a fifty-foot trained wisteria, before reaching our goal of Clifton Hampden bridge. It was now mid-afternoon and I felt like the Hunchback of Notre-Dame, bowing to the force of gravity. The wide water meadows stretched endlessly into the distance and I was beginning to imagine village church spires among the far line of poplar trees. Then two of the pollarded willows seemed to be walking towards us, and next moment we were embracing our good friends from Canada who just happened to be house-sitting in Oxford. In no time we had been driven back to their luxurious residence in Headington and I was lying, Ophelia-like, in the outsize bath strewn with bubbles with warm water lapping my chin.

I had known Ann since I was at primary school and we had lost touch for many years. We met up again in our late teens while working in a typing pool in the City. Sitting opposite each other addressing envelopes, we made a joint decision to get out. I had arranged a gap year in Canada working at the Banff Springs Hotel, and invited Ann to join me. While I was making club sandwiches in the snack bar, Ann was serving the great and the good in the grand dining room of this Victorian baronial hotel. It was here she met Rick, a dashing young air force pilot. At the end of the season we teamed up with two other English girls and toured the States in an ancient Pontiac, all chrome and fins. After driving down the west coast towards Mexico City, learning to use a stocking as a temporary fan belt and the importance of a universal joint before writing the car off in the Nevada desert, we could have graduated as mechanics. In December we boosted our flagging finances by waitressing in ski resorts in the Laurentians north of Montreal. Ann managed to get a job at the prestigious Mont Tremblant Hotel, while I was employed in the bar of a more modest Swiss-style resort. The bar was run by a charming gay (queer in those days) called Nicky who protected me from the wrath of the two professional French Canadian waitresses I was working with. After spilling 7-Up onto a lady's mink coat, I improved my bar skills sufficiently to pour three beers at once and mix a mean rusty nail and screwdriver. I worked from ten o'clock in the morning till the last customer left, often in the early hours, and my throbbing feet often kept me awake at night. However, it meant I had no time to spend my small salary, well boosted by tips, and returned home the following spring with two hundred pounds in my pocket. Meanwhile, Ann stayed on to see more of Rick and they married eighteen months later. I was held responsible for this enduring liaison. Since then we have never lost touch, and meet up every time they are in the UK. When they heard we would be almost passing the door where they were house-sitting, we were booked in to stay with them for three nights. Their hospitality was such that Ann had even phoned my mobile to find out what paper we would like.

Clean and refreshed, I sat in the conservatory watching the sun set over the towers and spires of Oxford. Rick was playing his beloved fiddle and the insistent notes of a Bach partita floated into the evening air. I finished writing my diary before we adjourned for drinks and a passionate discussion on how to end the messy war in Iraq. My progress report went as follows:

My rucksack gets heavier every afternoon and I dread taking on the extra weight when we reach the Pennine Way. We were off to a bad start as my beautiful new pack was permanently uncomfortable; nothing wrong with the pack, just my inability to fix the straps properly. My circulation has improved so much I hardly ever feel cold. I don't sleep much as my body thinks it has to keep walking, but I'm none the worse for that. Richard never complains and is eating and sleeping well. I manage to keep pace with him and we are now averaging about 3.5 mph [5.6 kph] over this easy stretch. In the ten days since we set off, Richard has lost 8 lbs [3.6 kilos] and I have lost 4.

If anyone wants to lose weight, all they have to do is to shoulder a large pack and walk fifteen miles (twenty-four kilometres) a day. They will feel not only a sense of achievement, but also a sense of well-being when they stop. Some would say it's akin to hitting your head against a brick wall, but as with any adequate form of exercise, the feel-good factor when you finish is reward enough for the effort made. The downside of this is the possibility of addiction, which makes people like us do crazy things like another marathon walk. If negative thoughts disturbed my dedication to the task for the last few miles of a day, they disappeared the moment I reached our destination, and I was as eager as Richard to be off the next morning.

Sir George Gilbert Scott, who must have been almost as busy as his contemporary Isambard Kingdom Brunel, built the handsome bridge at Clifton Hampden in 1864 to replace the ferry. Ann and Rick drove us back to the bridge and accompanied us for three of our next seventeen miles. The river, bordered now with pollarded willows, reeds and teasels, flowed softly past us carrying a few rowing skiffs. Swans and great crested grebes rode calmly over the wash. We had the woods and water meadows almost to ourselves until, across the river, we saw the almshouses at Abingdon, the oldest of these dating back to 1446. The spire of St Helen's church rose behind them and soon we reached the rebuilt medieval bridge. Abingdon and Wallingford have been arch rivals over the years. The old ford at Abingdon was long and difficult to cross so the town lost trade to Wallingford. The Fraternity of the Holy Cross built the bridge in 1422 in an attempt to win back trade lost to their rival.

No one can just bypass Abingdon. It has so much history: the old market place and magnificent county hall, and the abbey, once the most powerful church landowner in Berkshire. The town's riverside location helped it to become one of the chief centres of the Berkshire cloth trade. There was a time when the wharves would have been full of barges collecting locally produced malt bound for London and delivering Somerset coal brought along the Wiltshire/Berkshire Canal. We climbed the steps onto the bridge and crossed into the town to admire an assortment of buildings dating from medieval to Georgian. The Nag's Head was a must to sample the result of the locally produced malt.

Refreshed, we pushed on quickly to Sandford lock. Due to the steep gradient of the land below Oxford, this and the Culham lock just to the south of Abingdon, are the two deepest locks on the river. Sandford Lock has a fall of 8ft 10ins (2.7 metres) and the water from the pool thunders over the weir. It is known locally as the Sandford lasher. Just before meeting Ann and Rick at Iffley lock we had time to visit the beautiful little twelfth-century church at Iffley and admire the Norman pie-crust arches inside and out and the fantastic stone beasties under the roof. Iffley marks the beginnings of organized rowing races in Oxford. This was enough to make anyone feel thirsty, and the popular Isis Tavern had plenty of memorabilia in the several bars: oars, skiffs and black and white photos of stiffly posed rowing crews.

The last day of March dawned and it was time to say goodbye to the Thames Path, and the generous G&Ts of our Headington five star hotel. *The Trail Guide for the Thames Path* went home in a Jiffy bag, lightening Richard's load somewhat. To date we had had no setbacks and Richard's carefully planned itinerary was working well. Ann and Rick saw us off at Lower Heyford on the Oxford Canal and promised to meet us in Provence at the end of our walk to Nice. From now on we would be walking more north and less west, threading our way through the urban conurbations of Coventry, Birmingham, and Manchester.

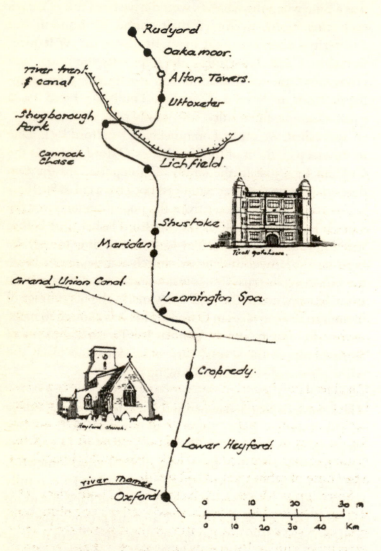

Rudyard
Oakamoor.
Alton Towers.
Uttoxeter
river Trent & canal
Shugborough Park
Cannock Chase
Lichfield.
Shustoke.
Meriden
Tixall gatehouse.
Grand Union Canal.
Leamington Spa.
Cropredy.
Heyford church.
Lower Heyford.
river Thames
Oxford

0   10   20   30 m
0 10 20 30 40 Km

3. The Heart of England.

Chapter Three

The Heart of England

After two weeks of perfect weather, rain was forecast. We had over seventeen miles to walk and so set off in good time from Lower Heyford. Below the old bridge the canal was packed with narrow boats waiting their turn for an outing. Boat names were carefully chosen: *Florrie*, *Daisy*, *Tinkerbell*, *My Rag Doll*. *Forget-me-not* came complete with smiling pansies on the roof. Further along the canal we saw a dumpy and down-at-heel motor launch named *Clarrie Grundy* and a narrow boat called *Saga* with *Darby and Joan* painted under a bunch of flowers on the side. The elderly couple sat under a sunshade on the bank and we gave them a cheery grin.

Canal boat holidays are for those who like slow-motion travel in tranquil surroundings. I know many people find them the perfect antidote to a stressful work situation, but they are not for the likes of me; I am far too impatient to sit in a queue waiting to negotiate a ladder of locks, and would certainly get a bad dose of cabin fever in bad weather.

Since it was Monday, we had the canal to ourselves. The day rolled by in a blur of fields, woods, villages and humpback bridges. A sleek mink nosed its way through the reeds and a grass snake slithered hurriedly into the water at our approach; harassed moorhens stabbed their beaks indignantly into the vegetation along the river bank.

By teatime I was always ready for a cup if not a pot. Banbury delivered the goods at the newly developed Castle Quay, a shopping centre and industrial estate cleverly incorporated on either side of the canal with Tooley's Boatyard and narrow boats advertising gifts, a chandler, guided tours and boat trips. We only had another four miles to Cropredy where we were meeting another Ann, our son-in-law's aunt, who knew the village and had arranged to catch up with us.

'Who's that?' I asked, watching a determined-looking lady bearing down on us from the bows of an approaching narrow boat. She was giving a passable impression of a windmill in a gale.

'No idea, but she seems to know us.' Richard can't have had his glasses on either, for the boat drew in to the bank and out jumped Ann.

'Too far to walk both ways,' she panted with a smile, 'so I thought I'd cadge a lift and come and meet you both.'

Cropredy, with a short o, is a small brick village which centres on the canal. As we crossed the bridge we noticed Coal Wharf, now only used by pleasure boats, but a reminder of Cropredy's working days. For us two it was the end of a long day and we climbed thankfully into Ann's car. Our farmhouse accommodation was at Great Bourton, a mile or so uphill from the towpath, and her taxi service was invaluable.

'It's shift work here,' said Brian cheerfully, appearing from a large shed which reverberated with pathetic bleating sounds. 'Peak lambing season for a month. I do the three a.m. shift but the wife and I share the rest.'

He looked remarkably lively for a man who was getting little or no sleep and he had enough energy left to be landlord, parish councillor and local historian. Out on his tractor in 2001, he found a boundary stone thought to pre-date the Civil War. It has been resurrected and re-sited on the verge near the ditch where he found it, and officially named the Cropredy

Boundary Stone. With his parish councillor hat on he regaled us with stories over the cornflakes.

'Take the new EU Health and Safety regs,' he said, passing Richard some toast. 'They can't leave anyone alone, even when they're dead and buried. The latest worry is gravestones. If they lean too much there is a danger that they could fall over and hurt someone. To test them, the verger has to go round the churchyard swinging a twenty-five-pound hammer onto every gravestone. If they don't fall over they're considered safe. How's that for common sense?'

'Gives a whole new meaning to the expression granny-bashing,' I said ruefully.

Rested and well ballasted with the Great English Breakfast, we set off along the canal towpath. The small garden of the lock-keeper's cottage at Bourton was full of daffodils and hyacinths giving off a wonderful scent as we passed by. We couldn't help noticing a large notice on the door: NO WAR IN IRAQ.

It was a day devoid of people, houses and boats; just miles of windy canal with intermittent showers. It was the first rain we'd had and we'd lost a rucksack cover. Huddling under a draughty bridge to eat our soggy sandwiches we missed our usual postprandial snooze in the sun. As far as the weather was concerned it looked as though the honeymoon was over. To cheer me up Richard informed me that we had covered one tenth of the walk: 260 miles (416 kilometres). A signpost showed that we were forty-six miles from Oxford and twenty from Banbury.

We were very happy to be met by Bron, an old friend and long-time patient of Richard's, at Napton Junction, where the Grand Union Canal meets the Oxford Canal, and taken to her home in Leamington Spa. Shortly after we arrived, pelting rain and roaring wind reminded us of what the weather can do in a normal English spring. The rucksack cover, I thought, would need replacing.

Bron was kindly hosting us for two nights, so the next day's scheduled twenty miles didn't seem too onerous as we had left our packs with her. It was a real April day, bright with a cold wind. The Grand Union Canal was wider than the Oxford Canal and beautifully tended with freshly painted lock gates, newly cut hedges and recently planted shrubs. A man was mowing the grass near a ladder of locks and here we gleaned some information about the Fosse Locks, so called because they take the Grand Union Canal over the Fosse Way, a Roman road. The construction of these twenty locks required vast numbers of bricks, three million of which were made in the area in 1795. History lives on in names, and we had walked past Brickyard Bridge and Folly Bridge on our way to Napton Junction. Although canals were a successful method of moving freight before the advent of the railway, there were problems in times of drought in summer and freezing temperatures in winter. Low water levels in recent years have been overcome by installing pumps, which can lift the 56,000 gallons (over 250,000 litres) of water needed to fill one lock in twenty minutes. A similar pumping system was installed in 1942 to keep the trading boats going during the Second World War. Knowing these facts, we were not surprised the coming of the railways quickly superseded the canals.

By late afternoon a sign welcomed us back to Royal Leamington Spa. Like our hometown of Tunbridge Wells, it has a Victorian gentility about it. The arrival of the Grand Union Canal in 1800 and the railway in 1852 lowered the tone and polluted the air sufficiently to reduce its popularity as a health resort. However, the advent of these transport routes to the manufacturing areas round Birmingham provided a new role for the town, which continued to grow and prosper. Today the watery periphery is struggling to emerge from its industrial past as the old houses along the deeply cut canal are being replaced with desirable waterside residences and high spec new estates. We felt obliged to try out a pub called the Dock, Lock and Barrel with a fair share of inebriates at the bar. The wall above our heads was covered with twisted aphorisms: *If a little knowledge is dangerous, better to be stupid and safe; Seek and ye shall find at the bar; Where there's a will there's a way to get home.* The inebriates were on the verge of picking a fight and the landlord had to throw them out. They would need plenty of will not to fall into the canal.

The snippets of history we gleaned were fascinating, and we learnt a little more about canals generally and this one in particular as we walked along. The commercial use of these eighteenth-century waterways gradually declined until the late 1920s, when the economic depression became the catalyst for giving new life to the run-down local networks. The Grand Union Canal took the opportunity to amalgamate eight companies to create a super waterway between London and Birmingham with links to Coventry and Leicester. The canals were widened, using labour under a government unemployment scheme, and a fleet of more efficient cargo boats was constructed. In spite of all this money and effort, the canal was never profitable, and was nationalized along with the railways in 1947. By the end of the 1960s, thanks to improved freight transport on the roads, the system had been virtually abandoned. It is only our love of heritage, and the leisure to indulge it, which has reversed the demise of our canals and turned them into popular tourist attractions and a resource for learning.

The Hatton flight of twenty locks is traditionally known as 'the stairway to heaven' and forms part of a twenty-one lock flight which ascends 146 feet (forty-five metres) over a distance of two miles (three kilometres). A line of black and white outstretched arms rose before us, with white uprights like Roman candles disappearing into the distance. From the top (a lot quicker on foot than by water), we had a distant view of Warwick castle, claimed by the citizens of Warwick to be the finest medieval castle in Britain. At Hatton Depot we passed a large Victorian building by the canalside, recently converted by British Water Enterprise into a Heritage School and Conference Centre; further proof of the new role the canal was playing in the twenty-first century.

Walking to Shrewley along the Grand Union Canal, Richard and I were beginning to feel a little less ignorant about the roller coaster history of our canal system. It was here we met our first canal tunnel. As we approached we saw a beam of light emanating from a dark cave overhung with trees, which soon became a bright telescope lit by the sun at the far end. The 433-yard (400-metre) tunnel was built in 1799 with the completion of the Warwick and Birmingham Canal. The guide described it as an exciting, but slippery, towpath tunnel allowing just two seven-foot wide boats to pass. It advised users to keep to the right. At that moment a narrow boat chugged passed us, lights blazing, heading for the tunnel.

After a further two miles, we left the canals for a while and joined the Heart of England Way, a very attractive designated footpath from Bourton-on-the-Water in the Cotswolds to Stafford. Richard now had to keep one eye on the waymarks and one on the map, as our path took us over stiles through fields and farms, woods and villages. We were always ready for a change of landscape and the joy of our route was that it was an interesting mix of varied scenery. The Heart of England Way lived up to its name, with undulating fields, copses of oak, ash and hazel, banks of primroses and a scattering of brick houses. The chunky eight-hundred-year-old Rowington Church stood on a carpet of golden celandines. It was hard to believe we were only fourteen miles from Birmingham.

Striding through a gently sloping field, we met a party of four retired gentlemen walking the Heart of England Way. It was their second day, and they were attempting seventeen to eighteen miles each day. Their average age was seventy-two and they had several artificial hip joints between them.

'I do have a little problem with the stiles,' confessed the old boy who was bringing up the rear. He looked uncomfortably warm in his tightly buttoned Viyella shirt, and seemed more than happy to stop for a chat. 'Of course, my old friend is a great help,' he added, patting his gnarled walking stick affectionately and leaning heavily on it. He jerked his head towards the comparatively youthful leader and confessed, 'When our George has the bit between his teeth, it's a job to keep up with him.' Then he pulled a hanky out of his pocket, wiped his damp brow, and muttered reluctantly, 'Better go. They're getting restless. Good luck with your walk.'

We congratulated them (and their orthopaedic surgeons), wished them well, and said goodbye. Four sticks waved and we watched them head off for the next stile and eventually a well-earned rest at the pub. Neither of us liked the stiles either, and Richard even suffered a minor groin strain swinging a leg while trying to avoid a holly bush.

Approaching villages and churches over the fields gives a sense of history and dislocates time. The church of St Michael, Baddesley Clinton sits aloof on a little hill surrounded by a sloping churchyard which was knee-deep in daffodils. A coachload of senior citizens crept up the path to enjoy the sight, before visiting the National Trust property of Baddesley Clinton itself.

Our progress through well-tended farmland coincided with muck-spreading, and for days we inhaled the rank smell of manure. Lambing was in progress, and one large barn was a busy maternity ward packed with ewes about to give birth. A couple of efficient-looking 'midwives' were keeping an eye on proceedings, and the tumty-tumty-tumty-tum of *The Archers* signature tune blared forth from radios into the surrounding countryside.

When I had booked up at a guest house in Meriden, I asked the landlady where the nearest town I might have heard of was. Back home, typing names like Meriden, Shustoke, Dimmingsdale, Rudyard and Compstall into our itinerary, I wondered where we were going. For me it was to be a mystery walk. In answer to my question, the landlady's tart reply was simply: 'Meriden *is* the heart of England.'

Suitably chastened, I didn't pursue the matter, and as we walked into the straggling town I wondered if it had a heart. While meeting friends at the pub that night we found it. In a courtyard at the Bull was a Land's End/John o' Groats-type signpost with CENTRE OF ENGLAND inscribed round the middle circle. London and Cardiff were written on the signs themselves and then, incongruously, Land's End to John o' Groats 700 miles.

At breakfast our landlady asked politely where we had walked from. We explained that we were on a sponsored walk from Dover to Cape Wrath.

'And where will you be going tonight?' she enquired.

There was an embarrassed silence. I looked at Richard. He looked at me. Although I didn't know much about the route, I usually supplied the names having booked the accommodation. Blankety-blank. The memory cells had crashed. Frantically I groped for some name, any name. Then I heard myself saying Shrewsbury.

'That's a long way,' she said, balancing four empty plates in one hand.

It was no good explaining that we were suffering from long-distance walker's amnesia. In our nomadic situation, time, days, dates, and names seemed unimportant. Places certainly mattered, but sufficient unto the moment to know them. Besides, there were so many that without a tape recorder and diary I should never have remembered them.

It was only eight miles (thirteen kilometres) to Shustoke (I knew it began with Sh), and this was one of our precious half-days. After a 48-hour blip, the weather returned to the sunniest spring on record, which was to see an astonishing 500 hours of sunshine and the highest maximum temperature of 26 degrees on 31 May. Although we didn't know it at the time, the warm spring was setting a trend for the summer. Our path that day picked its way through a green corridor between Coventry and Nuneaton and Birmingham. We even had distant views of the Exhibition Centre and high rise blocks of the big city. Yet the countryside was green and fertile with copses of oak and ash, prosperous dairy and sheep farms, sandstone churches and iron-red soil. Skylarks trilled and lambs bleated. The fan-like trees were beginning to flesh out and the woods were full of wild anemones.

Our bed and breakfast was the Old Vicarage at Shustoke run by a retired doctor and his wife. The rambling eighteenth-century house stood near the fourteenth-century sandstone church where John, our host, was churchwarden. The spire had been in danger of falling, he told us, and had to be rebuilt. Somehow the money was raised and it was finished in 1991. John felt it was unfair that the dwindling but loyal members of the congregation should have to be almost wholly responsible for the upkeep of the church.

'Everybody wants the church to be well maintained and they are quite happy to use it for weddings, christenings and funerals. I think everyone ought to have a share in looking after it.' he said with feeling. Then he opened the old oak door into the tower and invited us to follow him.

Having climbed a few Munros, I was surprised to find how unnerving it was to mount a series of smaller and smaller ladders to reach the top of the tower. John, less agile but more confident, disappeared well ahead of us. The dark enclosure was claustrophobic and between each flight we had to step on the beams. Gaps revealed the floor below, and above us were the great bronze bells. I couldn't begin to guess their weight, but one thing was certain, you wouldn't want to be underneath them if they fell. I wasn't sorry to squeeze through the low door out into the sunshine on the roof of the tower. Not so good for those suffering from vertigo, but we enjoyed a 360-degree view over red and green fields to another church tower, a disused coalfield and the urban conurbation in the distance.

Up here John told us a little about himself. 'I used to be a consultant physician at Birmingham's big NHS hospital. When I reached sixty I decided to retire. I didn't like the way things were going.'

He hitched his old jumper further over his shoulders and continued. 'Then I trained to be a GP. In some ways that was harder. Of the thousand children brought to see you every year, one would have meningitis. It was the GP's job to get the diagnosis right. In spite of that I stuck it for six years and even enjoyed it.'

He asked a little about our walk and the conversation turned to narrow boats. 'I spent four years as a student on one of those,' he said wistfully. 'Our first daughter was born on that boat. It cost me the princely sum of ten pounds. Much cheaper than digs. Now I think they're worth a thousand pounds a foot.' He smiled. 'At sixty to seventy feet they aren't called long boats for nothing.'

Shustoke must have been an important place in the Middle Ages for Henry II is reputed to have visited the village on his way back from Wales, and there was evidence of blue blood in the churchyard with a tombstone in memory of a certain Beaumont Albany Featherstone Dilke of Maxstone Castle.

Our choice of continental breakfast at the Old Vicarage was memorable. We came downstairs to the smell of home-baked bread and fresh coffee. The large Victorian table in the elegant dining room was groaning with apricot and prune compote, natural yogurts, croissants, and home-made jams and marmalades in cut glass jars. Thin slices of gammon were laid on a board with a Brie just beginning to bulge at the edges and a bunch of white grapes.

John's wife Mary was a radiographer and they had five daughters and a good clutch of grandchildren. We admired the house and Mary told us they ought to move, adding matter-of-factly, 'Someone else would be able to give this house all the care we can't afford.' She put a jug of fresh milk on the table and added, 'The trouble is we've been here a long time, we feel part of it, and one of our daughters lives in the stable block.' She smiled. 'Anyway, I like doing bed and breakfasts. I have one regular who comes for several weeks at a time.' Wiping the crumbs off my mouth with a linen napkin, I wasn't surprised.

After our restful stay at the Old Vicarage we had a pleasant twenty-one-mile (thirty-three-kilometre) walk to Lichfield through rich farmland and passed the Lea Marston Lakes. These are a testament to a successful purification system. The River Tame rises in the Black Country and passes through the West Midlands conurbation before its confluence with the River Trent. Water quality has been poor since industrialisation in the early nineteenth century. By the 1960s the water was so polluted that the River Tame was in fact dead and pollution was beginning to affect the River Trent as far down as Nottingham. In the late 1960s the River Trent Authority acquired the redundant gravel pits at Lea Marston and built a purification system that redirected the River Tame into the lakes where the solid impurities in the water sank to the lake bed and the purer water passed on its way. The cleaning process involved a regular dredging of the lake and disposal of the resulting waste, a bit like a cess pit. The system worked well, and a variety of river life returned to the Tame.

It's a positive story. Above the water line we saw swans, Canada and greylag geese, tufted duck, and a pair of kestrels mating. It was an easy walk through the Country Park, stopping briefly at Granny's Tea Rooms, before we reached the towpath of the Birmingham and Fazeley Canal.

Everything we walked through that day looked green and fertile. With arable and dairy farming and market gardening, it appeared to be the food basket of the West Midlands. A tractor was planting potatoes in the rich soil, a perfect moment after the recent rain.

The village of Drayton Bassett was obviously stockbroker

belt: expensively converted farm buildings, 4x4s with personalized number plates and large immaculate gardens. We looked down on the A5, which ran straight as a ruler across the surrounding plain. 'That's the Roman road – Watling Street – that goes to Chester,' Richard remarked. 'We were near the same road on the North Downs Way, only then it was the A2 route for the pilgrims going from London to Canterbury.' The North Downs Way seemed to belong to another world.

Lichfield certainly belonged to another era. The three graceful spires of the cathedral, even from some miles away, dominate the city. After a short walk through the squeaky clean suburbs which smelt of creosote, lonicera and window polish, we arrived in the pedestrian precinct of the old city. Our bed and breakfast in Shakespeare Avenue was over a mile from the cathedral and we were glad to get our boots off and our feet up. What we didn't realize was that there were no eating places nearby, so we had to drag ourselves back into the city to find food.

It was a Saturday night and Lichfield had metamorphosed in the two hours since we left it. Shoppers and children had been replaced by Beckham lookalikes. We passed several brawls and police were everywhere. I was starving and walked innocently into the first pub we came to. A gorilla on the door eyed me up and down and let me pass. I thought Richard was behind me. The room was lit only by flashing lights and loud music made the glasses at the bar rattle. A scantily clad girl was gyrating on the dance floor.

'No food here,' the barman told me briskly.

Someone touched my arm. It was my husband, being unusually assertive. 'Come on, we go now. This isn't what we want.'

As a granny with a sheltered upbringing, I was quite sorry to leave.

It took us twenty more minutes of tramping the charming old streets of Lichfield to find a suitable place to eat. When we eventually fell into the Gandhi Tandoori, Indian food, washed down with a Tiger or two, had never tasted so good.

Sunday morning. Apart from beer cans and crisp packets, the streets of the ancient city were empty. Lichfield's past was written on fine Tudor, Stuart and Georgian houses lining the paved streets with names like David Garrick, Samuel Johnson and Erasmus Darwin (Charles's grandfather). This gifted man was a much-loved doctor, philosopher, scientist, inventor, botanist and poet who belonged to the Enlightenment's Lunar Society. He would often hold meetings at his house with his friends Josiah Wedgwood, Matthew Bolton and James Wyatt. The Lunar Society historian, R. E. Schofield, described the Society as 'a brilliant microcosm of that scattered community of provincial manufacturers and professional men who found England a rural society with an agricultural economy and left it urban and industrialized'. In the next few days our walk would take us through the Black Country, the heart of the Industrial Revolution.

A peal of bells rang out as we approached the cathedral close and a small elderly congregation emerged from the great west doors. We spent as many minutes as we could spare admiring this 800-year-old building which took 150 years to complete. It was extensively damaged during the Civil War and the close was under siege three times. The cathedral was restored in the 1660s and the architect James Wyatt redesigned the choir and Lady Chapel in the late eighteenth-century. Our landlady at Shakespeare Avenue had recommended we look at a carving called the Hands of Life. The artist, she told us, sent a lot of his pupils to her. The series of outstretched hands, representing pain and anger rising to hope and peace, was carved out of yew wood. The choice of wood was significant, as in modern medicine a drug called tamoxifen, extracted from yew needles, is widely used in treating breast cancer.

We left with the cathedral bells pealing joyously over the city and headed towards Cannock Chase, a large area of open heathland and conifer plantations, often referred to as the green lung of the West Midlands. William I declared it a Royal Hunting Forest, but by the sixteenth-century the trees of the Chase were being felled to smelt iron and much of the land was rented out to charcoal burners. Thousands of acres were stripped of their trees and by 1610 the whole area was completely deforested.

At the south-east corner of the Chase we walked through the villages of Hammerwich and Burntwood; judging by their names they were probably centres for smelting iron. Today the neat brick houses have PVC windows and doors and their porches are decorated with pink candles, plastic flowers and sleepy cats.

On the highest point of the Chase we found Castle Ring, an impressive Iron Age hill fort covering fourteen acres. It was built by hunter-gatherers two to three thousand years ago and the huge triple ramparts must have taken a lot of muscle to construct.

Cannock Chase remained deforested, and in the nineteenth-century coal mines were sunk. An economic upturn and population explosion followed. At the outbreak of the first World War it was decided to use the now black and bracken-covered Chase for trench warfare training. The military hospital at Brindley Village received wounded from the trenches. We spotted the old railway line, which connected the two large army camps at Coppice Hill and Brindley Heath.

Trees were planted on Cannock Chase between the wars and the coal mining finally came to an end in 1993.

Today the Chase is once more dressed with conifers and hardwoods, bracken and scrub, and is criss-crossed with paths. The Marquis' Drive was heaving with cyclists, walkers and riders. Although it had only been a fifteen-mile (twenty-four kilometre) day, there was a knock-on effect from our twenty-one miles (thirty-three kilometres) the previous day, and my legs were letting me know all about it. However, help in the shape of John Higgins, who ran a bed and breakfast and walking holiday business, was at hand.

We had contacted John before we left home, to ask if he could give us bed and breakfast for one night. Not only had he agreed, but, even better, suggested that he put us up for three nights in a self-catering annexe at his home. He also offered to drive us to and from our destinations. We had just finished a welcome cuppa in the Milford Tea Rooms on the north side of Cannock Chase when John, an energetic man who had taken early retirement, scooped us up and drove us back to the Old Furnace, Greendale, Oakamoor, where his comfortable annexe gave us all mod cons with a boot-drying service thrown in. For two glorious days we were going to walk without packs and enjoy the privacy and comfort of our own place.

The next day John drove us the thirty miles (forty-eight kilometres) from his home in Greendale back to Milford. He was both enthusiastic and knowledgeable about the area, and confessed that Staffordshire had been voted the least popular English county in a recent *Country Life* poll. 'I'm not given to your disgusted letters,' he told us, 'but I had to let them know just how many fascinating things there are to do and see here.' To demonstrate this, he took us on a detour to Tixall Gatehouse where he parked his car in a lay-by and pronounced proudly, 'This is probably the finest sixteenth-century gatehouse in all England.'

We climbed out of the car to have a better look at this massive stone building with its four turrets and cupolas dwarfing the arched 'gate' itself. Nine mullioned windows covered the front, with supporting Greek columns. A stone balustrade topped the magnificent building, and we noticed a twenty-first-century man sunning himself on the roof. The house had been demolished in 1924 and the gateway looked surreal standing alone in the middle of a field.

'This is where Mary Queen of Scots was captured while she was out hunting in the remains of Cannock Forest. Elizabeth I had learned of the Babington Plot and thought Mary was implicated. She was held at Tixall for seventeen days without attendants or personal belongings. When she left, a crowd of beggars gathered at this gatehouse for charity as she passed by on her way to Chartley Hall. Mary had to tell the beggars that she was no better off than they were – rather worse, in fact, as she was executed at Fotheringhay in 1587.'

John ended his potted history and swiftly returned us to Milford ready to start the day's walk. The sun was shining and there was no weight on our backs. All was well with the world as we descended the now-wooded Chase and left the Heart of England Way for the Staffordshire Way. We soon found ourselves in broad acres of parkland belonging to Shugborough Hall, family seat of the Earl of Lichfield. The palatial house is now owned by the National Trust and a gamekeeper's fair was advertised.

Across the green fields of Shugborough Park we could see narrow boats moving slowly along the Trent and Mersey Canal, toys beneath the thickly wooded slopes on the far side. A pair of curlews were courting, rising and falling in balletic flights. We then crossed the longest medieval bridge in

England, built for the Earls of Essex to gain access to Cannock Chase for their hunting exploits. Its fourteen perfect arches spanned the river and we quite expected to see a packhorse.

The Trent and Mersey Canal was full of brightly painted narrow boats. It runs for ninety two miles (145 kilometres) to Manchester where it links with the Manchester Ship Canal to Liverpool. Birds were singing and the sun was warm on our faces; the only problem was the diesel fumes from the back of a narrow boat travelling at exactly the same pace as ourselves. We couldn't overtake and we were loath to hang back and lose time. When we left the canal at the next bridge, a young woman on board shouted: 'You're doing four miles an hour beautifully.'

To celebrate and wash out the fumes, we had a short intermission at Ye Olde Dun Cow at Colwich, before continuing on the remaining ten miles (sixteen kilometres) through undulating countryside and affluent farms. We were impressed by the new stiles and well-kept path of the Staffordshire Way.

Abbots Bromley was an interesting village with no less than five pubs. Our visit to St Nicholas church explained why: every September twelve stalwart locals dress up in medieval costumes and don a weighty pair of reindeer antlers. They proceed to dance through the streets followed by the villagers, dine with the local lord and dance back again. After this thirst-making exercise the entire village rounds off the day in all five of the local pubs. The irony of this wonderful pagan festival is that the reindeer horns are carefully hung up inside the church where they gather dust till the following September.

It was a real treat to be met by John in Uttoxeter at the end of the day, and driven back to our comfortable annexe. After writing up our walk in my diary, I made a note that I had paid British Gas £65.00 and put it on a direct debit account. We weren't entirely nomadic. There was no television but we heard the news on the radio that the coalition forces had toppled Saddam Hussein's regime.

Next day, after John dropped us back in Uttoxeter, we crossed the River Dove into Derbyshire and from rising ground we could clearly see the Weaver Hills. We had almost finished the flat part of the walk and from now on the E2 would be taking us into the Peaks and then onto the Pennine Way. The route would flatten out again between the Scottish Borders and Glasgow, but after that it would be uphill all the way. Little did I know what we were in for in the coming months.

In the village of Rocester (its name a Roman legacy), we found Tutbury Mill, a derelict cotton mill which was built by Arkwright in 1782 and until recently owned by the Courtauld company. Arkwright was responsible for the water frame that could spin 128 strong threads at any one time and did not require a skilled operator to run it; he also invented the carding frame. Together with his business partners, he set up a factory on the banks of the River Derwent in Cromford, Derbyshire, and from this foetus of the Industrial Revolution mass production was born. His factories and methods were widely copied throughout England and around the world, and with them came the notorious exploitation of the working classes and use of child labour, now only too familiar in the Third World. Our next glimpse of industry was a twenty-first-century quarter-of-a-mile oblong of green steel, complete with Geneva-Lake fountain in landscaped grounds. This was the JCB factory that would have helped our Iron-Age ancestors with their fort building.

From the stone village of Alton, we could see the turrets of Alton Towers perched on the edge of a wooded precipice high above the River Churnet. Arthur Mee described it as 'the Magic of Prospero', but today this Gothic-style mansion is best known as an adrenalin-releasing amusement park. The high-pitched sounds of terror from those enjoying the thrills of the park's Ripsaw and Nemesis rides echoed across the river; to us it seemed more like a scene from a Gothic horror movie or Tolkien's *The Lord of the Rings*.

The last two miles of our day's walk took us through the beautiful beech woods of the Dimmingsdale Valley. This enchanted place came as a surprise. Glades of beech trees with gnarled roots grew from the bare rocks beside the stream. Among the carpet of dead leaves we found deep pools, once used in the smelting process, and now it seemed waiting for elves and fairies to bathe there. We walked past the site of the first furnace in the county of Staffordshire, which dated from 1593, and noted an old carriageway. Later John Higgins told us it had been built by the Earl of Shrewsbury on his land so he could drive his coach and four to church every Sunday without being seen by the locals. From a National Trust viewing point at Toot Hill Rock we looked down into the Churnet Valley, tucked down amongst trees far below. The Weaver Hills, a smudge of grey on the horizon, marked the start of the Pennine chain. As our self-catering annexe at Old Furnace, Greendale, was only minutes from our E2 route, we had no need of wheels that evening.

The towpath along the Caldon Canal took us past the Churnet Valley Railway and Cheddleton Station. The railway had opened in 1849, and the last stretch of the line between North Rode and Macclesfield closed in 1988. It was saved by railway enthusiasts, and the first steam operated train ran again in 1996. The wood and brick station buildings, newly painted in maroon and white, were reflected in the still waters of the canal. The Consall lime kilns, hefty brick buildings, were well placed beside this integrated transport system and have also been rescued from decay. The seventeen-mile- (twenty-six-kilometre) long Caldon Canal was first opened in 1779 to bring limestone and flint from the quarries in the hills to the factories of Stoke-on-Trent. It drew its water from the Rudyard Reservoir, and survived until the 1960s. After a period of lying fallow, it was reopened for navigation in 1974.

At Cheddleton Flint Mill we felt the industrial revolution was really on us. This ghost mill dates back to the thirteenth century, and was converted for flint grinding around 1800. The flints were used to glaze fine bone china in the pottery industry. The ceramic colours were also prepared here by heating and grinding a mix of metallic compounds. The powders were then weighed and casked ready to be despatched to their customers by horse-drawn cart or narrow boat.

We wandered round the blackened brick buildings, silent water wheel and mill workers' cottages. Looking back from the twenty-first-century, it is hard to imagine this peaceful spot, set deep in its wooded valley, in the days of steam and coal. The noise must have been deafening: the loading of coal onto the waiting barges, the splitting and crushing of limestone from the kilns, the hiss of steam from the engines and screech of winding gear from the deep shafts of the ironstone mines. Add clouds of dust from coal mines and lime kilns, throw in dark smoke which hid the sun and then settled over everything, and you have a recipe for the Black Country. It is ironic that the end product should be intricately painted fine bone china, which would find its way to the most prestigious dining tables in the land.

The Victorians had some strange names, so I never thought anything about Rudyard (as in Kipling) until we reached Rudyard Lake. This attractive reservoir, known as the silver lake, was built in 1800 to supply the national canal system. It became a favourite Victorian holiday resort for, amongst others, Lockwood Kipling and his girlfriend Alice Macdonald. The story goes that he proposed to her here and she accepted.

Although their famous son was born in India, they named him after this romantic spot. Much more fun than the other story that Rudyard got its name from the ruddy soil hereabouts. From the many ostentatious mansions on the west shore, its popularity as a Victorian holiday resort is not in doubt. Two were particularly striking: Lady in the Lake, a boathouse built on stilts over the water with its own drawbridge, and further along a castellated mansion overlooking the lake and wooded hills that run down to it.

As we left the Staffordshire Way and joined the Gritstone Way we realized that our walk was changing. The path took us east instead of west and we had a good view of the Roaches, a dramatic rocky ridge, whose name is a corruption of *rocher*, the French word for rock. We were also at the corner of three counties, Staffordshire, Cheshire and Derbyshire. Moving from one county to another was always a welcome sign of progress. There was a chilling wind as we climbed the bare hillside to the communications tower on the top of Crocker Hill and looked down on the great spread of the Cheshire plain below us. To the west we could see the Prestatyn Hills in Wales, the River Dee and the Wirral. Manchester, the southern Dales and the Pennines were visible to the north. Richard was gazing thoughtfully into the middle distance.

'What's the date?' he asked suddenly.

'Thursday, April the tenth,' I replied, pleased that I had remembered.

'D'you realize,' he said slowly, 'at this very date on our coastal walk in 1995, we had reached much the same latitude as we are now.'

The cold wind was making our noses run; Richard groped in his pocket for a hanky and smiled indulgently at my puzzled face.

'The significant thing is that in 1995 it had taken us four

and a half months to reach this latitude. This time it has taken us under a month.'

'Something to do with ins and outs and rollercoasting foot paths,' I said, pulling on a pair of gloves and remembering the steep and tortuous paths of the south-west Peninsula.

The most striking feature on the plain below us was a giant edifice whose concrete arms were holding a great dish as if in supplication to the gods. It was Jodrell Bank, searching the frontiers of space. Our frontiers were different now. We were leaving the soft south behind and with it all the generous hospitality of friends and relations. The very next day we would be setting off on the backbone of England, as the Pennines are called. We would have to be strong and resourceful. I was still worried about carrying my pack across those notoriously difficult hills. Richard was worried about accommodation. He would be carrying our tent, which we had arranged to be brought up to Mankinholes by Richard's Rotarian friend. The tent was brand new and we would have sleeping bags, a cooker and fuel to add to the weight of our packs. The weather was crucial. So far we had been lucky, but we felt it couldn't last.

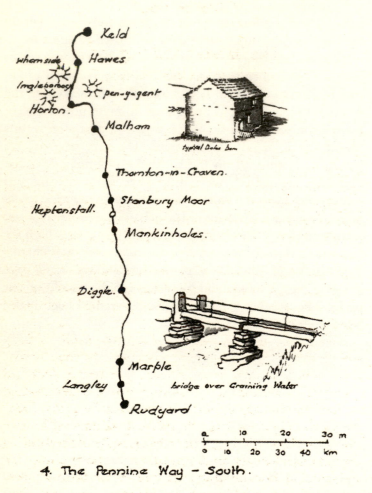

Keld

Hawes

whernside

Ingleborough

pen-y-gent

Horton.

Malham

typical Dales Barn

Thornton-in-Craven.

Stanbury Moor

Heptenstall.

Mankinholes.

Diggle.

Marple

bridge over Graining Water

Langley

Rudyard

a   10   20   30 m
0   10   20   30   40   km

4. The Pennine Way - South.

Chapter Four

The Backbone of England
– Pennine Way South

Leaving Langley village we passed a large dilapidated building, which was all that was left of the old mill, and a row of weavers' houses. Our landlady told us that the mill, founded in 1826, once employed up to a thousand people. The silk was imported from India, woven, then decorated using copper or brass pattern blocks. Mae and Peter had a beautiful example of one of these brass blocks mounted on the wall of their home.

'A few years ago they were chucking them out by the thousand,' Mae told us matter-of-factly. 'What wasn't taken was just burnt. We rescued this one, gave the brass a good polish and framed it. Lovely, isn't it?'

Standing proud, a rampant lion and the heads of King George V and Queen Mary on coins were displayed inside an intricately worked frame of brass. The entire block had been handcrafted and was a work of art in itself. We just wished we had been in Langley when they were up for grabs. Today the weavers' houses make desirable residences with three storeys and large windows under the eaves. Before and during the Industrial Revolution, family labour was utilized to weave and spin cloth from home in these well-lit garrets (penthouses today). Women could combine manufacturing with their household and childcare tasks to supplement family incomes. The advent of Arkwright's water frame in 1769 hastened the demise of this 'cottage' industry. However, spinning Jennies of up to sixteen spindles were used in domestic premises and some silk weavers in the 1840s and 1850s even had steam engines installed in the top storey of their homes: a good test for the floor boards. We were to find many more of these multi-storey weavers' houses in the valleys along the Pennine Way.

Our stamina was about to be tested with twenty-one hilly miles (thirty-three kilometres) in front of us. The first steep climb out of Langley was up a hill named Tegg's Nose. From just above his nostrils we had a good view down onto the rooftops of Langley and the old mill (about to become a housing estate) and on beyond Macclesfield to the Cheshire plain. We were standing on a disused millstone grit quarry. Traditionally, farm and quarry men would have walked to work and back daily and many of the routes they took have been incorporated into the public rights of way of the area.

The little round hills were fringed with copses of hardwoods, small villages with names like Rainow and Pott Shrigley hid amongst the trees. The fields were full of sheep and lambs. Farmers were out muck-spreading and liming the soil; this rural scene hardly seemed like the outskirts of Greater Manchester. Once up and onto Park Moor we had a good view of the bleak rolling moorland of the Pennine chain and then down we went again to the Peak Forest Canal. The glassy surface of this deserted waterway mirrored every bridge, tree trunk and twig. On the outskirts of Marple at the junction with the Macclesfield Canal, the ground dropped sharply. The sixteen locks here carry the Peak Forest Canal down 214 feet (66 metres) towards Manchester; it makes an interesting walk into the town of Marple where the canal merges seamlessly into the town, passing house backs, parkland, tall trees and steep hillsides. I was too tired to fully appreciate the wonders of Industrial Revolution engineering. A major canal aqueduct and an impressive railway viaduct spanned the valley at the foot of the locks where we crossed the River Goyt. I remember looking longingly at a refurbished mill hoping it was a tearoom.

'It's not far now,' Richard reassured me, knowing my late afternoon addiction.

We had booked our bed and breakfast before we left home and received some very clear instructions. 'When you reach Compstall, just go through the park down to the river and turn left along the main road. You'll find a restaurant there and you'll see Benches Lane on the right. We're number four.' Else Ramsbottom made it all sound so easy. We had imagined an urban park and a main road with terraced streets. Richard had a look at the map and found the park in question was a large country park in a very steep valley below the road.

As Communications Officer, I decided to ring our landlady again. The instructions were identical. We set off uphill along a main road, as Richard thought this would be quicker. It was half past five and the sun was low in the sky. The town disappeared behind us; we passed first the 40 mph limit sign and then the speed derestriction sign. The Etherow Country Park hung below us on one side and wooded hills rose up on the other. No terraced streets, no restaurants, nothing but miles of tarmac. It was a classic example of the nature of expectations. When they are not met, there is a tendency to go into emotional decline, enhanced by weariness if the body at the end of a long day's walk. Richard went on ahead, anxious to find the way. I plodded on as fast as my overworked and underpaid feet would allow. Eventually the figure at the top of the hill stopped, and when I caught up he was looking a little more cheerful. Pointing to an exit path from the Country Park he said, 'This is where she told us to leave the park. There's a restaurant further down the road and her house is up that lane. Look.' He pointed across the road.

Once in Benches Lane I was expecting a row of tightly

packed houses with number four near the main road. The lane took us up a steep hill for half a mile before we reached the fourth house. I came to the conclusion that our landlady had never walked it.

Else Ramsbottom was on the phone when we arrived. She put it down just long enough to open the door and tell us where to go. Our garret under the eaves seemed the height of luxury living. We had to stagger a further half-mile to the restaurant, but at least it was downhill and provided food, drink and entertainment. A lady with peroxide hair and a tight-fitting jumper was perched on a barstool talking at an audience of several attentive men. Her voice was clearly audible throughout the bar.

'If you want an efficient cremation,' she was saying, 'Stockport's the place for you.' Warming to her theme she continued, 'Even then they do take forty-five minutes, but no messing, they do a thorough job.' She paused for a sip of lager and lime and lowered her voice. 'You see, they even remove the titanium joints and bury them separately.' She stopped, listening to the silence, before adding, 'I should know, I sell the furnaces.'

When we returned to our room we saw the bright lights of Stockport over the trees.

After five days without news of the outside world, we watched the television and learned that although Saddam's regime had been overthrown, neither the dictator nor any weapons of mass destruction had been found.

Saturday 12 April and we were on our way to Diggle. Richard was doing some statistics. 'We've been walking four weeks, covered a distance of 425 miles [680 kilometres] since leaving Dover and only had three hours of rain.' It was our conversation hour and we were walking side by side.

'Fantastic,' I replied. 'Keep it up. By the way, where is Dover?'

Down in the Etherow valley on the outskirts of a town called Broadbottom (we had to be approaching Yorkshire) we found what looked like rows of stone coffins. They were silk dying vats near the river, dated 1802, more evidence of the once thriving textile industry in these parts. Climbing out of the steep valley we had a good view of Kinder Scout, a dome-shaped hill on the Pennine Way. Fortunately our E2 route eschewed the initial two days in these bleak hills. The twenty-eight-mile (forty-five-kilometre) stretch from Edale to Standedge is notorious for clammy mists and bogs over desolate terrain. We would join the Pennine Way when we left Diggle.

The landscape gradually changed from soft green hills and steep wooded valleys to open moorland, coarse grass, reed and blackened heather. A row of pylons stood like alien robots and a dark reservoir loomed in the distance one of the many sited on these bare hills to quench the industrial thirst of the towns and cities below. We ate our sandwiches by a peaty stream, watched by a pair of mallards on the far bank. As soon as we started eating, my lady swam smartly across the water and quacked noisily for food, leaving the embarrassed drake on the far bank. Like most men I know, he didn't 'do' begging. Our meal was accompanied by typical moorland sounds: the honking of Canada geese, the bubbling notes of a curlew, the startled mew of lapwings, lambs bleating and the tetchy cry of grouse. In this lonely place we saw a ewe with staggers, an affliction due to a calcium deficiency which makes the ewe unable to stand and eventually kills her. She was lying down, unable to feed her two distraught lambs. It bought home to us the vulnerability of all creatures up here; unless a farmer is at hand to help, only the fittest will survive.

The path took us through heather-covered slopes and dry stone walls. We looked down on lines of tightly packed houses,

Victorian churches, and the dark mills of Mossley. The shadow of the 'Moors Murders' hangs over the town like a shroud. The perpetrators, Myra Hindley and Ian Brady, were jailed for life in 1966 for the sexual abuse, torture and murder of three youngsters whose bodies were buried on Saddleworth Moor.

Richard had had to do some inventive planning at this point to get us through a network of different long-distance paths. From Mossley we left the Tame Valley Way for the Oldham Way and walked down to the Huddersfield Narrow Canal, which would take us to our destination at Diggle, one of the Saddleworth villages.

Uppermill was slowly making the transition from eighteenth-century industry to twenty-first-century tourism. Among the craft shops we found a very basic tea-room-cum-shop with a loo off the kitchen, everything the walker needs at teatime. The old mills were now smart new apartments, museums and a tourist office.

A couple of miles further on found me peering through the iron bars at the mouth of an endless dark drain. This was the Standedge tunnel on the Huddersfield Narrow Canal; an extraordinary achievement which took seventeen years to build and cost fifty lives. It was opened in 1811 and was recorded as the longest, highest and deepest tunnel in the country, taking the canal from Diggle to Marsden, a distance of over three miles. This awesome tunnel lies 600 feet (185 metres) below the moors. Before the canal was built, the only way to get goods and freight across the Pennines was by packhorse so, until the advent of the railways, the canal made transport much more efficient. The last commercial boat went through in 1921 and the canal closed in 1944 when it silted up and became a rubbish dump. Restoration work started in 1974 and the canal was finally reopened in 1997 at a cost of around thirty million pounds.

Suffering mild claustrophobia, I removed my nose from the bars and asked Richard, 'How did the barges get through?'

'The bargees would have to push it through with their feet against the sides of the tunnel. It's called legging it.'

I shuddered, thinking I'd rather leg it for any number of miles in the open.

Mr and Mrs Rhodes were entrepreneurial locals who farmed, ran a successful B&B, and rented their land out for caravans and their stables for horses. They were also a fund of knowledge. The Saddleworth area had once supported as many as thirty cotton and woollen mills and Samuel Rhodes, a relation, they told us proudly, operated the Dean Head mill in 1818.

'Early in nineteenth-century,' Mrs Rhodes told us, 'there were two thousand 'andlooms in Saddleworth weaving finest broadcloth in Yorkshire.'

She also told us that she was secretary of the Diggle Brass Band and that they were on a winning streak. They had taken a coach to Dundee last September for the National Finals. 'And,' she added, looking out of the window at the fields, 'we've 'ad no rain since beginning of March.'

Our fellow-lodger had his head down into his plate and said nothing throughout breakfast, apart from grunting an initial greeting. When he had gone Mrs Rhodes told us, 'Jim cumes down from Edinburgh for shootin' competitions. They call it Bench Rest Shootin.' She handed us our bill, adding, 'They're all crack shots. Jim's gun is so valuable, 'e brings it in at night and 'ides it under bed.' She sounded happy at the prospect. I wasn't sure whether that story was calculated to make fellow-lodgers feel safer or not.

As we set off Richard warned me that we were about to join the Pennine Way. Never mind sharp shooting, I thought, we had the backbone of England in our sights.

On 13 April, Simon, the son of our Rotarian friend Mike, met us near the youth hostel in Mankinholes and handed over the large roll bag full of camping gear and extras I had packed up before we left. I had piled in everything I thought we might need, sure that we would have plenty of time to sort the essentials from the superfluous at the handover. If we had taken everything in the roll bag it would have meant carrying another rucksack each. Simon, who was on his way to meet a girlfriend, had one eye on the clock, and one eye on our stooping backs as we struggled to decide how many more pairs of socks, cereal bars, deodorants, and T-shirts we really needed. We wrestled to put tent, cooker, fuel, sleeping bags, towels, midge nets, extra socks, deodorants and painkillers into our rucksacks on a muddy lay-by with cars whizzing past. Most of what was surplus to requirements went back with Simon, and more went home in a Jiffy bag which Leslie, our landlady in Mankinholes, was good enough to post for us.

That day we had been walking over bleak moorland, and now we had descended into a world of sheltered valleys, grey villages, grey walls and green fields. Little places like Mankinholes and Lumbutts are tucked under the bulky shoulder of the Pennine range.

Leslie, a handsome Mancunian woman, ran a bed and breakfast business while her husband worked a sheep farm. In the porch a lively golden retriever and a very dead deer greeted us. A stuffed peacock gave us a glazed stare in the wood-panelled hall, and several china Staffordshire dogs lurked under the nineteenth-century table. There was a beautiful patina on every piece of furniture and all the tables and sideboards were covered in antiques: French ormolu clocks, Chinese vases, thatched cottages, jardinières and lamps to die for. Persian rugs brightened the pile carpets and long case clocks ticked gently. A huge rhinoceros stood on the carpet outside our beautifully co-ordinated bedroom. Leslie was an interior designer who longed to leave the cotton, co-op and chapel ethos of these parts and find kindred spirits in Wiltshire or Somerset.

We walked half a mile to the little village of Lumbutts for our supper. Thinking it wise to reach the pub early, we were surprised to find it almost full at 6.45 p.m. No problem up here, for in Yorkshire they excel at hospitality. We had an excellent and very reasonably priced meal. By the time we had finished eating our hungry-walker-sized portions, the place was nearly empty. They eat early 'up north' and you don't go out in sloppy jumper and jeans; you dress up. The women wore low-cut tops and snugly fitting trousers or short skirts with plenty of leg on show. The men were in either suits or smart jackets, and favoured ties. Strangely enough we didn't feel underdressed in our lightweight walking trousers and fleeces; we were after all only transient observers. Service in Yorkshire is quick and efficient with good wholesome meals at reasonable prices – and I'm not in cahoots with the Tourist Board.

The next morning Leslie gave us a Yorkshire breakfast under a man-in-the-moon mobile, and made us some wholesome Yorkshire sandwiches. On the crest of Higher Moor we saw Stoodley Pike, a tapering monument to peace, originally built in 1814 to celebrate the defeat of Napoleon. However, celebrations were a little premature, for when Old Boney escaped from Elba in 1815, work had to be postponed and the monument was only completed after the Battle of Waterloo. It must have been a rushed job, for in 1854 the whole thing collapsed. The present solid edifice was built two years later and stands an enduring 125 feet (thirty-eight metres) high.

We walked down to the Rochdale Canal, an important one as it crosses the Pennines and empties into the Humber. We were now near Hebden Bridge, cradle of the industrial revolution. Wooded slopes rose steeply on the far side of the canal, but lines of industrial buildings stood on the towpath side. In this narrow valley there was just room for a transport system of railway, road, river and canal, a typical interface of industry and nature. There was a layer of ancient grime over everything: buildings, bridges, peat and the demonic-shaped boulders on the Pennine ridge. Even the sheep looked as if they needed a Persil dip.

Walking in bright sun high on the crest of a hill, we felt our feet bounding along as if on a trampoline. The peat on this degraded moorland was so dry a garden centre might have delivered it. Sphagnum (bog) moss is one of the few plants able to survive on this acidic soil and makes a thin crust of fragile vegetation. If this breaks down, deep channels or 'groughs' are formed and it only takes a few pairs of tramping feet to turn the moss into a morass.

'Hello!' shouted a pair of electric blue daddy-long-leg joggers. It was London Marathon day and they weren't going to miss out.

The Pennine Way, the first national trail in Britain, opened in 1965, has become a victim of its own success. Edale in the south to Kirk Yetholm on the Scottish border is a distance of 256 miles (412 kilometres) long. Every year, hundreds of thousands of people walk, jog, or cycle along some portion of it. No wonder it has suffered so much from erosion. In recent years, however, its popularity has waned. Miles of 'groughs' and peat hags, bogs and foul weather have turned it into an endurance test and deterred all but the most determined. We rarely saw anyone away from well-known beauty spots accessible by road. The erosion problem is now being tackled by laying paving stones and aggregate surfaces; new stiles and bridges have been erected and the path is well signed. These major repairs make for a much more enjoyable walk, yet ironically there are now far fewer long-distance walkers, and youth hostels are feeling the effect.

As we crossed the dam wall between the long narrow reservoirs of Walshaw Dean and climbed onto Stanbury Moor we saw a menacing blockhouse silhouetted on the skyline. We followed a line of broken wall and discovered that we had reached Top Withins, mythical home of the Earnshaw family in Emily Brontë's *Wuthering Heights*. Beside the unromantically restored house, the ghostly branches of two stunted trees fanned out against the grey sky, a reincarnation of Catherine and Heathcliff. Ghosts are internationally big business these days; a new Brontë Trail signpost near the house was written in English and Japanese. From this bleak hilltop we could see Ponden Reservoir, and our lodgings for the night.

Ponden Guest House was a converted barn next to Ponden Hall, allegedly the inspiration for Thrushcross Grange in *Wuthering Heights*. Richard and I sat on a pine bench in the hall and removed our boots. Something was tickling my hair. I looked up and saw a line of what appeared to be bare roots dangling from a balcony above. These botanical tentacles came from a tropical epiphytic plant, commonly known as an air plant, which derives moisture and nutrients from the air and purifies its immediate environment. The head and shoulders of a tinsel-draped plastic mannequin, with a sheep's wool wig and Victorian-style blouse, watched me pull my boots off. Then Brenda appeared from the dark recesses and showed us into the lounge.

'The first thing you need is a cuppa,' smiled our hostess, in homespun blouse, bright scarf and denim skirt. 'Just make yourselves at home while I get the kettle on.' As an afterthought, she added, 'D'you mind having an early meal? I'm going out tonight.' With this she disappeared.

We stood mesmerized. The beamed room had a Gothic arch over the fireplace and the walls were covered in original oils, watercolours and vibrant hangings. The most striking of these was a montage of Ponden Hall signed by David Hockney. An elaborate glass candelabrum with artificial flowers beneath a mountain of spilled wax stood beside fresh lilies on the large dining table. The battered copy of a Chopin étude rested on the upright piano. *Wuthering Heights* and a biography of the Brontë sisters had been carefully placed on the low coffee table. The antique sofa and well-used armchairs looked inviting. From the window the land fell away to the ruffled surface of the slate-blue reservoir.

Over the teacups we learned that Brenda's ex-husband had been at art school with David Hockney. The couple had lived in Ponden Hall for twenty years, providing accommodation for walkers on the Pennine Way in conjunction with their handloom weaving business. After their divorce, Brenda, with a lot of determination and virtually no money, created this extraordinary house. Until the Hall was sold she had no cash to convert the derelict barn. Friends lent her the money and nothing was wasted. The barn stands as a testament to recycling: the arch over the fireplace came from a nearby farm, the stone flags on the floor were reclaimed locally, and the cherry kitchen units were from trees cut down on the site. No wonder the house had so much soul.

There was a recycled element to Brenda's other guests that night. The youngish couple used Ponden Hall for their wedding reception exactly twelve years ago. Brenda, then in charge of the catering, told us they insisted on a chocolate cake (unheard of at the time). Their one bridesmaid was a black labrador.

Brenda provided us with a memorable supper of homemade parsnip soup, homemade bread rolls, chicken and lentil dhal with roasted peppers and red onions, broccoli, baked potatoes and gooseberry crumble with organic yogurt. She advertised weekend breaks, and we made a note to return.

We felt ready for anything after another great Yorkshire breakfast as we headed off past Ponden Reservoir to Thornton-in-Craven to meet a friend with whom we were to stay for two nights. Our Trail Guide gave us a 'toughness' forecast for the day: 'A grey day... over moors and mires and through the gritstone villages of Ickornshaw and Lothersdale, but by evening there will be green fields and firm footing to guide you into Thornton.' We were also given a warning about the boggy ground of Ickornshaw Moor, 'full of runnels and wet flushes'. This barren expanse of heather and bog, where once wolves and polecats roamed, is now home to red grouse, golden plover and curlew. Recently laid paving stones made the path both easy and enjoyable. However, the many ruined farms are testament to the toughness of subsistence farming in this hostile landscape; little wonder families opted to work in the mills, moving off the moor to villages like Lothersdale, which lies snugly in a deep valley.

Helen, my cousin's friend, looked after us for two nights in her house in Hellifield and met us in the village of Thortonle-Craven. The day we left she took our packs across to our next lodgings in Horton in Ribblesdale. Nothing was too much trouble. Her husband was a railway buff and she took us to see Hellifield station. While we stood on the silent empty platform, she told us a little of its history.

'Originally the station started life as the Midland Railway, Leeds to Morecambe line, and it was then at the bottom of our road.' Helen told us. 'When the Lancs and Yorks Railway started using the line, they moved the station here and rebuilt it. By 1875 the Settle and Carlisle line was finished, so this junction became even busier with three railway companies all using it. That's why it's a bit special.'

Special it certainly was. The great glass roof over the four stone-flagged platforms was supported with rows of soaring cast-iron pillars decorated with William Morris-style floral motifs. The platforms were long enough to accommodate a commuter rush-hour crowd; and, a mini St Pancras, it was more cathedral than station.

'It was at its busiest just before the First World War,' Helen told us as we admired the workmanship on the pillars. 'In its heyday it had two engine sheds and a staff of fifteen.' She waited patiently while I took some photographs, then added, 'Our terrace was built by the Midland Railway in 1899 and our neighbour's family bought their house that year and have lived in it ever since.'

It was a good example of the importance of the railway at the turn of the century. This junction was Hellifield's raison d'être; today it is just a rural village with a mini-market, a post office, a smart dress shop and a very magnificent station.

As forecast by our Trail Guide, the landscape changed to undulating fields, prosperous farms and cleverly converted barns. Swans were nesting on the banks of the Leeds and Liverpool Canal, a calm ribbon of water passing through green fields and beech woods. It is ironic that this canal is now an obstacle for modern trans-Pennine road traffic. The stone bridge has been fortified by putting a stronger bridge on top of the old to take traffic on the A59. This gave us a sense of double vision and we hadn't even had a beer for lunch.

At East Marton, the church of St Peter with its Norman tower stood among trees by the banks of the canal. It was open, and inside we met a local worthy doing a spot of touch-up painting. He told us the canal was built by Irish navvies, the JCB of the Industrial Revolution.

'Many of them,' he added, dipping his brush into a large can of paint, 'died of a plague-type epidemic. Being Catholics they were buried in a dark corner of the churchyard in unmarked graves.'

Gargrave on the River Aire treated us to a delicious slice of shoofly cake, the Yorkshire version of squashed fly, in the Dalesman Café, which invited 'walkers, cyclists and civilians'. It was like a scene from *Charlie and the Chocolate Factory*: a traditional red phone box was a chiller cabinet, the tables were supported by milk churns, rows of shelves were lined with jars of humbugs, barley sticks and sugared almonds. The waitress, all of twenty, enquired about our walk. When she heard where we were going there was a long pause before she murmured,

'It's all I ken do t' walk from car t' front door. That makes me puff an' all.'

A large sign outside read: Edale 70 miles, Kirk Yetholm 186 miles. We were now on the middle third of this giant backbone and would soon be in the Yorkshire Dales National Park and the start of real limestone country. We ate our ham and cheese sandwiches, made for us by the solicitous Helen, while we cooled our feet in the shallows of the River Aire watched by a pair of goosanders. Life was good and the real world seemed far away.

Malham has metamorphosed from a mining and milling town to a tourist honeypot, with Malham Cove and Tarn as major attractions. There was no shortage of pubs, tearooms, gift shops and tourists. The limestone landscape here has been farmed from medieval times. In twenty centuries the inhabitants of these parts have built many hundreds of miles of dry stone; wall, with careful rebuilding, much of these are still intact today. The old field systems (lynchets) are visible as long ridges along the contours, making oxen-ploughing easier for Anglian farmers in the seventh and eighth centuries.

In a temperature of over 21 degrees we climbed 400 steps to reach the famous tessellated pavements. The scarred surfaces of these giant slabs of limestone have been furrowed, ridged and pockmarked by the effect of water on their porous surface. When rock gardens were in vogue in the nineteenth century, Victorian opportunists removed hundreds of tons of limestone pavements. They can now be found in the local villages, along with some of the lime-loving plants such as lily of the valley, Solomon's seal, and dark-red helleborine.

Nowadays, although in season tourists' swarm like ants over the surface of this contorted pavement, it is at least protected from muscle-bound gardeners. On this Maundy Thursday we had the place to ourselves as we walked through the stony corridor of Watlowes Valley, dwarfed by limestone bluffs, to the open reaches of Malham Tarn, blue and inviting in the warm sun. In the late eighteenth-century, Lord Ribblesdale built the mansion across the tarn as a shooting lodge. The house is now a field centre with enviable views across the great expanse of water to the rolling limestone hills beyond.

'This was the path taken by the monks of Fountains Abbey.' Richard had been doing his homework. 'They used to farm sheep here in the Middle Ages and fished for trout in the tarn.'

'Monks weren't stupid,' I replied, thinking of the Friar Tuck stereotype. 'They chose their living quarters with one eye on the menu.'

Soon we had left the sheltered woods behind and reached the sandstone moorland of Fountains Fell. The summit lies in a field of cairns and the sad relics of an old colliery pit. Areas of erosion gaped like caries in a tooth, and there were plenty of peat hags to avoid. It was not a place to linger even on a good day, and we set our sights on the steep-sided bulk of Pen-y-ghent, which rises 2,227 feet (694 metres) above sea level. (I shall be sorry when we eventually lose our imperial measures as feet sound so much more impressive than metres.) This hill is the baby of the famous Three Peaks and we could see both Whernside and Ingleborough from its sandstone summit. Every year there is a Three Peaks race for those wanting to overdose on exercise and enjoy a mega adrenalin boost. As we wandered gently down the wide track to the little village of Horton in Ribblesdale, a thin layer of grey cloud lowered the sky.

Watching the local news on television that night from our swag-draped double bed, we saw that the peat bogland round Kinder Scout and Saddleworth Moor was burning and fire fighters were being flown in by helicopter. Peat fires are dangerous as they can burn underground for weeks, and there were fears that the Yorkshire Dales National Park might have to close. This was some indication of the exceptionally dry conditions on the Pennine Way in that year of unprecedented heat.

Horton in Ribblesdale gave us more than a comfortable night. A notice outside the Tourist Office was advertising a baggage courier service. 'Hurrah!' I said, hardly able to believe my eyes. 'My Sherpa at last.'

A quick phone call and all we had to do was leave our packs at the pub; Mike would fetch and carry them every day for the next seven days until we reached Hadrian's Wall. Richard kept his pack with our daytime essentials – lunch, fleeces, waterproofs – and decanted everything else into his pack liner; we left this next to my full rucksack in the utility room at the helpful Crown Inn.

Up on the bleak, empty hills of Cam Fell and Dodd Fell we felt a sense of vulnerability; only a handful of dwellings on the monotonous green of the wide dry valleys, and the dark squares of coniferous forests on the hilly slopes. There were also plenty of 'shake-holes' to avoid. These are conical depressions caused by underground subsidence and erosion of limestone. Some were quite shallow but it would not be advisable to put a boot into some of the deeper ones. All the calcerous underpinning of the Great Scar, the plateau on which those limestone pavements were weathered, has underground caves and cavities; paradise for the fearless potholer, but a stony downfall for an unsuspecting walker. The names we passed were revealing: Dismal Hill, Cave Hill, Ten End. Most of the day we were on grassy tracks, pack-horse roads and a Roman road. There were a few walkers where the Pennine Way and the Dales Way coincide. Several mountain bikes clicked and puffed on their way, followed by a roaring stream of motor bikes. We had noticed deep ruts from wheeled vehicles and soon knew the reason why; a handful of joyriding 4x4 vehicles with revving engines squealed past us, showering fragile peat in their wake.

It was Good Friday and the cobbled streets of Hawes were heaving with thirsty cyclists, walkers and sightseers. Tearooms spilled out onto courtyards and steam rose in the kitchens as gallons of hot brown liquid disappeared down hundreds of dry throats accompanied by scones, butter, jam, cream and cakes. For me, the Great English Tea has unique restorative qualities, enabling me to tackle even the last few miles of a long day's walk with renewed enthusiasm.

A quarter of a mile along the road we found ourselves at the youth hostel, queuing for a dormitory bed and a sheet. My pack was waiting for me but Richard's bag was missing. When I finally caught up with Mike on the phone, he told me he'd thought Richard's pack liner was dirty laundry and promised he would bring it round in an hour or two. Richard, unable to shower or change, decided that a short spell of sleep-filled oblivion would help, but someone else, busy at his ablutions, had appropriated his allotted bunk. Eventually, the weary Richard managed to find a free top bunk and gratefully put a tired foot on something lumpy which let out a furious grunt of displeasure; Richard's usual control snapped and he vented a volley of abuse. Two hours later, well fed and clean, he apologized.

Easter Saturday dawned and our spring heatwave seemed to be over. As we strode up Great Shunner Fell the wind dented our eyeballs and threatened to push stick or windward leg across the other one. The peat hags, usually black treacle waiting to suck your boot into pure gunge, were innocuous brown patches. We heard curlew, golden plover and red grouse; without the heat haze we could clearly see the Three Peaks. Paving stones had been laid near the summit where we met a family of three: mum and dad with sulky teenager. Mum was sitting down in the shelter of the cairn, bent forward, elbows on knees, gasping like an asthmatic. Dad kindly took our picture and then, looking at his wife, said ruefully, 'She's all in, poor thing. You wouldn't think she'd been training in the gym for weeks, would you?'

Our B&B that evening was supposedly just outside the tiny village of Keld, close to the Pennine Way. The trouble was that for pedestrians at the end of a long day, it wasn't near Keld. The unexpected mile and half uphill along the little road was an unforeseen effort. However, Mike and Jenny made up for it. Being walkers themselves they pointed us in the direction of a comfortable en-suite room with instructions to leave our dirty clothes outside the door for a quick march into the washing machine. A little later we were sitting on a leather settee by the fire, a glass of Black Sheep local ale in one hand and the newspaper in the other. Jenny cooked us a wholesome meal of soup, pork chops with apple sauce and three veg, and a treacle sponge. It was a husband and wife team; Mike had just sold his engineering business in Nottingham and purchased this lovely old house and their bookings looked good for a first season. We weren't far from the point where the Coast to Coast path meets the Pennine Way so hospitality was in demand.

We slept well under our duck-down duvet and set off next day in our detergent-perfumed clothes feeling as though we were starting a new school term.

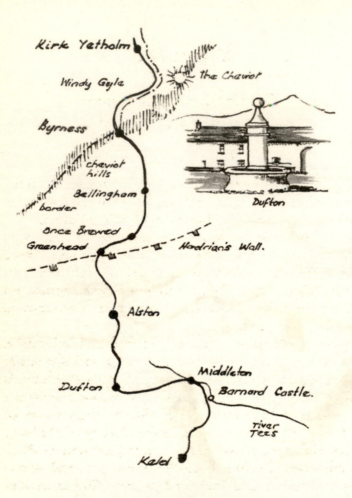

Kirk Yetholm

Windy Gyle

the Cheviot

Byrness

Cheviot hills

Bellingham

border

Dufton

Once Brewed

Greenhead

Hadrian's Wall.

Alston

Middleton

Dufton

Barnard Castle.

river Tees

Kald

5. The Pennine Way — North.

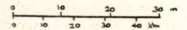

Chapter Five

The Backbone of England
– Pennine Way North

From the top of Kisdon Hill we looked down on the broad sweep of the Swale valley and the squares of dry stone walls with a lone barn or 'laithe' in each meadow. The Dales farmers erected these stone barns in the seventeenth century to minimize the distance they had to move their crop. Twice daily in the winter months, the farmer would walk from barn to barn feeding and milking his cattle and spreading dung on the adjacent fields; a seventeenth-century time and motion exercise.

As we moved north we gradually left these undulating fields and friendly copses of hardwood trees for packhorse trails across the sour vegetation of moorland. Ahead lay the isolated pub at Tan Hill, the Jamaica Inn of the north, and a sprinkling of disused coal pits and quarries. On the boggy wastes of Sleightholme Moor we were in the County of Durham, isolated in a wilderness of spongy peat and dark heather. Black clouds drained colour from the brown peat and straw-coloured rushes. Our Trail Guide warned: 'In bad weather this can be a dangerous place,' and gives an alternative route.

We seemed alone in the world apart from red grouse, a few solitary sheep and two hawks in aerial combat near Frumming Beck. The only sound was the lonely cry of curlew, and the only creatures that seemed happy in this wild environment were red grouse, their chestnut-brown plumage and scarlet combs perfectly camouflaged against the dark rust of the heather that protects them from severe weather and predators, as well as giving them most of their dietary requirements. Grouse shooting became popular following the invention of the breech-loading shotgun in the middle of the nineteenth-century. At that time, landowners excluded sheep and established a system of grouse husbandry, which is still in evidence today. Patches of heather were burned on a rotational basis to create a mosaic of different-aged growth for feeding, roosting and nesting. The grouse thrived and the shooters bagged over a thousand birds a day in the season. A precarious balance between heather, grouse, predators, keepers and landowners was maintained until after the Second World War when grouse shooting went out of fashion. In a recent revival, conservation groups have encouraged the re-establishment of heather moorland as a wildlife habitat.

The red grouse is a very British bird, solid, tetchy and conservative with a *go-back go-back go-back* call. They also have the British sangfroid, with an ability to lower their pulse rate from 150 to 20 beats per minute when sitting on eggs; in this hibernation mode they give off no scent, so even if a dog stumbled over a sitting grouse he would not be interested in disturbing her. If, on the other hand, a Pennine Way walker disturbs a red grouse, these versatile birds can accelerate their pulse rate to 600 beats in less than a minute, which makes Schumacher look positively slow. Walking along, we saw shooting butts, like military bunkers, scattered among the heather and peat. Although we found the man-made geometry of these carefully husbanded moors a minor irritant, we nevertheless enjoyed the sight and sound of these fascinating birds.

Our gradual descent led us to God's Bridge on the River Greta, a natural bridge over a puddle of water which quickly disappears into the limestone. The Way then took us through a tunnel to escape being run over on the A66, and soon we joined a few Swaledale sheep on the inhospitable wilderness of Cotherstone Moor. As we approached the Blackton Reservoir the low clouds seeped drizzle onto us and the soggy moorland was filled with bubbling, mewing and piping sounds from lapwing, curlew and sandpiper. The rambling stone farmhouse of Baldersdale Youth Hostel loomed out of the mist and on the five-barred gate was an old notice in the green paint I remembered from the bus shelters of my youth. On it was this mission statement:

This Youth Hostel is one of many both in this country and abroad where young people, regardless of race, or creed, may spend the night. The buildings are diverse in character but have a common purpose to help all and especially young people of limited means to a greater knowledge love and care for the countryside.

The accommodation was simple but adequate, uneven stone flags in the hall, a stone staircase, large kitchen and reception rooms, and the luxury of a room to ourselves with beds not bunks and a writing table. The seasoned warden told us that the Pennine Way is hardly used as a long-distance trail any more. Numbers, she told us, were dropping year on year.

'The few that do walk,' she said, 'are solitary folk, usually men with old-fashioned frame packs, heavy duty jackets or army fatigues. They keep themselves to themselves and don't want to socialize.' She closed her booking ledger and continued in a schoolma'am voice, 'Very different from the Coast to Coast walkers we had at my previous hostel. They were a competitive lot who dressed in all the latest gear and enjoyed a good natter. The only problem at that hostel was' – she tapped her pen on the desk top – 'the walkers brought their walking sticks into the lounge to see whose had the most spring. I then had to clean the little dents their feasibility studies left in the floorboards.'

Later she told us that if you book into youth hostels along the entire length of the Pennine Way, you are likely to be sharing it with the same walkers for over two weeks. Fine if they are kindred spirits, but if you are lumbered for twenty four hours a day with a real bore, you could find your holiday quickly becoming an ordeal.

'Two men who were walking the Way were booked in here for the same night,' she told us. 'Only one man arrived and announced that his companion had got lost. When there was no sign of him in the morning, the Mountain Rescue Service was alerted. The missing walker had found his companion so irksome that he gave him the slip and escaped to Middleton for his lodgings that night.'

Trying to sleep that night I fantasized about the Pennine Way walker: a dull two-legged insect perfectly camouflaged against the bleak moorland, scuttling off into the distance, while groups of brightly coloured Coast to Coasters, (C2Cs) were bouncing over the heather in large groups on their spring-loaded sticks. Meanwhile the grouse were screeching *go-back-go-back-go-back*.

The youth hostels along many of our long-distance footpaths were well placed for the walker and we had hoped to use as many as possible. Where else could you get a home-cooked evening meal for just over a fiver? Family rooms are available and a drying room is often useful. If you are in the mood you can socialize in the evenings providing you don't do feasibility studies with your new walking stick. The Youth Hostel Advance Booking Office failed to tell us that the Pennine youth hostels took their weekly day off in sequence from south to north. As fast as we booked at one hostel we would find the next one closed. However, having heard the warden's stories we felt it might have been a blessing in disguise.

It began to rain next morning as we passed the Blackton Nature Reserve, set up to protect this wetland habitat and its associated life. Sandpiper, common toads, water avens, birch, tufted hair grass, soft rush and sweet vernal grass were all enjoying the wet day. Rain does change the goalposts when you are a human out in the wilds on your feet; once your glasses get wet you either hide them irretrievably under your anorak and wander myopically along, or you have to wipe them every few minutes and that means getting a hanky out of your zipped Gore-tex pocket. This involves removing a glove with your teeth (not recommended for those over sixty) and attempting to unzip the pocket with one cold wet hand. When eventually you get in there, the hanky is almost certainly in the other pocket. By this time my trailblazer had disappeared into the mist and I gave up.

Somehow I managed to decipher a notice with the words Hannah's Meadow inscribed on it, fortunately in large letters. Hannah Hauxwell was a tough Yorkshire woman who had farmed this land all her life without the benefit of electricity or running water until she retired in 1988. Her unchanged lifestyle was broadcast on television and she wrote several books about her life. We were looking at a rare example of a traditional northern hay meadow, where no fertilizers, pesticides or herbicides had been used. Meadow flowers that would be blooming in June and July were woodcranes, globe flower, ragged robin and adder's tongue. Sheep and cattle graze on the meadows at different times of the year, which keeps the 'sward height low and reduces the organic matter entering the soil'. The wild flowers are allowed to grow and set seed before the hay is harvested in late summer.

Comfort stops (otherwise known as peeing) on the Pennine Way might have been a problem before the numbers of walkers declined. It is an area where there is no hiding place. However, I could usually dive behind a clump of reeds or a stone wall. One particular day it was not so easy; the only other walkers we saw all day were brightly coloured C2C types who headed straight for my chosen clump of reeds. I just had time to straighten up, pretending I'd been examining some rare plant, and grin at them. I fared no better at my second attempt. A man appeared from nowhere driving a mini-tank as if it was a Formula One racing car, leapt out just in front of my cover, stapled a lamb's ear, and roared on up the hillside. A metal crook stuck up like a flagpole from the back of his truck.

Our bunkhouse at Holwick was on a working farm that also ran a campsite, a holiday cottage and a restaurant. Our lodging was a converted farm building in the middle of a field with sheep and lambs all round and a view of the River Tees. Hay was still stored in the upper storey so we felt like the cattle beneath, but we had comfortable bunks, and a basic living room and shower all to ourselves. Supper was courtesy of Jane the farmer's daughter, who ran the on-site restaurant. She gave us the largest portion of home-reared lamb we had ever eaten, followed by the largest helping of rice pudding. She had just finished serving us and a party of eight when she had to go and help her dad find a lost lamb. They were a hard-working and enterprising family; qualities which help today's farmer make a living. The bill was £11.00 for the bunkhouse and £8.50 each for the meal.

Soon after leaving our bunkhouse at Holwick on 22 April we had our first sight of the whin sill, a dramatic outcrop of basalt extending across northern England, which forms some of the most impressive scenery of the Pennine Way. At Crossthwaite Scar a line of quartz dolerite projected from a row of dumpy hills and sparkled in the sunlight.

The Teesdale National Nature Reserve incorporates a river walk that wouldn't have looked out of place in a stately home. The River Tees runs through a natural rock garden; the winding gravel path is lined with juniper bushes, wide ones, tall ones, big ones, little ones, all with a smell that reminded me of London gin. This wasn't surprising as the berries were harvested to flavour that particular beverage. Less frivolously, the wood, known as savin, was once used to make the best charcoal for the gunpowder industry. The shallow Tees splashed and eddied on its rocky bed and we saw dipper (the James Bonds of the bird world in their smart tuxedos), sandpiper, oystercatcher and grey wagtails. I was roused from this rural idyll by what sounded like a motorway; all that being behind us, the roar turned out to be a foaming band of water crashing down from a shelf of dolerite over a vertical band of shale. It hit the dark pool beneath with the force of a high-speed hose. We had High Force, as it is called, to ourselves at this time of year, but in summer the far bank would be buzzing with tourists who arrive by road and have to pay for the privilege.

We noticed that the houses on the slopes of the far bank were all painted white and looked strangely conspicuous in this grey part of the world. We had been told that Lord Raby of Raby Hall was caught in a storm while out hunting and needed shelter and refreshment. If you were a lord in the nineteenth-century you didn't have to wait until you reached a hostelry, you just went into one of your tenants' houses and demanded food, drink and lodgings. On this occasion his lordship was told that the house he had entered was not one of his and the owner sent him packing. He was so furious at this slight that in order not to make the same mistake again he had all the houses on his large estate painted white, and the tradition continues today. The Earl of Strathmore owns the south side of the dale, where the buildings remain traditional stone.

The sun brought out the colours as we walked along the winding river: olive greens, russet browns, and darker patches of heather on moorland that was littered with rocks and lined with stone walls. Upper Teesdale is a unique environment, which has remained a grassy island in what was once a sea of forest. It has therefore been able to retain fragments of the tundra vegetation that covered most of Britain after the Ice Age. We were thrilled to find some rare arctic-alpine flowers: brilliant blue spring gentians, lilac bird's eye primroses, and deep blue violas. We put up snipe, grouse, and partridge (how they must have cursed us) and Richard spotted several ring ouzel and a pine marten.

We had to watch our step over the slippery rocks and the steep cliffs or 'clints' along by the River Tees. The Trail Guide warns that years of wear by walking boots have polished the boulders and regularly twisted ankles and broken hips.

Fortunately we managed to reach the dramatic waterfall at Cauldron Snout without being helicoptered off to the nearest Accident and Emergency department. The falls surprised us; as we rounded a corner we saw a snaking band of white water roaring between black rocks and the torrent widened into a fan of demonic foam before a pool subdued its fury. We climbed up the steep rocks at the side, deafened, showered and exhilarated.

At Maize Beck we crossed into Cumbria. It was then an easy climb along an old miners' track with long views of fells and moors to reach High Cup Nick, a mini rift valley named after the devil. Nothing prepares the unsuspecting walker as he approaches this geological wonder. From an opening in the basalt wall the ground disappears into a great scooped valley with the silver thread of High Cup Gill far below. A sheer curtain of the whin sill guards the upper reaches of this giant hollow where grass and scree curve inwards. In the distance the valley merges with a fertile plain and melts into the horizon. It is a Biblical scene and no surprise that we were looking at the Valley of Eden. A fellow-walker at Baldersdale Youth Hostel had told us that when she arrived here she thought she had died and woken up in heaven. Our descent into Eden was as gentle as it was beautiful. Gorse blazed in the low sun and the pastures were lush and green. Further down a lime green haze covered the larch trees and pink and white cherry blossom dripped from cottage gardens. Roses were pushing out fresh copper leaves and the air was filled with the scent of new-mown grass.

The village of Dufton goes back to Saxon times and its name means settlement of doves. The Quakers, who owned a lead mine in the area, improved the village in the 1730s after the Jacobites had destroyed the old wooden dwellings. This gives the sandstone houses and tree-lined green a pleasing sense of cohesion. We sat in Eden, outside the Stag, quenching our thirst and inhaling the scent of hyacinths. I wrote in my diary 'best day yet'.

Mandy Foster was a self-reliant woman who had lost her husband a few years ago. She ran a smallholding, ten sheep, eight chickens, five goats (which she milked twice a day) and a comfortable B&B. She had only just given up running the village shop.

'It did get a bit hectic,' she admitted. 'I had to milk in the morning and feed the animals, then off to work and milk and feed them when I got back. Then there was my bed and breakfast business. I can sleep five. There just wasn't time for anything else.'

She didn't milk us, but she certainly fed us a delicious meal and imparted lots of interesting snippets about the area.

'It may look idyllic here,' she said cheerfully as she placed a steaming casserole in front of us, 'but visitors don't know about the wind. It's called the helm, comes without warning and blows everything that moves. It can last up to two weeks.' She was holding a corkscrew in one hand and a bottle of wine in the other. We nodded enthusiastically at her unasked questioned while she continued her story. 'One day the wind blew up just as we were shutting the big shed door out there. My husband was alive then and even the two of us couldn't manage to close it so we had to use the tractor. That's how bad it can be.' There was a soft pop from the cork and Mandy put the bottle between us on the table.

'How did it get its name?' I asked.

'The helm?' She thought for a moment. 'The name comes from the helmet of low cloud that hangs across Cross Fell. It can be really bad at times.'

I had a sleepless night thinking I could hear the helm (it turned out to be the hot water tank in our room) and listening to Mandy's rescue dog doing a Hound of the Baskervilles impression when he found a hedgehog. My subconscious knew that tomorrow we had a big twenty-mile (thirty-two-kilometre) day to Alston across the notorious wastes of Cross Fell.

We enjoyed fresh eggs for breakfast and Mandy provided a packed lunch. She also fed us at 7.30 a.m. which meant we could have an early start, psychologically important on a long day's walk.

The weather was good with a slight heat haze. We strode briskly along the tree-lined lanes back to the Pennine Way and gradually ascended a conical hill called Dufton Pike. Once on the harsh moorland grass, we began climbing the flanks of a hill called Knock Old Man and enjoyed good views of the Eden Valley; Richard could even make out the hazy outlines of the Lakeland fells. Ahead, on the broad summit of Great Dun Fell, a giant had carelessly dropped several golf balls. This radar installation acts as an excellent waymark. At the cairn on the summit of Knock Old Man, walkers in other years would have been pulling on fleeces and anoraks against the elements; we were in T-shirts sunning ourselves in a small shake-hole.

'D'you know,' Richard said, reading from the Trail Guide through a mouthful of chocolate bar, 'Cross Fell is *"generally buried in snow for ten months of the year, and eleven in clouds"*.' He stowed the chocolate paper carefully in his pocket and added, 'That was written in a magazine in 1747.'

From Great Dun Fell, Cross Fell dominated the skyline. It is the highest point of the Pennines at 2,930 feet (900 metres) and we scrunched rather than squelched up its broad incline, rejoicing in our good fortune. Skylarks and pipits trilled happily. I was bouncing along, in the lead for once, when I spotted a pair of handsome birds with chestnut fronts, pot bellies and stylish black and white stripes on head and chest. I stopped in my tracks and waited for the expert.

'Dotterel,' murmured an excited voice behind me. 'Unmistakable. They're quite rare.'

I bounced along even more after that until we reached the summit of Cross Fell and then realized the world had gone quiet. The atmosphere was palpable even on a fine day, for there was nothing in this pagan landscape; no birds sang on the stony plateau, and the only sound was the sighing wind. Cross Fell was once called Fiend's Fell, and was not a place to linger. We descended to the corpse road, passing a disused lead mine, and spent a few minutes in Greg's Hut bothy, once used by workers from the mine. It is now a very basic shelter. In the visitor's book we noticed that a Dutchman was also walking to Nice, presumably on the E2. After our short break, we continued along the stony track through desolate moorland for many miles, occasionally stepping on fluorspar chips and pebbles, and noting that some of the heavier stones appeared to contain galena (lead ore). At a place with the inauspicious name of Black Gut, we spotted a hen harrier flying low over the boundary posts and I recorded the notes of a strange bird; Richard reckoned it was a curlew with a sore throat. Our sore feet were not enjoying the miles of boulders on this old miners' road, which stretched monotonously into the far distance. I looked at my watch; three o'clock and we still had nine miles (fourteen kilometres) to go before we reached Alston and a bed for the night. We were working hard for our rewards.

Garrigill revived us. This little village had a post office on the green that could have come straight out of a Postman Pat book. POST OFFICE was written on the wall in very faded letters. The creaky door led into a flagstoned passage with a post office counter on one side where there was hardly room to lick a stamp. A few newspapers and a tray of chocolate bars lay on a small counter extension. A handwritten sign advertised the magic word TEA. Five minutes later we were sitting at a table outside sipping real tea out of real cups and munching Mars bars. Back on the Way, I was happily recording the piping song of golden plover and curlew when Richard dropped behind for a comfort stop. On my own in the lead, I found myself approaching a wall with stone steps on it. On autopilot, I eschewed the path and clambered over the wall. I was halfway up the field when I realized there was no sign of Richard so I sat down on the ground (never stand with a heavy pack if you can sit). Eventually I heard someone hailing me.

'Shally! What on earth are you doing up there?' You've gone the wrong way!' Richard was peering anxiously over the wall, convinced that I must be in serious trouble. Physically I was fine, but mentally he may have had a point; after all I'd only been ahead for five minutes. My place was definitely in Richard's wake; that way at least we had a chance of getting to the right place at the right time. Single file at a distance of three metres or more could pose a problem; if Richard heard me shouting into the wind, he didn't answer, and I certainly couldn't hear his dulcet tones from the rear. I got tired of bellowing, 'Can't hear you! What was that?' Anyway it disturbed the wildlife and made me feel like a deaf old biddy. My only hope was to reduce the gap between us sufficiently to be on his heels, or, if the path allowed, to walk beside him. This was fine until I wanted to record something or take a photo, or just dream away, when my pace automatically slackened. During our round Britain walk I often had a job to keep up with his long stride, especially on the flat, but this time either he was walking more slowly or I was better able to keep up the pace, so, unless he dived down a side street or into a building, I was usually able to keep his back in sight. There were moments when I thought of giving him the book

Why Men Don't Listen and Women Can't Read Maps but I had a sneaking feeling it would just sit on the shelf and gather dust.

The last four miles (six kilometres) beside the South Tyne were soon behind us, and just after 6 p.m. we walked up the steep cobbled streets of what is reputedly England's highest market town. Alston is not set in aspic; it just hit a backwater and stayed there. Rusting enamel signs advertised Oxo and the *Daily Telegraph*. The shop names painted on boards had a pre-war look: the Alston Clock Shop ticked away, King Arthur Cycles and the Alston Village Stores. My grandmother would have felt quite at home here.

We approached from the cemetery, a highly recommended place to re-enter the 'comfort zone', and walked into this English version of a provençal village: a delightful place that would be missed by the road traveller whizzing past on the A686 below. We wandered past the tall, square seventeenth- and eighteenth-century houses of the old Market Cross and into the alleyways behind the church. These were known as the Butts, so called because archery (compulsory before the reign of Henry VIII) was practised there. We were searching for our guesthouse.

'Can you tell me where Nantholme is, please? It's supposed to be in the Butts,' I enquired of a friendly-looking lady with man in tow. She looked puzzled and turned to her man. He mumbled something and suddenly her face cleared.

'Oh, yer meen the Berts,' she cried, happily pointing us in the right direction.

Nantholme was an elegant house advertising vegetarian food. The bell was still ringing when the door opened and a man in neat shirt and trousers stood on the threshold with a welcoming smile.

'Hello! Shally and Richard, isn't it? So pleased to meet you.' Now it was our turn to look puzzled. 'I've read your book *The Sea on our Left*,' he told us, 'so I know all about you.'

Tony was running the business with his wife; they had a toddler with fair hair and an angel face, very like our own granddaughter. His wife worked, so Tony was left literally holding the baby. Next morning he served a delicious full breakfast to four of us and one screaming toddler strapped to a high chair. The dining room furniture could have come straight out of Charles Rennie Mackintosh's house in Glasgow. The elegant long table and high-backed chairs, sideboard and cabinet were exquisitely crafted in Art Nouveau style. Knowing that I was writing a book, Tony would not be drawn on their provenance.

According to our Trail Guide bible, we could expect a disappointing day's walk through Slaggyford and Lambley to Greenhead. The weather was in agreement, with low cloud and threatening rain. The path, along the tree-lined banks of the South Tyne, rang to the sounds of birdsong and bleating. At the grassy ramparts of Whitely Castle we met the Romans; this fort was built to defend a road linking the Stanegate at Carvoran with Watling Street at Kirkby Thore. It was known as the Maiden Way, probably built in 80AD after Agricola had marched north to quell the barbarians. Road building played an important role in the conquest of Britain. In 300 years the hard-working Romans built 6,000 miles (9,600 kilometres) of road to control the locals, unify the country and develop trade and industry.

Slaggyford (meaning muddy ford) was a pretty place in spite of its rather unprepossessing name: old stone cottages, postage stamp gardens filled with daffodils and a village green strewn with dandelions. On our way to Blenkinsopp Common we marched along the Maiden Way, and met our third Methodist chapel conversion, an indication of the popularity of the Methodist Movement up here. Then it began to rain. This time the smudges were too much for Richard's map reading and we lost the way. While he wiped runnels of moisture off his glasses and map case, I tried recording the thrumming of the many macho snipes that we could hear, but not see, all around us. The eerie noise comes from the bird's tail feathers as he vibrates them in the breeding season. Apart from the bleating of a few soggy sheep it was the only sound we heard as we stumbled around in the mist looking for a triangulation point. There were no landmarks and few walls or fences, just the wind-scorched grass waving like anemone tentacles when the tide comes in.

Having no sense of direction myself, I had chosen my trailblazer carefully. While I have problems finding a superstore on the outskirts of a town, Richard can find a stile, cairn or trig point in almost any weather conditions. After some deliberation, and a few moments sniffing into the wind, we ducked under a wire fence and headed up an incline where the blurred outline of a white block soon became visible.

Our baggage carrier hadn't let us down either, and we found our rucksack and 'laundry bag' waiting in our B&B in Long Byre near Greenhead. We would now be carrying our packs for the duration of the trip, and, although it took us a while to get used to the extra weight, they became less irksome as our fitness levels improved.

After two long and tiring days we had a mere eight miles (thirteen kilometres) to go to reach the youth hostel at Once Brewed, just off Hadrian's Wall. Typical Pennine weather hung round us and it began to drizzle. Thirlwall Castle, an ivy-covered fortified tower house, now as bleak a ruin as any eighteenth-century artist could have wished for, was built in the early thirteenth-century by John Thirlwall using recycled stone from the Wall, and the nearby fort of Carvoran. Although Edward I stayed in the castle during his wars against the Scots, its usefulness was shortlived, and it has been gently declining for the past 300 years. What hasn't fallen into the burn is inhabited by birds and bats.

There was some excitement locally as the new Hadrian's Wall Walk was about to open at the end of May; we passed a smart new Interpretive Centre in the Northumberland National Park complete with information boards and pictures of busy Roman soldiers building forts. When the Walk opens, the really keen pedestrian will be able to follow the line of Hadrian's Wall from Bowness-on-Solway in Cumbria to Wallsend in Tyneside, a distance of eighty-four miles (134 kilometres). The Countryside Agency has spent time and money opening up new gates and public rights of way and generally enabling the route to be walked. As I write this in 2004, the Wall Walk has been so successful that people have been asked to keep away during the winter months to allow the fragile ground to repair itself and long-term diversions may be needed in some places; the price of commercial success in the natural landscape.

Up on the rollercoaster whin sills of Hadrian's Wall, known as the Nine Nicks of Thirlwall, rain pattered on our Goretex and the wind buffeted our creeping forms. We empathized with the Roman soldiers who built this extraordinary wall, which was originally ten feet (over three metres) wide and sixteen feet (five metres) high. Along with the eighty mileforts it took them eight years to complete and used more than a million cubic metres of stone. The miracle is that they achieved all this in skirts and sandals on a diet of mainly bread.

We slipped and slithered in our strong boots and were glad to arrive at Once Brewed, our centrally heated de-luxe youth hostel, promising ourselves a trip to Twice Brewed, the nearby pub, after supper. However, by the time we had eaten home-made soup, lasagne and chocolate pudding and I had sent some e-mails courtesy of the hostel's cyber facilities, we were ready for bed. This was worrying as the day had only been eight miles (thirteen kilometres) and once again fears nagged me of not being able to manage the Cape Wrath Trail. The well-appointed late-twentieth-century purpose-built hostel had plumbing that Hadrian would have been ashamed of. The family rooms were down a long corridor, each with its own washbasin; one push on the taps and they roared and wheezed like an asthmatic lion before a moment's respite was followed by a blood-curdling shriek, then blessed silence until the next room's occupants decided it was time to clean their teeth. This serial torture went on until after pub closing time when the Twice Brewed contingent arrived in good spirits and it started all over again.

Next day Hadrian's Wall sparkled in the sunshine, and from Winshields Crags we had uninterrupted views of a switchback that would be the envy of Alton Towers. Even though today the Wall is much diminished in height, it gives the spectator a glimpse of the power and discipline of the Roman Empire.

It loops along the precipitous band of whin sill, an added deterrent to any barbarian with ideas above his station. At High Shield Crag, a vertical chasm of rock rises above Crag Lough, a peaceful lake used by a handful of swans and geese and a lone fisherman. We could see the wide expanse of Blenkinsopp Common, benign in the bright sunlight, and at Rapishaw Gap we gave the Wall its valediction and dropped down into featureless marshy ground edged by square blocks of dark spruce trees. Apart from some long-tailed tits in the plantation, we had the Way to ourselves, until a couple of male masochists came charging towards us wearing only black loincloth shorts, skimpy T-shirts and large packs. At that moment Richard announced that he could see the Cheviot Hills, gateway to Scotland and the finale of the Pennine Way.

During the walk Richard would phone his 94-year-old mum every week to reassure her that we were fit and well and on schedule and reassure ourselves that all was well. Although incontinent and nearly immobile, she still has all her wits about her and faces old age with commendable stoicism. She followed our progress with interest and was always glad to hear our news. As we came down off Hadrian's Wall Richard found a convenient rock on the draughty hillside and, holding his hands to his ears as if he had earache, pressed the Madge Hunt button. When he enquired how she was the accusing reply came: 'Yes. I'm fine, but why is it you only walked eight miles yesterday?'

We were now in the land of the reivers, an old name for robbers or bandits. These were ruthless men who carried out raids on the local landowners, stealing cattle and sometimes killing if anyone got in their way. The area north of Carlisle was known as the 'Debatable Lands', where the line of the border between Scotland and England was not clearly defined. If the rightful landowners were to sleep safely at night, they needed protection, and so built themselves fortified houses known as bastles (pronounced like castles with a b). Some of these had Pele towers, small stone buildings with very thick walls designed to withstand short sieges. We passed several ruins and one sixteenth-century fortified farm called Lowstead. Our path took us right through their grassy yard where the old stone and slate farm buildings, like the house, were in perfect condition

'The walls are four feet thick and would have allowed the farmer and his family to sleep secure from "reiving, riding Scots".' Richard was reading from the Trail Guide for my benefit.

'Why do they have steps leading to the first floor and no door on the ground floor?' I asked, looking hard at the house.

'If you open your door to an unwanted guest, it is better to be above them, a bit like Horatius defending the bridge over the Tiber.'

I took Richard's word for it, and we crossed the reedy moorland, reaching Bellingham (pronounced Bellinjam) without as much as a skirmish. The little town was silent, grey and foodless. We called in hopefully at the mini Co-op where there was no room for even two shoppers to pass down the aisles, let alone a woman with a pack. Like the Romans, we wanted some bread to fill our stomachs.

'We've got nowt at moment but cume back later. The sandwiches should be 'ere by half past seven. We close at eight.'

We returned at closing time.

'Sorry. Naw sandwiches kem in today. Thur'll be nowt till Monday,' the shop assistant assured us.

'Don't worry. Thank you so much. Goodbye.'

We were in Northumberland, land of the Geordie, and we were now the outsiders with our clipped vowels and exaggerated diction.

Bellingham Youth Hostel had just celebrated its golden jubilee and looked exactly like a Boy Scouts' hut. However, the warden was no Baden-Powell. There was one living area with Formica-topped tables and a few armless chairs near the wood-burning stove. Ted, the warden, was counting cash at one of the tables where a queue of black Lycra legs and Day-Glo zipped cagoules waited to be allocated a bed. 'Men' on the right, 'Ladies' on the left. The party of cyclists from Sunderland was in trouble. The warden was trying to work out how many men, women and under-eighteens there were, and each one was paying cash up front for their family. It took a good twenty minutes to sort out. Then Ted rose to his feet with a sigh and said to us, 'Does yer 'ed in, don't it?'

All sixteen members of the cycling club were in the pub and having a good evening. We were back in the 'Scouts' Hut', all tucked up in bed (Men on the right, Ladies on the left), when they came in at pub closing time. Now it was party time and wine and Geordie mirth flowed far into the night. When the Ladies finally came to bed, they had forgotten the party pooper. Dirty jokes time was laced with lots of giggles. As the laughs got louder, the jokes got worse. The conversation turned to the problem of snoring and the teenager opposite my bunk said, 'If sumwon snores we can blame that lady wot we don't know.' That lady wanted to shout 'Shurrup!' but she controlled herself and just snorted, 'Chance would be a fine thing.'

It was mixed weather as we walked to Byrness; heavy showers and sunny intervals over rolling moors which stretched to every horizon. The clear visibility showed miles of dark heather speckled with grey boulders, geometric patches of firs, and our little path rising and falling across the gentle hills. Cloud shadows teased the bleak moors and led us on to the beckoning Cheviots.

Byrness was more road than village; apart from an old stone chapel, it consisted of utilitarian 1930s houses built by the

Forestry Commission for their workers. The youth hostel had appropriated two of these and a voluntary warden ran them. Food should have been provided, but in the circumstances it was self-catering only. Fortunately the one hotel, half a mile down the busy road, was open. We had a welcome meal in front of a roaring fire and shared the large bar with one golden retriever.

The next day did not dawn; it rolled in like a wet dog and shook itself all over us. My mobile weather line promised improving conditions and good visibility, but as we left the hostel sodden clouds hung over the hills like wet washing. The First and Last Shop in England was our last hope for food. It only sold fizzy drinks, crisps and sweets. I grabbed two pot noodles, two packets of crisps, a handful of Mars bars and a pint of milk to see us over the Cheviot traverse.

After a steep pull up, we footslogged in wind, mist and rain for seven hours. The peat hags were death by chocolate. My boots, unhappy with bogs, sikes and burns, started to leak. The best thing about the day was the York paving slabs laid over the worst stretches by fit young volunteers. At Yearning Saddle, we stopped in the mountain rescue hut, glad of some shelter for lunch. One Rousseauesque figure we had seen writing poetry by the banks of the Tees had overtaken us somewhere and had written a few euphoric lines about the joys of life in the great outdoors in Greg's Hut on Cross Fell. Jon, as he was called, must have been just ahead for these were his words in the hut visitor's book: 'Sod the aesthetics. I've nearly finished the PW and all I want in Yetholm is a limo and a crate of champagne!'

We covered the fifteen miles (twenty-four kilometres) surprisingly quickly, seeing little but our feet. It made us realize what an endurance test the Pennine Way could be in continuous bad weather. The odd time we raised our eyes all we could see were Ministry of Defence warnings: DO NOT TOUCH ANYTHING. IT MAY EXPLODE AND KILL YOU. The MOD owns twenty per cent of the Northumberland National Park. Over the high ground at Ogre Hill, we descended into blanket bog where the well-worn path hugged a wire fence. Richard stopped, wiped the map cover with a dripping sleeve and announced that this was the boundary with Scotland. It was dreich (dreary in Scots). Richard had planned to camp at Windy Gyle, 'one of the most elegant and enigmatic of the Cheviot summits at a very respectable 2,030 feet [625 metres]'. We reached a mound of dull grey stones and Richard told me these were Russell's Cairn, a medieval meeting place for the appointed Lords of the Three Marches. If there is verbal cut and thrust in the Commons today, this was literal cut and thrust, with frequent bloodshed. Lord Francis Russell, who was murdered on that spot during a wardens' meeting in 1585, gives the Cairn its name. Strong gusts of wind snatched at waterproofs and spat raindrops in our faces.

'I don't think we'll camp just here,' I said uneasily. It was going to be a sleepless night without ghosts.

We descended thankfully from the summit, and soon found a more sheltered place to pitch the tent. Banks of piebald clouds threatened renewed downpours, but Lord Francis must have been looking after us, for it held off until the tent was up and we were safely inside. While Richard went on a water search, I unpacked the sleeping bags stored neatly in the bottom compartment of our rucksacks. Unlike the main compartment, they were not in a waterproof liner, and were far from dry. We had forgotten that rain has a tendency to dampen more than just the spirits.

It was our first night in the tent, and we were determined to keep morale up. This was greatly helped by a pasta meal washed down with the last of the whisky Richard carries for 'medicinal' purposes, finishing with an apple, a chocolate bar and coffee. At this point we heard the revving of an engine, and, looking out, saw a rosy-faced young man on a 4x4 go-kart.

'Have ye seen ma quad?' he asked cheerfully.

Thinking one of his sheep had produced four lambs, and silently congratulating him on the fertility of the Cheviot ewes, we shook our heads. It was only later we discovered that shepherds have traded in their boots for these four-wheel drive quad bikes which roar over everything this hostile landscape has to offer.

The wind rose and was gusting at 50 mph as forecast. We battened down the tent and climbed into our soggy sleeping bags with most of our clothes on. For hours the windward side of the tent flapped like a loose jib in a storm. Eventually the wind eased and we slept surprisingly well; it must have been the whisky.

When we woke there was no patter of rain on the nylon, and although the sky was overcast, it was dry. With only twelve miles (nineteen kilometres) to go and our baptism by wind safely over, our steps were spring loaded as we headed for the wide whaleback of the great Cheviot itself. Thin blue patches appeared in the sky and soon the bald rolling hills and wide valleys were lit by bright sun, darkened only by fir plantations and chasing clouds. We debated whether to tackle the detour up the 2,674-foot (820-metre) Cheviot summit and decided to conserve our energy for the Schil, our last big hill. The wind had freshened again and was doing its best to prevent us from completing the last obstacle on the Pennine Way. It was a memorable struggle battling up the steep hillside, but we were rewarded with views that made every step worth while: on the horizon lay the shimmering coastal plain with Berwick-upon-Tweed and Holy Island, behind us the dark spread of the Kielder Forest, and below the green and gold blanket of lush pastures and flowering oil-seed rape of the Tweed Valley. On the horizon we could just make out the Southern Uplands and the Lammermuir Hills.

We dropped down into Scotland, glad to be off the windy tops. Soon we were back on a small tarmac road with just over a mile to go to the finishing post at Kirk Yetholm. For some strange reason, for us, it was the longest, hardest mile of the entire Pennine Way. Kirk Yetholm hides itself from weary walkers for as long as possible, and gives them an unexpected tarmac hill to climb. Fortunately someone had put a seat at the top, and we lowered our weary bodies onto it like Darby and Joan. Just as we were catching our breath, my mobile sprang to life with a text message from our two small granddaughters: *We miss you ganny and poo. Hold tight. Good luck. Love Ella and Molly.*

Sitting by the welcoming fire, under a fine set of antlers and a swathe of tartan, we toasted our supportive family and our good fortune; even the most demanding vertebrae of the backbone of England had been kind to us.

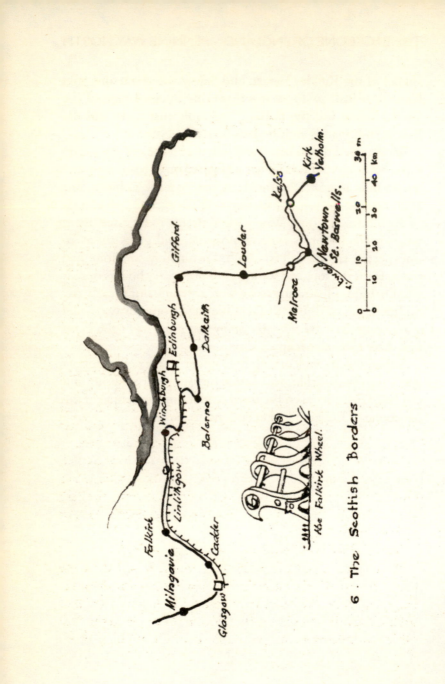

The Falkirk Wheel.

6 . The Scottish Borders

Chapter Six

The Scottish Borders

Sitting in a little cart behind the smooth brown rump of Ben, the Clydesdale, was a novel experience. Katherine Ponsonby Talbot, alias Spud, and her bull terrier Tess (yes, the names are the right way round) walked round the coast of Britain together in 1993/4 and we met up when we had finished our walk in 1995. Spud was then a feisty girl of twenty-four and the 4,500 mile (7,200 kilometre) walk was a very courageous thing to do alone. Nor did she just walk; she spent time and energy fundraising on the way, which included helping in a soup kitchen in Glasgow on Christmas Day. On her return she wrote a book about her experiences called *Two Feet Four Paws*. Now she lives with her husband and six-year-old son Barney in an old mill house near Kelso in Roxburghshire.

Ben clip-clopped into a small car park, we climbed out, and Spud tethered him to a lamp post. She then took me to a bungalow with the Post Office logo outside and rang the bell; after a short pause the door was opened by a cheerful lady in flowery apron and slippers.

'Hello, Spud! And who have ye brought today?'

We chatted about our walk for a moment and then she went behind a small table in the hall; it was littered with forms, ledgers, papers, stamps and a computer. A delicious smell of baking wafted from somewhere. Jean had been with the Post Office for twenty-seven years and there was nothing about the postal business and the village she didn't know. I presented her with a Jiffy bag of superfluous maps.

'Can ye wait just a minute, please? I've been cooking chocolate buns and the scales are in the kitchen.'

Richard and I had planned not to take any days off, but, when washed and rested, my body was not anxious to cover the twenty-five miles (forty kilometres) from Kirk Yetholm to St Boswell's the next day. Spud, who had collected us from the pub at Kirk Yetholm and brought us home for two nights of pampering, must have been a thought-reader:

'Why don't you let Richard do the walk tomorrow on his own?' she said firmly. 'You can stay here and rest.' Her hand was hovering above the phone and she was smiling mischievously, 'And while you're at it, how about a massage? I know a sport's masseur; he's got all the right qualifications and has helped me a lot.'

So when a slightly chocolaty Jiffy bag had been despatched on its way, I found myself lying face down under a photo of Roger Bannister receiving his medal after his record-breaking four-minute mile.

'He was my hero when I was a kid. I've done a lot of professional running myself and I know what it's like.' Tony was busy squirting oil on my back and running his palms over the muscle groups, releasing tension and improving blood supply. I hadn't had this sort of treatment since I was a physiotherapy student when massage was still on the curriculum. Shortly afterwards, this mental and physical tonic was discarded in favour of the machine; after all, you could treat more patients if you just plugged them in. That too fell from favour, and now joints are mobilized and the patient does the rest. I am a firm believer in the placebo effect. Our experiences with expectations on our long walks have taught me not to trivialize the psychological side of the equation. I came out feeling like Bionic Woman; next stop Cape Wrath.

The little town of Kelso has plenty of history to boast about: a castle, an abbey, a John Rennie bridge, and the largest market square in Scotland complete with town hall dating from 1816 with imposing octagonal belfry. I wandered round the wide Georgian and Victorian streets searching for an outdoor shop to purchase a replacement for my bandanna, which had disappeared into the mists of Blenkinsopp Common. For me, this earmuff-cum-hair band is a must in bad weather as it keeps the hair out of the eyes, warms the ears and controls the flow of moisture that falls onto the specs. Kelso was unable to help.

Back at the mill, Spud showed me her livestock. It was the breeding season, and multiple births were imminent. Six plump sheep waited patiently to drop their lambs; a black-spotted sow rolled over to show off her pregnant belly with its rows of expectant teats. She grunted with pleasure as Spud gave her the massage treatment; as a veteran mum, she knew these were the last few days of peace before a dozen or more squealing piglets would be fighting to pull a pint at the milk bar. Contented chickens clucked in the barn crowed over by a handsome cockerel; Ben whisked his great tail and champed happily at his hay bag. Tess, an old lady now with coast-walk arthritis, lay snoozing in front of the wood burner. In the garden, Barney was giving a Braveheart impression on the swing with blood-curdling cries that even scared the dogs.

The phone rang; it was Richard from St Boswell's, on time and in good spirits. Spud went off on four wheels to collect him.

'It was a great day,' he told us. 'After a few heavy showers the sun came out. I was on St Cuthbert's Way – we'll be on that tomorrow as far as Melrose,' he added looking at me and gulping down a second mug of tea. He rhapsodized about trout and salmon jumping in the River Teviot and the impressive ruins of Cessford Castle, once owned by the powerful Earls of Kelso. Unencumbered by rucksack or wife, he had marched along Dere Street, the Roman road we met on the Cheviots before we camped at Windy Gyle, and then followed the River Tweed from Maxton to St Boswell's. He had the look of a tired but rewarded walker.

Somewhere I felt a twinge of regret. I had hesitated about taking the luxury of a day off, and now, rested and relaxed, I almost wished I hadn't missed out. Those were my cerebral thoughts; physically my body was feeling as rewarded as Richard's.

Over haggis, neaps, tatties and quantities of Cab Sav, the four of us celebrated shared memories of the great outdoors. The next day it was *au revoir* and not goodbye.

St Cuthbert's Way is a sixty-two mile (ninety-nine kilometre) walk from Melrose to Lindisfarne on Holy Island. St Cuthbert had done a good job, for the path along the bonny banks of the Tweed was easy underfoot and well signed from Newtown St Boswell's to Melrose. Mature oak, ash and beech trees dressed the banks in fresh foliage. The woods were either white with wild garlic flowers or carpeted with bluebells; clumps of primroses hid in nooks and crannies. Spots of rain and a few trout ringed the slow wide river, where swifts and martins swooped low for insects; buzzards soared on the thermals and the air smelt of garlic and wet grass.

Beyond the river lay the bare slopes of the Eildon hills, volcanic triplets, and a stone marking the site of the Eildon Tree where, legend tells, the thirteenth-century poet Thomas the Rhymer met the Queen of the Fairies. She entranced him and led him away to the Elfland where he stayed for what he thought was three days but was in fact seven years. When he left, he was given the gift of prophecy. His legacy, apart from prophesying that there would one day be a bridge over the River Tweed visible from this spot, was some of the earliest examples of Scottish poetry.

'Wonderful things fairytales; sort of thirteenth-century spin on doing a bunk with a fair lady on a white horse.'

'Never believe anything you are told,' Richard replied wryly, 'especially if it comes from a politician. Many of them think they're latter day prophets.'

Richard was certainly a doubting Thomas, and I had to prove myself by producing either verbal or material evidence for almost everything I did or said. This created a certain amount of resentment on my part.

The sandstone houses and ancient abbey of Melrose catered largely for tourists; tea shops, pubs and gift shops for sensible people under umbrellas in tweeds and wax jackets. The Tourist Office was extremely helpful. Richard, a belt and braces man, was concerned about accommodation on our next stretch up to Glasgow. After a few miles on the Southern Upland Way we would be diverting from the E2 route which goes to Stranraer in south-west Scotland. Richard's plan was to walk north over the Lammermuir Hills, turning west to skirt Edinburgh, over the Pentland Hills and then along the Union Canal to Linlithgow, Falkirk and Glasgow. From here we would take the West Highland Way to Fort William and finally the Cape Wrath Trail.

'We're looking for accommodation in Dalkeith, Winchburgh and Falkirk,' I volunteered in answer to the 'Can I help you?' from a smart lady in tartan waistcoat, crisp white blouse and silk scarf.

Richard had been correct in his assumption that accommodation along this lesser known route would be a problem. However, Janet was a Scot with determination. Twenty minutes of thumbing through accommodation books and telephone directories, asking colleagues, and ringing landladies, and we were sorted. Anxious to complete our sixteen-mile (twenty-five-kilometre) day into Lauder before dark, we left the cultural delights of Melrose Abbey for another time and headed north across the River Tweed.

Our flirtation with the Southern Upland Way was brief and unremarkable and we arrived in the no-nonsense stone ribbon town of Lauder in a cloudburst. Fortunately we were booked into a comfortable B&B run by a widower. It obviously met with the approval of a South African widow touring the Scottish Borders; she had booked herself in for one night and was still there four years later. Over tea in the lounge I asked her how she was coping with the Scottish climate.

'Ya geet used te anytheeng,' she answered, settling her ample frame on an equally ample armchair. 'Ah do embredery and tepistry and that keeps me beesy in the winter.' I then noticed the fire screen, a riot of French knotted hollyhocks surrounding a thatched house with 'Home Sweet Home' at the bottom. 'Ah did thet,' she said proudly adding, 'Ya. Jim an' I geet along just fine. Ah do the cooking and cleaning and he does all th' odd jobs'. She looked lovingly at her partner who was balancing precariously on a ladder fixing the curtain pelmet.

The Lammermuir hills did not live up to their beautiful name; it was dreich and only the grouse on the foothills were enjoying it. At the summit of Lammer Law, Richard told me we should be able to see the Firth of Forth and Edinburgh in the distance. As it was, only the highlighter yellow of rape blurred the Scottish mist.

The Pishwanton Community Wood caught my eye. This was a Live Science Trust project aimed at exploring ways of developing creative and sustainable interaction between people and their natural environment. It had been purchased by the Trust in 1996 and was gradually developing a woodland based working community with small-scale agriculture, horticulture, and craft activities. Richard waited patiently while I read the information board. He was longing to reach the home comforts of our hotel; I was longing to try the thatched compost toilet, but Richard's face had the sort of expression men wear when they are waiting for women to finish their shopping, so I abandoned the eco loo and we trailed Indian file to our hotel in Gifford.

I opened a glass door with ENTRANCE on it, and found a small room filled with cardboard boxes and piled up with chairs; a black cat on the reception desk greeted me with a startled 'miaow'. I returned to the rain and checked the grinning goblin on the hotel sign. We walked along the glazed frontage and found a door leading into a Scottish-Conran-style dining room and bar. Fires blazed at each end of the long room and a bar ran along its length. A smart young lady in black was putting coals on the fire at one end. She straightened up as we approached and looked at us with thinly disguised horror.

'Jest how canna help yew?' she demanded, holding the poker like a sword; drips from our Gore-tex were audible on the shining floor boards.

'We're booked in for tonight,' I said firmly. 'We paid a fifty-pound deposit back in March.'

'What's the name?' She frowned. 'We're no' expecting anyone in tonight.'

We gave our name. She disappeared and returned with a tall gentleman in a black waistcoat. 'Y'are booked in,' she said with disbelief. 'The only problem is the room's no' ready.'

By this time I had removed my Gore-tex and sat myself by the fire.

'John'll check the room.' Her voice was more civil now.

'That's fine,' I said, relieved that we weren't out in the rain. 'Could we have a cup of tea while we wait please?'

Our experience had led us to expect that anything having

the suffix hotel or guest house asked more and gave less than a no-frills B&B. It looked as if this would be no exception. After a cup of luke-warm tea, John took us through the silent reception and up several creaky flights of stairs to our room. He gave us strict instructions on what to do in case of fire and apologized for the upheaval.

'We're having work done here at the moment. Do let me know if there is anything else you require.'

The room was small with partitioned en suite facilities; chintz swag curtains with matching fabric on an easy chair gave an upmarket feel. The heating wasn't on, a pile of superfluous sheets lay on the television, drawing pins were heaped on the dressing table and the bedside lamp didn't work. I could have forgiven all this if the bathroom had had any towels.

Gifford was enchanting in the bright sun of the following morning. The model village with rows of vernacular eighteenth-century houses lined the wide street from the T-shaped church to the Market Cross. The village green, with an avenue of lime trees, ran at right angles to the main street. The village is named after the Gifford family who owned the castle in the twelfth-century; the Goblin Ha', an underground chamber reputedly the work of fairies, still remains. In the sixteenth-century the lairds built themselves a new mansion, enclosed the park and moved the inhabitants to the present village.

We walked out beside the high stone wall of the park, behind which magnificent oak, beech and lime trees showed off their fresh new leaves to passers-by. It was May but we were having the sunshine and showers of an April day. There were good views of the Firth of Forth and King Arthur's seat, a solitary hill of basalt just outside Edinburgh. We could even spot the Bass Rock, a 350 feet (106 metres) high volcanic plug rising out of the sea off the coast. East Lothian was a colourful striped canvas: cattle and sheep grazed emerald fields, neat hedges separated the rich brown of ploughed earth from strips of Day-Glo rape, and Scots pines reached up to a blue and grey awning of sky.

We felt euphoric. The walking was easy, Glasgow wasn't far, the weather was fine, and we'd ticked off the Pennine Way. Friends from Kent were going to collect our camping gear from Spud on their way up to Lochgoilhead, before giving us hospitality for two nights on the West Highland Way.

From West Saltoun we were able to walk along the Pencaitland Railway Walk, a seven-mile (eleven kilometre) disused railway track which offered a pleasant alternative to the metal road for cyclists, walkers and riders; a green regeneration after the demise of the coal mining industry. Coal mining in this area dates from 1841 and the railway walk fringes the East Lothian coalfield. Goods traffic continued on this section until 1964 and its closure was due to the shutdown of all mining works in the area. Remnants of the once flourishing industry are now only visible from the walk; a series of memorial tablets sit like gravestones among the brambles giving information about each pit: the date it was sunk, the number of men employed and the amount of coal produced. We noted that some pits produced as much as two to three thousand tons per day and one, in 1943, employed 193 men. Now the few remaining pits and sidings are resting in strangled peace, and Mother Nature is being actively managed to encourage a richer variety of wildlife.

From our high point above Dalkeith we could almost touch the Firth of Forth and the grey sprawl of the docks at Musselburgh. King Arthur was sitting on his hill with the old city of Edinburgh deferentially at his feet; with a bit of imagination we could make out the Campsie Fells and the beginning of the Highlands. Our next obstacle, the Pentland Hills, looked green and inviting in the afternoon sun.

If our usual approach to villages was through the churchyard, in big towns it was often the industrial estate. Not much here to lift the spirits, especially at the end of the day, and from the notices on the wire gates of Dalkeith industrial estate we realized that most of the factories were either closed or about to close. We were on the wrong side of the town for our B&B, but after crossing the River Esk, we found the chalet bungalow ankle-deep in wallflowers on a modest-looking housing estate. We were shown to a self-contained upstairs flat with a comfortable lounge between two bedrooms. The sumptuous bathroom had more towels, bathrobes and shower gels that we knew what to do with. Lilian, our landlady, had thought of everything: hair dryer, games, magazines, cut glass tumblers, digital bedside clock, and our own stationery. The next morning, enjoying more breakfast than we could manage, we discussed the comparative evils of midges and cleggies (Scottish horse-flies) with a vet from Wester Ross, while Lilian told us of an octogenarian she had put up who was doing the Land's End to John o' Groats walk, admittedly with day pack and support; stories like that give us all hope. When we left, Lilian, who could give me a few years, threw her arms round me in a motherly hug and said, 'Haste ye back.'

It was a bank holiday weekend and families milled round the visitor centre near the Glencorse Reservoir: mums, dads, grans, children and baby buggies all getting a lungful of fresh air. The reservoir, fringed with Scots pines, arched south towards the Pentland Hills Regional Park as we climbed gently up and over the saddle towards Balerno. The wind had freshened and sudden gusts tugged and buffeted our anoraks, making us feel the pull of the Highlands and a taste of what might be in store. Our one stick was a useful tool both for forward propulsion and as an anchor. On the Cheviots we had seen a sturdy young couple in shorts, batting along with two sticks apiece as if they were cross country skiing. We decided there and then to purchase another stick each in Glasgow.

We walked straight past our B&B in Balerno. We were after all looking for the usual modest house with a sign up, but having found the right road the right house didn't seem to exist. It was hiding behind a high stone wall, and we felt a little uneasy as we crunched up the gravel drive towards the substantial Queen Anne façade and rang the brass door bell. While we waited in the ample porch we had time to admire an array of broad-brimmed and panama hats resting jauntily on a pair of antlers, and a medley of walking sticks in a battered brass jug. A young woman opened the door and explained that the owners were in Portugal but they were happy for her to let us in as they'd be back later that night.

We removed our boots before stepping onto the polished old boards of the spacious hall, and followed our guide up a graceful staircase to a large airy room on the third floor.

'I'll be off now to collect my kids,' she announced briskly. 'I'll leave a key for you on the hall table so you can come and go as you please. Enjoy your stay.' And with that she disappeared.

As we looked east from a sash window, King Arthur's seat was now no more than a somnolent lion, and the Forth Bridge a line of Meccano. Two more windows on the southern aspect showed a row of topiary yews cut into spades, hearts, diamonds and clubs. Beyond a green baize lawn lay a well-marked tennis court. There was an antique teddy bear on the armchair in our bathroom under the eaves that was reminiscent of Aloysius in *Brideshead Revisited*. Lying horizontal on the brass bedstead we could admire the eighteenth-century chest of drawers and the nineteenth-century washstand. The Chippendale chairs were too good for our grubby garments which lay in a pile on the carpet.

On our way out for a meal, we met a man on the stairs and I asked if he was the owner. He explained in a broad Australian accent that he and his wife were also guests. At breakfast we learned that they were from the Blue Mountains near Sydney on an eight-week European tour mainly in the UK. Richard noted the difference between car and feet: our walk for the day was fourteen miles (twenty-two kilometres) along the Union Canal to Winchburgh, whereas that evening they would be in Inverness having done the Cairngorms and the eastern part of Scotland; by the time we reached Falkirk twenty-four hours later they would have done Skye, and when we reached Glasgow in three days' time they would be on their way down to the Lake District.

Balerno was long on pavement and short on food. The recommended pub did not serve meals, and, although there were several takeaways, we felt the general ambience of our lodgings did not fit with cold tandoori or pizza eaten out of cardboard. We finally settled for a seat in a pub willing to serve us crisps, cheese toasties and lager. We were hungry enough to have eaten our boots, which was just as well, as the toasties were plastic cheese oozing yellow frills over burnt bread, coyly covered with a paper serviette.

The refurbished Union Canal waited expectantly like a restaurant before opening time; everything was ready but there were no punters. Built in 1822 the canal was originally linked with the Forth and Clyde Canal to provide a seventy mile (112 kilometre) waterway crossing from the Forth to the Clyde, linking Scotland's North Sea and Atlantic coasts. In its heyday it carried about 200,000 passengers a year as well as coal, whisky, stone and other freight. The advent of the motorways drained all the life out of the canal, ironically once a watery version of the modern motorway with service stations at places like Ratho where horses were rested, barges loaded and tolls paid. After 150 years of useful life it degenerated into an overgrown rubbish tip. The Union Canal then lay remaindered, a depository for supermarket trolleys, rusty bikes and beer cans. Many of the locks leaked, three were buried under a Glasgow housing estate, some of the lift bridges were replaced by infill road embankments, and others became fixed crossings, offering just sufficient headroom for a British standard swan.

It took a brave and visionary man to resuscitate the Union Canal for a new role, not merely for leisure, but also as a 'corridor of opportunity' for waterside developments. Jim Sterling, director for British Waterways Scotland, with chief civil engineer George Ballinger, not only met this gargantuan challenge, but completed it in two of the planned five years at a cost of £78 million. It was opened in the spring of 2001.

As tourists, we were determined to enjoy this rejuvenated canal as it flowed through fields of yellow rape and beech and oak woods, and under stout stone bridges. The banks were high with comfrey and cow parsley and tufted duck and swans were busy feeding from the ruffled water. There was a chill wind and we had time in hand. The Bridge Inn at Ratho was too tempting to walk past, and we presented ourselves expectantly at the bar in a snug room with a blazing fire.

'If ye're just after a drink,' the young barmaid said tartly, 'move through to the Public Bar.'

Meekly we obeyed, and asked another harassed girl in the barn-like room for two glasses of wine. Without looking up, she put a stainless steel goblet under a pump on the bar, and out came a strange Ribena-coloured liquid which then frothed all over the mahogany counter. The girl sighed loudly, drew a second one, and then mopped up the red lake with a cloth.

We didn't improve her temper when we asked for a bowl of chips.

The old village of Ratho hid among trees on the far side of wheat and rape fields, while the canal by the bridge was filled with narrow boats offering cruises, floating restaurants and wedding receptions: all part of the vision to make the canal become an income-generator. The banks here were neatly landscaped with daffodils strewn over the grassy slopes and wooden seats under newly planted prunus and silver birch trees. The summer season had begun and the ducks waited expectantly.

We continued on the towpath under a green canopy of beeches, sycamore and oak trees, following the blue ribbon of empty water that stretched between Edinburgh and Glasgow. Yellow marsh iris softened the banks and the birds were in good voice.

The River Almond chuckled under the long stone arms of the Almond aqueduct and curved its way through mature woodland between shingle islands. It felt strange walking on an aerial pavement beside the elevated canal. Apart from birdsong and the raucous quacking from tufted duck and mallards, the only other sound was the distant roar of the M9.

Accommodation here was scarce and the B&B in Currie (recommeded by the tourist office in Melrose) was full. They gave us the telephone number of a modest B&B in Winchburgh. No meals and the local eating house was closed on Mondays. Thanks to the Yellow Pages a pizza was delivered to the door saving our stomachs and our feet.

Along the section from Broxburn to Linlithgow the towpath took us past lines of sandstone hills that rose impressively on either side of the canal. These were remnants from the shale oil industry developed by James 'Paraffin' Young in the nineteenth-century. At one time, this industry employed 13,000 people in 120 separate works; digging the shale out from dripping underground caverns must have been employment for desperate people. The men would have been soaked to the skin every day with no chance of drying their inadequate clothes properly. Many died in their forties from respiratory diseases. James Young made so much profit he was able to help finance Dr Livingstone's expedition to Africa, and push out the boundaries of an already extensive British Empire. The fifteenth-century castle of Niddry stood on its little hill dwarfed by an Ayers Rock of shale bings. It was once the home of Mary Seton, one of the 'Four Maries' who served Mary Queen of Scots.

Just before we reached Linlithgow and made contact once again with Mary Queen of Scots, we saw a pair of swans nesting on the tarmac towpath. The female was sitting uneasily on her eggs, while 'himself' marched wearily up and down hissing hoarsely at all who walked past. Someone should have told him that, when it comes to homes, location is everything.

The substantial remains of Linlithgow Palace and the parish church of St Michael were just visible above the chestnut and oak trees as we walked into this sophisticated town with its Palladian town hall and Scottish baronial buildings. We spent a pleasant 'tourist' hour in the draughty palace where Queen Mary was born and spent the first seven months of her troubled life. The elegant façade is in the Renaissance style and was built between 1618 and 1624. The solid sandstone walls give a sense of presence and the Great Hall is considered amongst the finest medieval rooms in Britain. Feasting, music, theatre and even a meeting of the Scottish Parliament took place here. Draughty it might have been, but starved the guests were not. During just one feast in 1528, when James V was in residence, his guests consumed 95 loaves of bread, 23 gallons of ale, 40 white fish, 40 codlings, 200 herrings, 4 salted salmon, 1 halibut, 2 pike and unspecified quantities of scallops, cuttle fish, butter, cheese and apples.

The thought of all that bread, fish and ale made us head for the nearest hostelry to consume macaroni cheese, chips and beer before heading back to the towpath. The Linlithgow Canal Basin has a stable block where once the horses were changed, now a museum and tearoom; several red and black narrow boats livened up the grey water. The low arch of the Manse Road Bridge showed grooves in the corner stones left by the rubbing of the ropes between the barge and the horse. Behind an old cone-shaped 'doocot' the metal prongs of the controversial crown of thorns on St Michael's parish church pointed heavenwards like crossed swords.

In the Muiravonside Country Park we found a magnificent aqueduct: twelve graceful arches spanning the River Avon at a height of eighty-two feet (twenty-five metres). We scrambled down the steep bank to the river, and were then dwarfed by the stone stilts and vaulted roof of the viaduct which was mirrored in sunlight at our feet. The cost and work put into this canal made us realize the importance placed on these waterways by contemporary engineers.

Andrew had taken early retirement from teaching and was helping Helen, also a teacher, with a B&B business in Laurieston on the outskirts of Falkirk. We spent a night in their comfortable Victorian house and had time when we got in to take stock of our progress. As always, I was finding walking on the flat gave me leg cramps which worsened as the day went on. Richard found it alarming that I was having difficulty on a canal towpath. 'How are you going to manage the Cape Wrath Trail, or on some of the long days in Holland and Belgium?' he asked accusingly.

I began to feel I was physically not up to the task; already I had taken a day off at Spud's and had then arranged for Alan and Felicity (our friends from Kent who were going to host us in their cottage on the West Highland Way) to collect our camping gear from Kelso on their way north. The plan was that we would pick it up when we stayed with them at Lochgoilhead, as we wouldn't need to camp until we left Fort William. It meant going many miles out of their way, and Richard, who was carrying the extra weight, was not happy with this at the time. We had a heated discussion on the subject but I bulldozed through his objections and made the arrangements. Later on I think he appreciated having a lighter load and Alan, when lifting the dustbin bag bursting with cooker, fuel, pans, sleeping bags, tent and inflatable mattresses, understood perfectly.

Richard's metaphorical glass is always half empty, and he really believed I would not be able to do the toughest part of our walk on the Cape Wrath Trail. I began to feel more of an encumbrance than a walking partner. We were resting on the large double bed, Richard's head in a map while I gazed listlessly at the ceiling with doubt and resentment nagging at me in equal measure. After a long while, having rejigged our itinerary, Richard looked up and gave me my marching orders.

'We'll catch a train from Croy into Glasgow tomorrow which will mean only 14 miles instead of 19. After that,' his voice trailed off as he carefully folded the map, 'we'll have to see how we go.' He sounded like a doctor who was giving the patient a poor prognosis as diplomatically as possible.

It was a silent half-mile walk for our lasagne and chips and I went to bed promising myself I would meet the challenge whatever fate held in store.

Andrew, in blue-and-white-striped apron, cheered us up over breakfast.

'I'm very happy with this life,' he said, in answer to our usual question. 'I do part-time lecturing at Sterling University to keep the brain cells ticking over, and I really enjoy meeting my guests.' He put a plate of grilled bacon, tomato, and perfectly set scrambled egg in front of us and went off for a large cafetière of delicious-smelling coffee. Then he leant on the ample Victorian sideboard, and told us that the area round Falkirk and Bonnybridge was world famous for its sightings of unidentified flying objects.

'UFO enthusiasts come from all over the world. We had one Russian self-styled expert who rang me on his way here to find out where we lived. Our conversation ran something like this: "Where are you?" "On a motorvay." "Yes, but where?" "No sure. M50 per'aps." "Where are you near?" "I just pass Wales."' Andrew came over and gathered up our empty plates. 'Heaven knows how he got here. He was ringing me up every few miles. The poor chap was having no luck with his UFO sightings so, in desperation, he asked a bouncer outside a nightclub if they had noticed any unidentified flying objects; needless to say he almost became one. Not a man to give up easily, he then asked the police and nearly got arrested. When he left I gave him detailed directions on how to reach London.' Andrew, plates in one hand and toast in the other, had a twinkle in his eye, 'Some time later the phone rang and a familiar Russian accent asked: "How I get to London?" "Where are you?" "Don't know. Motorvey hard shoulder." "Just keep going south."'

Gradually we left the town and its growing suburbs behind and joined the Forth and Clyde Canal heading towards the Falkirk Wheel. We caught a surreal glimpse of a boat travelling on a high-columned aqueduct above the trees before we saw the Wheel itself. This rotating boatlift was the most futuristic piece of functional sculpture I'd ever seen; when vertical there appeared to be two steel turkey-heads with large beaks and huge iconographic eyes. Each circular 'eye' holds a gondola, each one lifting around 300 tonnes of water and boat; when activated, the arms rotate, and the upper and lower gondolas remaining horizontal on their gimbals as their positions are reversed. They are lifted and lowered a height of eighty feet (twenty-five metres) from the Forth and Clyde Canal to the Union Canal and vice versa. This whole operation takes forty-five minutes and less energy than six toasters. The Visitor Centre, a large slice of glass and stainless steel, lies beside the round pool in which the Wheel operates. No wonder this Millennium Link between the Forth and Clyde and Union Canals is more tourist attraction than boatlift. It was still early in the day but coaches were already arriving in the large car park.

The empty Forth and Clyde Canal ran geometrically mile after straight mile. My aching legs sent my morale, temporarily restored by the wonders of the Falkirk Wheel, into sharp decline. I needed to stop every hour and stretch my thigh muscles by squatting down, glad that I was unobserved either by Richard's retreating back or any other walkers. I amused myself by trying to take photos of the many swans landing and taking off from their watery runway. Although Croy railway station was a mere fourteen miles, it seemed much further, and I was happy to let the train take the strain into the centre of Glasgow. Here we were met by my godson Simon, who greeted us warmly and escorted us back to his student flat for a welcome bath, food and bed. Richard's plan was to return to Croy on the train the next day, pick up our route where we had left off, and walk fourteen miles to Milngavie, avoiding a dreary plod through the urban sprawl of Glasgow by catching a train into the city centre. It was a mini-cheat for weary wives and would be followed by a welcome rest day in Glasgow.

We set off in the rush hour next morning to catch the train back to Croy. After so many weeks of solitude we felt disorientated in this ant hill of human activity, inhaling the smell of armpits in the crowded tube, and fighting our way up and down escalators. Back on the towparth I forgave the Firth and Clyde Canal its monotony and just enjoyed being in the fresh air.

It was eerily empty, except for a couple of fishermen near a car park where a board reassured us that the water was now clean enough to support perch, pike and roach. We met the Romans again west of Kirkintilloch in the shape of Roman camps and forts, built near the often invisible earth mound of the Antonine Wall. This thirty-seven-mile (fifty-nine-kilometre) frontier defence extended from the River Clyde to the Firth of Forth. I couldn't help feeling sorry for those Roman soldiers, marched from their native land flowing with sunshine and wine to the bleak northern climes of Britain where it rained incessantly and the natives spoke gobbledygook, ate raw oats, and threw tree trunks over their shoulders. The Antonine Wall had a short defence life; it was continually being breached and repaired until it was finally abandoned. The guerrilla tactics of the Celts and the hostile Scottish environment were too much even for the disciplined Romans. Today any pedestrian needs a pair of binoculars and a good map to locate the diminished remains of the most northern point of the Roman Empire.

Nor were these the only ghosts: on the outskirts of Cadder

we found an ivy-clad derelict church with a graveyard waist-deep in nettles and surrounded by rowan, ash and oak trees. This was described by the Canal Pleasure Steamer's Guide of 1907 as 'sylvan loveliness' in their publication *Shadowy Walks – a Shady Past*. Graveyards like this were perfect for the brisk trade in body snatching, rife during the eighteenth- and nineteenth-centuries, being close to the canal so that the robbers' gruesome cargo could be transported to Edinburgh in just a few hours. The Edinburgh Medical School was constantly in need of bodies for dissection; Robert Knox's anatomy classes at Surgeon's Hall attracted hundreds of students and they were always looking for fresh cadavers. Body snatchers (sometimes known as resurrectionists) grew in number and became more unscrupulous. Two notorious Irish immigrants called Burke and Hare came to Edinburgh to work on the New Union Canal. They were quick to see a niche in the market for grave robbers; they worked hard on the canal by day and robbed graves by night. Demand outstripped supply and Burke and Hare became serial murderers, their victims ending up on the anatomy tables of Dr Knox, who paid them and asked no questions. Burke was caught and hanged in 1829 and Hare died penniless in London in 1858. Ironically, Burke's body was donated to the medical school for 'useful dissection' and his skeleton is still on display at the University Medical School.

The church we were looking at was surrounded by iron railings, and we learned from our Pleasure Steamer's Guide that after Burke and Hare's depredations fresh bodies were bolted into iron coffins and the graveyard was watched over from the stone tower. A stiff breeze rustled the trees and the long grass swayed over the tombstones beside the grey water of the canal. We hurried on along the towpath. Glasgow was seven miles.

Sauchiehall Street was a blur of self-assured shoppers, cars, buses, traffic, lights, pedestrian crossings and plate glass windows. Sauchiehall is Gaelic for 'Avenue of the Willows' but I confess this took a lot of imagination. We spent several weary hours purchasing an extra telescopic spring-loaded walking stick each and a rucksack cover. When we returned to the flat and examined our sticks we discovered we had two left 'hands'. It was the wrong season for bandannas.

Simon was in his penultimate year at Mackintosh School of Architecture. He had generously given us the use of his room in a block of circa 1900 sandstone tenements in Woodlands Drive. He also gave up his afternoon to take Richard on a pedestrian sightseeing tour of Glasgow: St Mungo's Cathedral, the Necropolis, the Provost's House, the Toll Booth, the Clyde, Strathclyde University and Glasgow Infirmary. When they returned Richard reckoned it had been the most tiring day yet. I was sorry to miss the tour, but glad that I had given myself a chance to catch up with washing, writing and phoning. From now on we wouldn't be near 'civilization' until we reached Fort William at the northern end of the West Highland Way.

Simon cooked us a deliciously cosmopolitan chicken and then entertained us with the help of his flat mates, Yena, a Danish girl studying photography, and Ronan, a hopeful architect. We discussed the cons of the Iraqi war: Yena enlightened us on the delights of Copenhagen with her mobile phone, constantly in use, clasped under her long blonde hair like an outsize earring, while Ronan's stories of rock climbing exploits made us wonder how anyone could enjoy such suspended danger.

'It's the adrenalin flow,' he told us. 'It's addictive.'

Wine, whisky and lively discussion made a very pleasant interlude before we shipwrecked ourselves on a futon island among files, models, paper, computers, cast-off shoes and faded jeans; the high sash window mirrored the sandstone tower, mullioned windows and a dunce-hat roof of our Glasgow palazzo. Outside, bursts of wind shook the trees and blurred the glass with sleet.

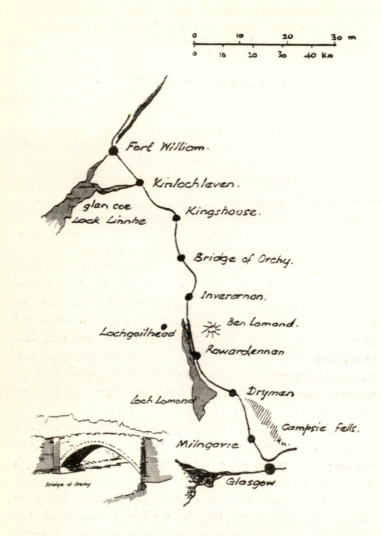

Scale markers: 0 10 20 30 m / 0 10 20 30 40 km

Fort William.

Kinlochleven.

glen coe
Lock Linnhe

Kingshouse.

Bridge of Orchy.

Inverarnan.

Ben Lomond.

Lochgoilhead

Rowardennan

Loch Lomond

Dryman

Campsie fells.

Milngavie

Bridge of Orchy

Glasgow

7. The West Highland Way.

Chapter Seven

The West Highland Way

'Two singles to Milngavie please,' I asked a glass screen on Glasgow's Queen Street Station.

'Ye meen Mul-guy,' replied a dour face busy punching out two tickets. We were in Scotland.

The train slid effortlessly past the old tenements, office blocks, and red brick Victorian buildings of the big city and soon reached the empty green spaces of East Dunbartonshire. It was Saturday, and we found the square in 'Mul-guy' filled with C2C-type walkers all busy having their photographs taken in front of an imposing granite obelisk with a thistle-in-the-hexagon waymark. They milled around in twos and threes, ages ranging from 30-something to 70-something; one group was happily dumping their packs into a large van advertising a baggage carrier service. Unlike our walk to date, we were not going to have the West Highland Way to ourselves.

The WHW goes from Milngavie to Fort William, a distance of ninety-five miles (152 kilometres) and was opened in 1980. Starting on the periphery of Glasgow, the Way passes through the gentle pastures of the Lowlands, along the shores of Loch Lomond, through the blanket bogs of Rannoch Moor to Glencoe and Ben Nevis. It uses abandoned coach roads and railway lines, old drove roads and military roads. English troops were sent in to quell the Jacobite uprising and, unlike the native Scots, the English were unable to move easily over the harsh terrain. In 1974 General Wade was sent to report on the situation and there followed many years of road construction so that English solders could patrol the Highlands efficiently. The West Highland Way walker is truly grateful for the excellent military road between Bridge of Orchy and Kinlochleven which was built by Major William Caulfield after the 1745 rebellion.

We followed the thistle waymark and a string of coloured Gore-tex along the banks of rivers, over streams and across green fields to reach open moorland. From here we had a good view of the rocky hump of Dumgoyne, the end of the line of the Campsie Fells. These hills were formed from layers of volcanic lava which erupted through the old red sandstone laid down millions of years ago; during the Ice Age a glacial finger dug a long trough which eventually filled with water and became Loch Lomond. We had tantalizing peeps through to the steely waters of the loch and beyond. The bigger hills, draped in grey cumulus clouds, waited.

It was easy walking through the lush lowland scenery but the downside was the three mile (five-kilometre) slog along the A811 to the only B&B with a vacancy; May was a popular time to walk the WHW as it was usually midge-free with fine weather.

Richard spread maps over the acres of carpet in our comfortable room and invited me to see what was in store; a series of pink highlighted blobs stuck out among a sea of brown contour lines threaded with blue rivers and lochs. These maps showed the real challenge that lay ahead, walking unsupported and wild camping in the Scottish wilderness. We planned to book into hotels wherever we had the chance, but these would be few and far between. It was a sobering moment.

We lost sight of the Campsie Fells as we climbed Conic Hill, described in the Trail Guide as 'the first significant climb of the walk, with a total rise of over 500 feet or just under 200 metres'. From the summit we looked down on the flotilla of green islands that marks the position of the Highland Boundary Fault: a diagonal line from the Firth of Clyde in the south-west to Stonehaven in the north-east, separating the Scottish Lowlands in the south from the Highlands in the north. It was an exhilarating moment as we looked north and saw Ben Lomond, the most southerly of the Scottish Munros; weather permitting we had allowed a 'rest' day to climb it.

A variety of dense coniferous forests, wooded knolls, and mature oak woods bordered the east side of Loch Lomond; grey water slurped round gnarled tree roots and the woods were filled with bluebells, primroses and shepherd's purse. The lochside resort of Balmaha was in summer weekend mood, there were more cars than we had seen since we left the M25 and a boot fair was in full swing. Clinker built fishing boats and expensive yachts bobbed up and down on their moorings in the little bay.

In Blair Wood we discovered the importance of farming woodland; here a habitat restoration programme was being carried out with financial assistance from the EU. In the nineteenth-century these oak woods were all bustle and noise, as men felled the trees and women and children stripped the bark and stacked it to dry; the bark was then taken by boat, ground up and used to tan leather in the tanneries of the Clyde. The peeled timber made excellent charcoal either for gunpowder or for use in smelting iron. In 1995, some of the oak from these woods was removed and used to reroof the Great Hall in Stirling Castle.

We were told to look out for pied flycatchers, redstarts and blue tits. Richard spotted redstarts and blue tits; the pied flycatcher was not on view. The coniferous forests of northern England and Scotland are home to the pine marten, but this little creature comes with a warning: they may look cute and cuddly but they are fierce predators, living off smaller mammals, young birds, eggs, fruit and berries. They are also adept at scavenging scraps of food left by untidy visitors.

Our path curled round short sharp hillocks, through woodlands and over rocks gripped by twisted tree roots in a ball and claw effect. Every now and then an enlarged Ben Lomond appeared through a gap in the trees. By teatime we had reached Rowardennan and the Scottish baronial shooting lodge built for the Earl of Montrose which was our youth hostel for the next two nights. After supper we watched a grey mist settle on the hills as day drained from the loch; pinpricks of light appeared on the far side and it began to rain.

It was still raining as I made porridge for our breakfast; undeterred we decided that our plan to climb Ben Lomond would go ahead whatever the weather. By the time we set off the rain had stopped, the air was keen and fresh and the dark summits of the mountains surrounding the loch were dusted with snow. In the hostel drive, a large lady with a large voice was busy leading a group of middle-aged walkers in a series of warm-up exercises: 'Bend, stretch, up, down, stamp those feet, swing those arms!' The woods and hills were alive to the sound of Elvis emanating from a large transit van marked Ptarmigan Tours.

As we emerged from the wooded skirts of Ben Lomond we looked down onto the grey waters of Loch Lomond, where islands basked like prehistoric monsters. A curtain of rain was moving slowly but surely across the rippling surface, but the visibility was good enough to see the icing sugar summits of the Campsie Fells and Conic Hill to the south, the Arrochar Alps to the north-west, and Loch Katrine and the Trossachs to the north-east. The great bulk of Ben Lomond rose before us like a beached white whale. It was an easy climb up the well-marked track until we neared the summit, when we entered a monochrome world of slippery black rocks and mini snowfields. There were no footprints in the crisp white snow and no view, just a strong wind throwing icy moisture in our faces; in this strange blanketed world, we saw ptarmigan, a bedraggled lamb, and a young man in jogging pants. I was happy to descend the slippery rocks and leave behind the cloud and snow of that eerie black and white world. On the way down, we met a straggling party of red, yellow and royal blue anoraks. A red face under a black fleecy hat handed me a large slice of fruit cake. I was wondering what I had done to deserve this when she asked me if I could give it to Big Dave.

'He's down there. Bit slow. Trouble with his knees,' a red anorak with grey beard explained, shouting into the wind.

I took the large chunk of cake rather hoping that Big Dave wouldn't materialize. We found him half a mile further down, gave him the cake and warned him that there was snow at the top.

The mobile phone is a blessing and a curse for the walker, the intrusive jingle always coming when you are puffing up a steep hill or battling with wind and rain; trying to locate the phone, remove its case with cold clumsy fingers, and press the right button in a myopic fog, is a skill in its own right. More often than not our caller had given up. We loved to hear from family and friends, but voice mail and text messages are best, as these can be read or listened to at personal convenience. However, without a mobile phone we would have been unable to cross stretches of water, keep check on the family and book accommodation. Even then, it is only as good as the signal and, as the beauty of the Scottish Highlands is not marred by phone masts, I often found the 'No Network' message. These days it is not unusual to see people perched on little hillocks, at the ends of drives or leaning in suicidal poses out of upstairs windows frowning over their clenched left hands.

After our descent from Ben Lomond, I was standing on a raised portion of the Earl's spacious drive in a biting wind, attempting to get a signal to book one of our planned hotels. With my mobile clamped to my right ear, I was wrestling with credit cards and itinerary sheets, when the polite voice from the recesses of the Highland hills started to break up. Hoping my message had been received I turned back to the hostel and saw an elderly walker slumped, half sitting, half lying, on a garden seat. He was dressed in a thin cagoule, tracksuit bottoms and what looked like gardening boots. Although his face was blue with cold, and one wet leg was supported on a gnarled walking stick, he was a picture of dignified resignation. Traditionally youth hostels don't open their doors till five in the afternoon and it was only half past four. We exchanged smiles and I told him that the door was open and he could wait in the warmth of the reception area. Nodding politely, he creaked slowly upright, hefted his small pack and walked stiffly through the welcoming doors. Later Richard found him in his dormitory, washed, changed and snoring gently on his bunk. It transpired that he was 88 years old and had walked the rocky six-mile (ten kilometre) section from a favourite hotel at Inversnaid. He planned to make the return journey the following day.

'I joined the Youth Hostel Association in 1936, the year they started,' he told Richard. 'No in-house meals, central heating or showers then.' He bent down slowly and drew a diminutive towel and soap from his pack. Straightening up he added, 'I was pleased to see there were no cars in the drive either. None of those in the old days.' There was a twinkle in his eye as he headed off to the washroom.

He set off next morning like a well-seasoned tramp; polythene bags wrapped round his inadequate boots, a Viyella shirt and tie under the flimsy pack-a-mac, and ancient skiing gloves. We met him halfway along the steep path where he stood aside and politely waited for us to pass.

'I have to take it a bit easier these days,' he acknowledged. I offered my hand and congratulated him on his achievement. It took him some time to remove the tight glove but he managed it and gave me a firm handshake. He had all the hallmarks of an aristocrat and was a master of the understatement.

'I'm from Bedford,' he told us, 'with an ongoing love of Scotland. Ireland is my real home. I gave up an estate there and now I just have a caravan and some trees.' His estate, I thought, was definitely not of the housing variety. He paused to regain his breath, leant on his stick and gazed over the loch. We stood silently for a moment and then he added, 'I thought I had the best view in the world in Ireland until I saw this.'

'Have you had trouble with blisters?' I asked looking at his polythene-wrapped Doc Martens.

'Blisters? No. These are my son's boots, size ten and I've worn them in gardening.'

So far, the walking on the West Highland Way, including our ascent of Ben Lomond, had been easy. Day three was different. Sunshine and heavy showers meant we had clear views of the rising hills ahead on the few occasions when the path left the trees. Most of the day we were scrambling up and down steep inclines, fording brooks, and slithering over black rocks on a rough track hugging the loch shore. We passed Rob Roy's cave, an unlikely hideout in a gloomy cleft amongst boulders perched on the steep slope. In the eighteenth-century, Rob Roy MacGregor was a brawny outlaw who fell foul of the expansionist policies devised by the legal brains of the Campbells. He ran his own cattle droving business until 1711, when his head drover ran off with all the cash for the main cattle sales leaving MacGregor in debt to his former friend and ally, the Duke of Montrose. The Duke turned against Rob, and not only outlawed him, but turned his wife and family out of their home at Inversnaid and burnt it down. After this Rob Roy became the Robin Hood of Scotland, stealing the Duke's cattle, kidnapping his men, and holding them to ransom in his two cave hideouts along the West Highland Way. Of such stuff myths are made. It is perhaps surprising that this outlaw died peacefully in his bed at the respectable age of 63.

The oaks and birches were lime green with new leaves, and from a gap in the trees we saw a ferry crossing the loch, vibrating to the sounds of Abba. Blackbirds and thrushes added their delicate notes to the sound of boots and sticks tramping the woodland paths.

Walking behind a line of people along a narrow path is like driving along a busy road; if your stride is just a little quicker than the person in front, overtaking is a major problem. Pedestrians don't have wing mirrors and the person you are trying to overtake is often blissfully unaware that there is anyone on their heels. You have to wait your moment, hoping the walker in front will stop for a breather, hear you and pull over, or that the path will widen. If the person or group you are hoping to overtake are walking at a similar speed as yourself, it requires a lot of acceleration and an embarrassing amount of time to complete the manoeuvre. In addition, you are thinking of something suitable to say as you pass: 'Thanks so much. Got a train to catch' doesn't sound quite right; 'So sorry, my friend's on ahead' is patently not true. In the end you just puff a feeble 'Excuse-me-please-thanks-lovely-day-isn't-it' and use your acceleration calf muscles for all they are worth; so far so good, until you meet a gate, a stile, or steps up a stone wall. The problem gets worse when you need to stop for a pee; it may take a while to find a good hiding place.

First check the path is clear both ways before diving off into the trees; then, by the time you have taken off your pack, seen to yourself, slung it back again, and rejoined the path you will probably hear the happy chattering sounds of the party you have just overtaken striding past.

The old door of the Drovers Hotel creaked as we entered a large flagstoned hall where we found ourselves eyeballing a stuffed bear on its hind legs. The walls were littered with antlered deer heads and candle sconces flanked the empty stone hearth. A medieval-sized log fire at the back of the candlelit bar welcomed visitors and rough tables and benches were scattered beneath stuffed birds in glass cabinets. It was here we met our friends Alan and Felicity, who were not only going to put us up in their house at Lochgoilhead, but had driven many extra miles from the Scottish Borders to collect our camping gear so we didn't have to carry it unnecessarily. A Rob Roy lookalike in kilt and sporran served us tea and biscuits from behind the ample bar and some of his clan sat on bar stools; the loo only catered for slim-line walkers.

Alan, an architect friend of thirty years standing, had designed a small eco-friendly house on the shores of Loch Goil; patio doors led onto a small terrace from where the ground fell away to the wooded loch whose motionless surface mirrored the green hills above. There was a smell of seaweed from the tide line and we could hear the piping notes of redshank and oystercatcher. In Victorian days steam boats from Glasgow would bring tourists to the loch, and those with enough money left a legacy of Italianate villas there.

Felicity had taught our younger daughter at primary school. Jo was then a shy little girl with glasses; under Felicity's guidance she metamorphosed into a happy and confident person, perhaps something to do with being given the lead in the form play, Pandora's Box.

Thanks to Alan and Felicity we enjoyed an eighteen-mile (twenty-nine kilometre) pack-free day from Inverarnan to the Bridge of Orchy. The sun shone on broad splashes of white water as the River Falloch spewed over rocks in a headlong rush between the birch trees. With Loch Lomond behind us we were walking in more open country and the going underfoot was easy. We ate our sandwiches on a grassy summit looking down on the river, which meandered through a broad valley below the massif of Ben More. Coniferous plantations were strewn across the lower slopes of these hills like bottle-green pieces of jigsaw.

At Kirton Farm we met St Fillan, yet another Irishman who settled here and spread the teachings of a Christian way of life to the heathen Scots and Picts. A pious reminder on a 3D information board was a gentle warning to the walker: 'All travellers who use this wild and beautiful place will do so in peace if they tread their path lightly'. A pile of moss-covered ruins lay in the damp shade of a copse of birch, ash and oak trees; a little graveyard stood behind a stone wall with the tombstones leaning at crazy angles. I remembered the story of our parish councillor at Cropredy, whose churchwarden had to bash the tombstones with a large hammer to see if they could continue to rest in peace. I felt sure these drunken tombstones would not stand the hammer blow of the new EU health and safety regulations. I comforted myself that we were in Scotland where the laws were different, and hoped they might be allowed to bow gracefully to the force of gravity.

At Auchtertyre Farm we found a shop selling ice creams, and sat on the steps taking a childish delight in our chocolate and vanilla cones while we admired the centrally heated wooden wigwams which make simple but adequate accommodation for walkers or holidaymakers.

The West Highland Railway is one of the most scenic in the British Isles and the metal tracks snaked gently through the valley alongside General Wade's military road. Richard and I recalled a recent journey from Glasgow to Mallaig on this line; it was a beautiful day in March when bright sun sparkled on the snow-covered mountains and a white blanket hid the brown wastes of Rannoch Moor. For passengers (or should I say customers) on the train, the spectacular views were invisible behind the layers of dirt and grime on the windows. I improved my field of vision by jumping out at the first station armed with a packet of tissues and some elbow grease. At Rannoch Moor a small party of cross country skiers alighted, and, as our train pulled away across the white wilderness, we watched a line of brightly coloured Lowry figures disappearing towards the snowy giants of Glencoe. This magnificent railway, a boon for many West Highland Way walkers, was opened in 1894, but today its future hangs in the balance.

Our Trail Guide gave us an interesting anecdote about the first railway surveyor's excursion across Rannoch Moor. In 1889, Robert McAlpine, with three engineers, a solicitor and two factors, set off from local estates. Two of them, prepared for the rigours of the Highland weather, carried umbrellas. It was a disastrous journey; the boat to take them up Loch Treig was late and leaked, the hunting lodge which had promised hot food and a bed gave them cold food and thin blankets. The following day they set off with sleet stinging their faces to walk the twenty-three miles (thirty-seven kilometres) across Rannoch Moor. They were offered shelter halfway but refused. One of them collapsed with exhaustion and was left with two others and one umbrella. The party was split, and those still able wandered off into the cold night. One of the engineers collided with a fence in the dark, and knocked himself out; when he came to he realized that a fence meant habitation and followed it to a shepherd's hut where he raised a rescue party. McAlpine eventually got off the moor after walking all night and the main group were brought to safety before a real blizzard struck.

Our experience that spring afternoon was very different: warm sun lit the snow-dusted peaks of Beinn Dòrain and the Glencoe mountains, and thanks to General Wade's excellent road we reached the Bridge of Orchy in time to have a swift pint before the taxi we had ordered took us the forty-five tortuous miles (seventy-two kilometres) back to Lochgoilhead.

Felicity and Alan drove us back to the Bridge of Orchy station, a long building in brick and timber covered with a slate roof that could have been a life-size model on a toy railway. Here we said our goodbyes, and set off for Glencoe across the infamous Rannoch Moor, with the added weight of our camping gear.

High cloud with pale blue strips hung above the loch-strewn peaty wilderness of the moor. The lonely silence was broken only by our boots and sticks thumping along the well-made track. We were in a desert of heather, peat, reeds and water with patches of light and dark strobing the surrounding hills. The snow-capped whalebacks of the Glencoe massif rose to the north-west, and ahead lay the white rump of Ben

Nevis. Climbing up from Ba Bridge to the summit of a hill, the views stretched to the distant Grampian mountains and the hills of Glencoe, dominated by the sheer cone of Buachaille Etive Mor. Far below tiny beetles moved along a thin grey string which stretched across the peaty wastes; the very presence of this road enhanced the bleakness of these surroundings. The great glens of Etive and Glencoe lay temptingly before us, wide scoops through flanks of ancient rock etched with a thread of river.

I had imagined the Kingshouse Hotel to be in a small Highland village, but it was just a lonely white building under a slate roof. No rooms were available, but permission was granted to camp by the river. As we pitched our tent on one of the few dry spots, we noticed that we were not alone. One hour later there were two tents, and by the time we had eaten our meal a host of coloured mushrooms had sprouted along the river bank. Dutch, German and English walkers, cyclists, and motorcyclists were all enjoying the traditional hospitality of this 200-year-old hotel which lies at a lonely crossroads and was built as a barracks and safe house for travellers. Donald McGuiness took over this drovers' inn after a distinguished career in the King's Army. He found life in Civvy Street harder than he had imagined and resorted to the illegal selling of whisky and salt. After chilli con carne and rice in the hotel bar, we sat by the rock-strewn river. As the warm light seeped away into the west the great mountains darkened to silhouettes and an army of storm clouds massed above our heads. The slug of legal whisky in our coffee warmed our souls.

We woke to damp grey skies and the sight of a German disappearing into the heather with a catering size toilet roll. I brewed a good helping of porridge, and we ate some bread I had stashed away during our evening meal washed down with a mug of hot chocolate. The only problem was the kettle, which took fourteen minutes to boil. In spite of this delay we were among the first to leave, happy to have stowed the tent, before the first drops of rain made little rings in the river.

We had a taste of real Scottish weather as we climbed the 849 feet (261 metres) military road, known as the Devil's Staircase, and just managed to catch a view of the precipitous bulk of Buachaille Etive Mor before cloud enveloped us. The wind got up, the rain came down in sweeping sheets of water and we saw only the path ahead and one little tent perched on the heather, shades of things to come. At the top we glimpsed the Blackwater Reservoir, built to power the aluminium smelter at Kinlochleven. This is now closed, but the power station continues to send electricity to the national grid. Rows of giant steel tubes plummeted down the mountain as we wove a tortuous way through dense birch woods to the 'model village' of Kinlochleven, built to house the workforce. It was paradise for wet walkers. We found an excellent hotel which advertised a camping site with views of the Pap of Glencoe. The cheerful bar was walker-friendly with tiles on the floor and a roaring cosy stove. A strange octopus-shaped machine stood by the door with tubes coming from a central fan heater; perfect for drying sodden boots. The friendly man behind the bar offered us a camp site for £10 or a heated cabin for £24. There was little hesitation, and soon we were showered and dry in a snug four-berth cabin with our wet clothes happy in a purpose built drying room.

During the night the wind buffeted the cabin and squally showers spat on the glass window. We slept well, glad we were not in the little tent on the top of the Devil's Staircase.

Stretches of Major Caulfield's military road made easy walking for our last day on the West Highland Way. The climbs were well graded and the forest paths springy underfoot. The bulky flanks of Ben Nevis, with its summit shrouded in mist, appeared from time to time, and soon we were descending into the Alpine scenery of Glen Nevis. We walked through dense pine forests, lush grass, primroses and a few straggling bluebells. Streams, swollen by the recent rain, tumbled down the hillsides as if a series of giant hosepipes had been turned on. From our last hill we had a good view of the metropolis of Fort William, the last town until we reached home.

My dormitory at the youth hostel was empty, but two rucksacks and several pairs of very large trainers indicated that I would not be alone for long. After a shower and some tea I had a quick snooze, and woke to the sound of male voices from two young lads in the bunks opposite mine.

'Is this a mixed dorm?' I asked, wondering if I was just dreaming.

It was apparently a lassies' dorm, but the lads had been told to use it; I was issued with another key and ended up with the luxury of an eight-bedded room all to myself.

Ben Nevis eluded us thanks to the Scottish weather. Rain fell in stair rods all day long so we took a trip to Safeway instead. That evening Richard told me a fit young man in his dorm had just returned after climbing Ben Nevis, and had crashed out on his bunk without even washing. We felt vindicated when we heard there was four feet of snow at the top and the going was tough. That evening we built ourselves up for the Cape Wrath Trail with steak and a bottle of wine.

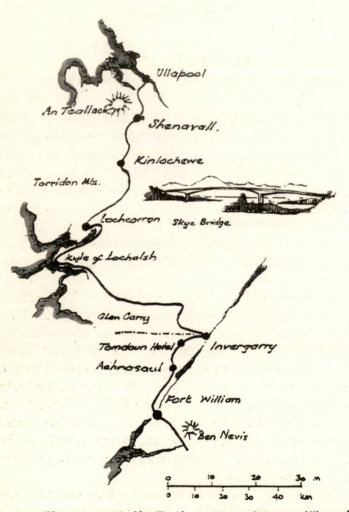

Ullapool

An Teallach

Shenavall.

Kinlochewe

Torridon Mts.

Skye Bridge

Lochcarron

Kyle of Lochalsh

Glen Garry

Tomdoun Hotel

Invergarry

Achnasaul

Fort William

Ben Nevis

8. The Cape Wrath Trail. – Fort William - Ullapool.

Chapter Eight

The Cape Wrath Trail

We left the West Highland metropolis of Fort William in sunshine and showers and headed off up the Caledonian Canal from Banavie Bridge (where the canal meets the Atlantic Ocean) towards Loch Lochy. The empty grey water ran straight as a ruler into the distance and trees screened us from any views. It was a long eleven miles (seventeen kilometres). We were surprised to meet a steady trickle of walkers in both directions and later discovered that Fort William was the start or finish of the Great Glen Way, a long-distance footpath from Inverness to Fort William via Fort Augustus. It was, I felt, an inauspicious start, but Scotland doesn't disappoint for long; by the time we reached the River Lochy, dazzling yellow gorse and broom alternated with may trees dripping white blossom and clumps of wild lupins splashed mauve across the shingle. Further down the river, swathes of beech, chestnut, oak and willow hugged the banks and fish ringed the water like large raindrops. We could hear the piping of sandpiper and redshank, and the mournful honking of greylag geese. The snow-capped bulk of the Mamore mountain range, crowned by Ben Nevis, filled the horizon to the south-east.

The sun came out and we found a little campsite and pitched our tent below what had once been the platform of a railway station. The warden allowed us to use a white plastic table and chairs and we were soon basking in the welcome sun in total comfort. A gaggle of young ladies doing the Great Glen Way came in to use the excellent facilities and asked us how we managed to get the table and chairs into our rucksacks. We told them it was wonderful what they can flat-pack these days. Our only problem was food. The nearest pub was two miles down the road, and the campsite didn't sell anything. However, our luck was in; Richard looked up from the paper and announced that the closed hamburger and chip van, conveniently parked in the campsite, was about to open. We enjoyed every mouthful of our high-cholesterol feast prepared by a lady from Essex who had moved north two years ago. We asked her how she was getting on.

'Love it,' she said, shaking vinegar over a huge pile of chips. 'We wouldn't go back now. It's so quiet up here, no traffic, and a slow pace of life. Only trouble is,' she paused, wrestling to get an oversized burger into an undersized paper bag, 'the rain. It does rain a lot.'

'What about the dark winters?' I enquired, holding my burger and chips reverently and watching Richard's nose twitching like a rabbit's as his nostrils inhaled the scent of forbidden fruit.

'No problem,' she said briskly. 'It's only the four weeks up to Christmas and then the evenings get lighter. Enjoy your meal.'

We munched happily as we watched the world go by, the world being a balding gentleman with long legs and short trousers, carrying a caber over one shoulder. He turned out to be the local schoolmaster, another ex-pat Sassenach. Shortly after this a 4x4 drove up and parked next to our little tent. Four fit-looking men catapulted out as soon as the doors were opened, released from sharing space with a large tent, camping gear, rucksacks and several crates of beer. They were a jolly group, on the last lap of the Great Glen Way, heading for journey's end at a Fort William pub. They enjoyed their penultimate evening, and when finally they retreated to the tent I thought they had brought a sleeping Loch Ness monster with them.

We woke early on a perfect spring morning to the sounds of a Scottish dawn chorus. Tackling the final and most demanding section of our walk to Cape Wrath was a daunting prospect, for this was no waymarked national trail, more an idea in the mind of David Paterson to extend the West Highland Way to the lonely north-west of the Scottish mainland. In 1993 he set out to walk cross country for over 200 miles (320 kilometres) through the north-west Highlands to Cape Wrath, on a route he himself had devised. This took him through spectacular scenery, away from roads, but using existing paths and old drovers' tracks where possible; he also included a few villages, hotels or hostels for the walker to rest and re-provision. The result was the seductive little book we had seized on when browsing through the Aladdin's Cave of Stanford's map and bookshop in Covent Garden. For us, the idea was about to become reality.

Crossing the Caledonian Canal, we took a path through beech woods by the shores of Loch Lochy on our way to Achnacarry. This was the soft side of Scotland, carpets of moss under the beech trees whose tangled roots stretched to the slurping loch where clinker built boats waited patiently by a landing stage. Our road to Achnacarry was a cul de sac with only a couple of houses, a Norman church and the Clan Cameron Museum. From here we walked through the broad acres of the Cameron estates before crossing Loch Arkaig to Achnasaul.

Once round the head of the loch we started our 2,000 foot (615 metre) climb through birch, rowan and pine trees and in time we left the tree line and were off the path on the heather and peat hags to the pass, in Gaelic called Bealach na h'Urchaire. It was a long pull up with our heavy packs and the change from lush green pastures to harsh mountain vegetation was mirrored by the weather. Big clouds swallowed the sun and there were intermittent heavy showers. Pausing for breath from time to time we could see into the deep recesses of Glen Tarsuinn to the east, and the dark waters of Loch Arkaig to the west. Except for the gusting wind as another shower approached, it was awesomely silent; we looked and listened in vain for some signs of life, a deer, an eagle, a cuckoo, anything; all we heard was the strange thrumming of snipe.

It seemed as if we should never reach the saddle, but once on the crest we forgot fatigue and were rewarded with panoramic views of the great mountain ranges which lead to Knoydart in the west, and Glen Quoich and Glen Shiel beyond Glen Garry to the north. The elusive Ben Nevis, well behind us now, had its head in the clouds. A steeply shelving brown carpet of heather, bog and rocks spread before us backdropped by ancient mountains. We sat humbly taking in the grandeur, until the cold wind chilled our overheated bodies and we started our descent by the roaring waters of the Allt Ailein river. It was only 4.30 p.m. and Richard wanted to get right off the mountain before we camped. The ground was very boggy and you can't put a tent on heather or peat hags, so we were lucky to find a small patch of coarse grass by the river firm enough to take the tent. Another squall was on its way and in a very few minutes we were cramped but cosy inside our tiny home, while heavy raindrops spat on the nylon. We had a tot of whisky, cuppa soups and savoury rice with added ham and carrot, followed by hot chocolate and Mars bars. Perhaps not so strangely, we discussed the trials of Captain Scott on his ill-fated Antarctic expedition; no real comparisons except we were now a little nearer the edge. It made us aware of how privileged we were in our everyday lives, and now, many miles from a shop or house of any kind, we had to rely on our own resourcefulness and know that our rations were finite. Perhaps this is one of the attractions of living beyond the 'comfort zone'. We managed to wash ourselves and our mugs and pans between heavy showers and then slept fitfully until daybreak.

The morning dawned dry with small patches of blue between the heavy white clouds shrouding the higher peaks. I made our usual porridge for breakfast and, thinking we would reach the Tomdoun Hotel for lunch, we gobbled up our meagre supply of bread rolls. Then we were off down the mountain and could soon see Loch Garry far below; we knew our night's lodging was the other side and, although there were several rivers to cross, from above it all looked easy enough. Richard managed to pick up a rough stalkers' path which might have been good a hundred years ago, but now was almost indistinguishable from the heather and bog of the mountainside. The recent rain had made the going very soft underfoot and great concentration was needed to avoid shipping bootfuls of peaty water. Richard was happy to be back on any sort of path as he knew it would lead to a bridge where we could cross the river. Then we saw it: a rustic affair of poles and planks but a bridge nevertheless.

'There it is,' I yelled excitedly and surged in front. However, all is not what it seems, especially in the Scottish mountains; it was an old bridge, some of the planks were missing and the poles sagged alarmingly towards the turbulent water. It was tempting to go ahead and cross it, but if it had collapsed under our weight we should have been dashed to pieces on the rocks beneath. We decided not to risk it, which meant there was no choice but to cross the river itself. Richard took off his pack and walked upstream to see if he could find a suitable crossing place. I watched the tumultuous water roaring and foaming over rocks and waited nervously for his verdict; rock hopping was not my favourite pastime.

'OK, a quarter of a mile further up. The river is narrower and we can cross on some stones. Come on. I'll take your pack.' Richard looked relieved. I followed him upstream and watched enviously as he strode over the racing water on some precarious boulders. 'See,' he shouted triumphantly, 'it's easy!' I calmed myself with some deep breaths and concentrated on the stones and not the water, glad of my two sticks to steady me. I had to leap from the last stone to the bank, but Richard held my stick and I made it. He went back for my pack and we set off again, having covered only two miles in as many hours.

For a while we made better progress, squelching along the nearly invisible track and into a plantation of firs. I was thinking lovely thoughts about hotel lunches and hot baths when we met another river, wider and fuller than the last. The last few days of rain had melted the late May snow on the mountains and all the rivers were in spate. We searched for a suitable crossing place but there was no way anyone could have forded this roaring demon. Eventually we found the remnants of a flimsy wooden bridge which had plunged into the water at one end and was non-existent at the other.

Richard looked concerned. 'We have to cross this river if we are going to reach the hotel as planned.' He pointed across the loch. 'It's just across there.' Drops of moisture fell silently from his moustache as he gave a frustrated grunt.

It was becoming clear to us that the Scottish wilderness makes no concessions; the terrain is hostile, the going underfoot is difficult, the rivers rise and fall according to the rainfall, the weather is unpredictable, and your twenty-first-century mobile is unable to pick up a signal. It is one thing to know these things and quite another to experience them.

'There's only one thing we can do,' Richard said, having

realized that short of a Bailey bridge there was no way we were going to cross this torrent. 'We'll just have to walk to the road bridge at the far end of the loch. I'm afraid that means an extra eight miles.'

We sloshed along the boggy loch side. Unable to avoid the worst of the pools we often went ankle-deep into peaty water; at one stage Richard's stick would not come out of a bog and it took him ten minutes to extricate it. Finally there was a loud slurp and he triumphantly held up a metal question mark. It was then he told me that, never mind Jordan, there was one more river to cross to reach the loch road bridge. I began to catastrophize: what if we couldn't cross the next one? With an inert mobile and very little food we could be in for a miserable night, and this was only day two. I found a sizeable piece of blue nylon rope on the ground and picked it up thinking it just might come in handy.

Adrenalin drove us on and we made good time in spite of the terrain and found a bridge that was after all strong enough to hold our weight. Breakfast seemed a long time ago so we stopped for a hot cup of soup. While I changed my sodden socks, Richard pulled out the cooker but found the screw top wouldn't budge. We ended up drinking burn water to go with two cherry tomatoes and half a protein bar each. Then we set off for the last five miles back to civilization and were soon on the narrow road to Tomdoun. Where the track merged with the road there was a notice board which read:

Take care! You are entering remote, sparsely populated, potentially dangerous mountain country. Please ensure that you are adequately experienced and equipped to complete your journey without assistance.

We walked silently along the road for two and a half miles (four kilometres) to the Tomdoun Hotel, a solid brick building under a slate roof, sited on a grass-covered rise, the long sash windows looking over the lush valley of Loch Garry to the hills beyond. The string of tarmac snaked on past the hamlet of Tomdoun, along the banks of the River Garry to the dark and desolate waters of Loch Quoich and the treeless wilderness of the Glenquoich Forest. It ended at Kinloch Hourn, an even more remote hamlet on the shores of Loch Hourn which joins the Sound of Sleat.

We sat down on a convenient bench on the veranda to remove our boots. It was five o'clock and we had left our mountain camp at 8.30 that morning. The smell of our socks must have alerted a small white hearthrug on four paws and a bloodhound whose sagging jowls slurped to and fro as he walked. Satisfied that we had reserved a room, they left us alone and we went sideways through double doors which might have accommodated a bag of pheasants, but not a full rucksack. The hall had a fine mahogany staircase, antlers and stuffed fish decorated the walls, and the wooden floor was strewn with Persian rugs. There was no reception desk and no one around; we began to feel we had entered a Victorian sporting lodge without a visiting card. I tripped over a sleeping whippet in my search for someone, and finally discovered Laura in the kitchen. There was a faint smell of damp dog and onions. Yes, she was expecting us, and when I muttered something about the Cape Wrath Trail and unfordable rivers, she paused on her way up the stairs.

'Sure,' she remarked, 'the TGO [The Great Outdoors] Challengers who have just passed through said the same. It's often the case at this time of year.' She made it sound as commonplace as a traffic jam in the south-east. We reached the top of the stairs and she unlocked a large mahogany door and opened it with a flourish. 'We've upgraded your room and let you have it for the same price. Supper is from seven p.m. in the bar. I hope you'll be comfortable.'

The large window looked over the quiet waters of Loch Garry and the very hills we had struggled over that morning.

After a much needed shower and several cups of tea we lay on the bed and reflected. Our first day on the Cape Wrath Trail had taught us that it was going to be even tougher than we had imagined. Every mile was hard won, even in reasonably good weather, and if you walked ten long miles and found a river you couldn't cross you had to retreat the ten miles back to your starting point. Richard knew that the next day he had planned to take us through the vastness of Glen Loyne and across the River Loyne which was much bigger than the ones we had met already.

In his book *The Cape Wrath Trail*, David Paterson compares this walk with the West Highland Way. Apart from being twice as long, the main difference, he felt, was in the quality. While the WHW had good lodgings every night, enabling the walker to carry less, his Cape Wrath Trail was more physically demanding with a 2,000-foot (615-metre) ridge to climb on day two. High ridges and fair-sized rivers to ford were normal, and there were fewer comfortable places to spend the nights. The walker needed to be self-sufficient for several days at a time, which meant carrying heavier packs with camping gear and food. There were no Sherpas on this route, yet he described it as 'measuring up to the best in long-distance walks anywhere, and for scale and grandeur it will bear comparison with almost any Himalayan trek'. Richard felt it was to be the dramatic finale to this UK section of our E2 walk; to be thwarted on day two was frustrating.

'I think we had better give up,' he said suddenly. 'If I make a plan I stick to it. I don't want compromise.'

I was silent; as the weaker member, it was on my account any compromise would have to be made. We were tired and morale was low. This was not the moment for decisions; our dejected descent of the grand staircase was reflected in a large mirror on the wall.

The bar was a cosy room with a coal fire at each end and long windows looking out over the loch. We sat by one of the fires and relished a large bowl of carrot and orange soup followed by venison casserole, several pints of beer and a malt whisky; so much for roughing it. A middle-aged couple sat at the table opposite us with a young man in running shorts and a ponytail. He wasn't eating with them and he sounded like a Munro bore (someone who bags mountains over 3,000 feet and brags about it). We wondered where he fitted in, but we had to wait for breakfast to find out. Removing our feet from the attentions of a black labrador, we returned to our room and flattened ourselves on the bed. Rehydrated and well fed, Richard's brain was busy making an alternative plan. He sat up and produced maps to illustrate his thoughts.

'We can walk from here into Invergarry on the forestry track, that's about fourteen miles [twenty-two kilometres], and camp there. Then we can catch a bus which will take us to Kyle of Lochalsh.' His finger moved over the map to show me exactly where he meant. 'From there we can take the train to Strathcarron, via Plockton, and walk on to Lochcarron. We'll spend the night in a B&B there, then pick up the Cape Wrath Trail again to Torridon, walking over the Coulin Pass into Kinlochewe.'

He paused and waited for my reaction. The words bus and train jarred for both of us. After all this was a sponsored walk and we felt it was somehow cheating. Moreover the walk into Invergarry was going east, not a pleasant prospect. I nodded and mumbled, 'Sounds like a good compromise.'

Richard spread another map on the bed and pointed to a sea of brown contour lines near Kinlochewe. 'We could do the Letterewe and Fisherfield forests, wild camp near the bothy here at Shenavall, then pick up the track that leads round the base of An Teallach to Dundonnell. Then we'll catch the ferry at Altanaharry which should take us across Loch Broom to Ullapool. I just hope it's still running. If not, we'll have to walk all the way round Loch Broom which is about twenty miles [thirty-two kilometres].' The kettle had just boiled and he made himself a cup of coffee before settling himself back in front of the map. 'After Ullapool we can take a path around Beinn Mor Coigach to Achiltibuie and from there the coast road to Kylesku and Rhiconich. I know we've done it all before but I think we should skip climbing Foinaven with heavy packs. The last two days will be off the roads to Sandwood Bay and the Cape.' He folded the map up carefully and had a sip of coffee.

I gazed out of the window at the wilderness beyond the loch. I knew he was doing this rejig for me. I also felt it was the right thing to do. Taking big risks when we still had the European part of our walk to do was not sensible. Still looking out, I asked him if it was really necessary to make these adjustments; I had to know what he really felt even if it hurt.

'We need local knowledge about the rivers but we can't get it here. If you really want the truth I feel responsible for you. It's hard,' he replied, measuring each word carefully.

It was hurtful: I had not lagged behind; when we used the tent, it was teamwork; I cooked the food and did my bit to keep morale high and I didn't complain. There was a long pause before I felt able to reply, 'OK. I'll ring the Cluanie Inn and cancel tomorrow.' Glad of something to do, I rang them and tried to sleep. Sometime during that long night I recalled Wainwright's words on a remote part of north-west Scotland: 'Weaklings and novices must expect to perish. Once committed there is no easy escape.'

Dawn brought a sky full of fat rainclouds. Breakfast was in a large airy dining room at a long table covered in a spotless white cloth. An imposing stone fireplace was flanked by

Chinese vases and the deep blue walls were dressed with Victorian watercolours. We spooned our cereal from crystal bowls and sugar from Bristol glass encased in filigree silver. A round table, with a silver urn overflowing with hydrangeas, filled the bay window.

The trio from the night before sat opposite us, and we soon discovered that Ben the ponytail was a rent-a-guide and knew the area well. Local knowledge, it seemed, came with the cornflakes. He told us he had spent the winter making deer fences on the north-west of Knoydart. The winter, he said, had been so mild that there was very little snow on the mountains. The late fall that contributed to the swollen rivers was not unusual. When we quizzed him about the River Loyne he admitted it would be a problem when in spate, but added cheerfully, 'Rivers soon go down here and having come this far I think you could give it a go.' I wished we hadn't asked him.

The Glen Garry forest looked like the no-man's-land of the First World War: felled trunks littered the hillside like giant matchsticks scarring the landscape. The Glen Garry Forest Enterprise was involved in a harvesting scheme; this was the first step in the attempted restoration of the native trees which had been threatened by the underplanting of different productive conifers; these specialized trees were currently being removed to allow the natural ground flora to recolonize and the native pine woods to regenerate naturally. 'The Great Caledonian Forest grows again', was written both in English and Gaelic. Walking along by the river on a carpet of springy moss drenched in the clean scent of pine, we saw siskin and the diminutive goldcrest, our smallest bird. The contrast of the sheltered green glades of the conifer forest with the bare windswept mountain we were on only yesterday illustrates how the landscape in the Highlands can change dramatically within a few miles.

We camped at Invergarry and walked the mile and a half to find the pub, a tourist office, a salmon hatchery and a garage/shop strung along half a mile of road. Under the fresh new leaves of mature beech trees we watched two kayaks tossed like ping-pong balls by the churning water of the river, swollen to bursting point by the melting snow on the mountains and the recent heavy rain. It was a sleepless night in our tent; gusts of wind roared through the trees like a train, and squalls of rain hailed down like bullets.

The bus into Kyle of Lochalsh shot along the little roads and squealed round bends while Richard and I clung to our upholstered seats high above the road. We had a bird's eye view of Loch Garry; the shape, we were told by the lady in the garage/shop, was like the map of Scotland, and she was right. Our great chariot whisked us past the Cluanie Inn, a deserted building on the road and the Sisters of Kintail, their five peaks softened by heavy black clouds, to Shiel Bridge and Loch Duich. From time to time, rays of light pierced the gloom, illuminating deserted valleys that once formed the Great Caledonian Forest. This enforced road journey was hard for Richard; he so longed to be out in the stormy wilderness which, from behind the warm glass of our coach, looked temptingly dramatic.

Kyle of Lochalsh was all bustle and noise as tourists milled round the little town between showers, wondering what to do next. We booked a B&B at the Tourist Office, and lunched on sandwiches, beer and chips while we waited for our train to Strathcarron. Then we walked over the graceful arc of the Skye toll bridge (costing drivers the controversial price of £5.70 one way). On the gate of Eilean Ban, the house on an island where Gavin Maxwell nurtured his wild otters, we saw the words 'Uniting Community Interest with Wild Life

Conservation'. There is a delicate balance between the needs of local people and tourists and the need for wildlife to be left undisturbed. Gavin Maxwell's otter island is now a sanctuary for these beautiful creatures, which can no longer thrive so near the noise and traffic.

From the bridge, the panoramic view in bright sun between banks of cumulus clouds was too good not to savour; we reminisced about our coastal walk in 1995 as we spotted the island of Raasay, the Applecross Corries, and the Torridon Mountains. To the west the jagged teeth of the Cuillins of Skye rose above the Sound of Sleat where a group of fishing boats, flying the blue and white flag of St Andrew, were moored to the jetty. Gulls mewed and screeched round the fishing fleet, while bright sun sparkled the water and lit the yellow gorse and the springy tufts of sea pinks beneath the bridge.

Lochcarron, according to our landlady, is the second longest village in Scotland; when we reached the first lamp post, a sign advertised the Spa supermarket as being one mile further on. The little village of traditional whitewashed cottages under slate roofs was strung out along the loch side, and our room for the night was a further half mile from the Spa at the centre of the village. Our diminutive landlady was very friendly, and her cottage spotless and comfortable. She insisted on giving us a towel to rest our rucksacks on, exclaiming, 'I'm no' houseproud, mind.'

Her husband was an old sea dog who went into fishing when he came out of the Navy. 'Now uh do a wee bit of gardening for folks, cut grass and sech like, and the wife runs the bed and breakfast.' He looked at us knowingly and added, 'As for that farmed salmon, I wudna touch it with a barge pole, and ye wudna either if ye knew what goes into them.'

We took pains to avoid salmon on the pub menu but couldn't resist a bowl of cullen skink, (haddock soup).

At breakfast we met two men who had been walking through the Glenaffric Forest which we had eschewed. They told us it had been hard going and the youth hostel (the most remote in the UK) was cold, damp and very run down. They hadn't had to cross the River Loyne. Dave and Brian told us that their friend George, a mere 78-year-old, had spent the last thirty years walking from Dover towards Cape Wrath in 'bite-size' portions. Now he was only a few 'bites' from his goal. He had been sleeping in his camper van outside and we managed to shake hands and exchange addresses before the taxi arrived to take us to our rescheduled starting point at Achnashellach. From here we planned to walk over the Coulin Pass to Kinlochewe.

It seems that everyone in these remote places needs to be an entrepreneurial general factotum. Our 'unofficial' taxi driver was a good example: he was born and brought up in South Wales, lived for thirty years in Birmingham, then moved to Lochcarron where he drove the school bus, gave people lifts in his 'taxi' and let out self-catering holiday accommodation. He also knew how to get free venison.

'If you run over a deer it's no' yours to take away,' he told us, drawing his car into a layby, 'but the drivers behind you ken.' He turned off the engine and continued, in a Brummy accent tinged with Scots, 'One day uh was the lucky driver be'ind, and uh whipped out me knife, carved off a haunch and put it in the boot of ma car. When uh came to open it, a trail of blood was dripping out ma boot onto the road.'

We clambered out of his warm car in seriously wet conditions and walked a quarter of a mile uphill to a tiny station surrounded by mauve rhododendrons and heavily scented yellow azaleas. Two people were waiting on the platform. We followed a broad forestry track, arriving at the top of the pass soaked but elated. Our reward was a break in the clouds giving long views of rolling moorland dotted with copses of stunted birch and Scots pine; the familiar shapes of Beinn Eighe and Liathach loomed ahead. At Loch Clair, a collage of blue sky, white clouds, grey mountains and dark firs layered the still waters. A cuckoo announced that spring had really come and the piping call of a sandpiper drifted up from the loch. Beside the rocky path we found the violet-spurred flowers of the carnivorous butterwort, marsh orchids, golden guineas and even a few clumps of primroses.

Our proposed campsite at Kinlochewe only took caravans, so we had to walk several miles up the road to reach an area of grass with a tap and loos for those who were self-supporting. It was the 2 May bank holiday weekend and we were not alone. One neighbour had a very loud voice and we knew exactly how many baked beans were on his supper menu. We turned in early, as the midges were out in force, and slept at once. I dreamt that there was a thunderstorm and our tent had been struck by lightning. Orange flames licked the flimsy walls and the ground shook with a monstrous roaring sound. I heard the lady in the next tent scream.

'Fire! Fire! We must get out!' I shouted, scrambling from the downy confines of my sleeping bag and attempting to unzip the tent. Richard's calm voice told me not to worry; a JCB truck had just trundled down the track and its powerful lights were my imagined flames.

The next time I woke it was to hear the incessant drumming of hard rain, so hard it was impossible to strike camp, so we waited patiently hoping the weather would improve. We finally got off in monotonous drizzle, and stopped at the garage café in Kinlochewe to tank up with a large slice of cake and a mug of hot chocolate before tackling the Heights of Kinlochewe, Loch an Fada and the Fisherfield Forest.

On the outskirst of Kinlochewe, we passed a small tin tabernacle belonging to the Wee Frees and a notice on the door told us that it served Applecross, Lochcarron, Torridon and Kinlochewe, literally hundreds of square miles. We hoped the minister was given a mileage allowance.

Once out of the village, we found a path signed to Dundonnell, a reassuring start. Our track through the Heights of Kinlochewe was easy underfoot but the drizzle turned to rain. We made good time until the path petered out near Loch an Fada, a slate grey sheet among the dark heather and bruised hills. Here we met a young man with piercing blue eyes descending from a tough Munro called the Mullach. His fair hair was dripping under a saturated hat, but his face shone with exertion and excitement. 'I couldn't see a thing but I've done it,' he cried triumphantly.

Now we were once more on the heather, scrambling round great peat hags and clambering up and down small hillocks; after three hard miles we finally found the path along the frothing snake of the River Nid in the Fisherfield Forest. It was hardly a path, at times a stony stream and at times a green boggy strip beside the racing water. It began raining and the wilderness enveloped us; water streamed off the smooth grey flanks of Sgurr Bhan across the dark waters of Loch Nid and off our clothes and faces; our feet were always under inches of water. At one point I noticed a sheep's skull lying in a black pool beside a stump of the Old Caledonian Forest: a telling memento mori. We splashed and squelched along like insects under the shadow of the frowning hills until we reached the end of the valley. A ruined croft just off the path at Achneigie a mile short of the Shenavall bothy made a perfect camping place; now we were only half a mile from the good track which leads round the base of An Teallach to Dundonnell. The air was damp and silent; wild empty valleys stretched to the south and west as far as the eye could see; meandering rivers flanked by bright green vegetation wandered along the valley floor. As I cooked supper Richard told me it was one of the most isolated places in the UK; like the young man we met earlier, we felt exhausted but jubilant.

We had a good night in our ruined croft, no ghosts, and no rain. After tea and hot porridge I put on my last pair of dry socks and hoped we would get to Ullapool in the dry. We still had the Shenavall River to cross, but fortunately the rain held off during the night, and we managed to splash through the shallows to reach Destitution Road, so called because during the Clearances the Highlanders were herded down this road to Gairloch where they emigrated. This desolate track took us round the base of An Teallach and across wild moorland and brown locheens to the soft green estates of Dundonnell.

'We need to know whether there's a ferry to take us across Loch Broom', said Richard anxiously; he was having visions of us walking twenty miles (thirty-two kilometres) round the loch to reach Ullapool. I rang the Tourist Office on my mobile.

'Can you wait a moment, please? I'll just have to ask a colleague,' said a polite voice in my ear. My mobile batteries were running low and it seemed a long wait.

'Hello? I'm Sheila. What was it you wanted to know about ferries?'

I explained as briefly as I could.

'OK. I've the timetable right here. The ferries leave once a day at ten a.m. from Ullapool.' Richard was hissing in my free ear. 'We don't want a car ferry. We want the little boat from Altnaharry.'

I relayed this vital point to Sheila.

'Sorry,' she said. 'I've no idea. I can no' help ye there but I'll try and find out and ring ye back.' I hadn't time to explain that my battery was so low I would have to turn the phone off.

However, being a female, I wasn't afraid to ask. We met a steady stream of walkers on their way to climb An Teallach but they had all come by car to Dundonnell. The only sign of life in this minute hamlet was a picture gallery with an OPEN sign on the gate. We walked into a warm well-lit studio, full of paintings, cards and wee gifts. A beautiful lady at the till with shoulder-length dark hair and big brown eyes smiled knowingly when we asked about the little ferry from Altnaharry to Ullapool.

'Och yes, that'll be Jimmy,' she said, 'he'll take ye across no problem.' She looked at her watch. 'His next scheduled trip is one thirty so if you hurry you'll catch him.' She looked hard at us for a moment and then added, 'Here's his mobile number, and I'll give him a ring meself.'

I could see Richard thought she was a goddess.

We put on a spurt for the six miles (nine kilometres) along a small road through the wooded valley of the Dundonell estate, protected from the prevailing winds by the great bulk of An Teallach. The sky remained sullen, but the temperature rose, and our wet socks steamed as we pounded up the metalled road under the steep side of Beinn nam Ban to the ridge where we could see Ullapool, a sprawl of white, on the far side of Loch Broom. It was nearly one thirty and we scanned the empty water looking for Jimmy's wee ferry. Nothing moved on the grey-blue expanse. We raced down the track, where a couple informed us that the road to the loch was impassable as they were rebuilding the drive. Taking no notice, we stumbled down a precipitous slope where a JCB had churned the peat into giant peaks and troughs; it was worse than battling across heather and peat hags, we were tired, and I slipped and fell. Unhurt, I got to my feet but something in me had snapped; I was anointed with peaty mud from top to toe and I screamed with fury. It was one forty-five and there was no sign of Jimmy; we were out of food and water sitting on rocks at the loch edge, and once again the creature comforts we craved were just a stretch of water away.

I wiped my messy hand on a sodden hanky and dug the mobile out of my pocket, hoping there would be a signal and enough battery to call the ferry. The phone lit up, there was a signal, and with shaky fingers I dialled the number our goddess had given us.

'Halloo! Are ye there?' The Scottish voice sounded amused. 'Jeannie let me know ye'd be along. I'll be with ye in ten minutes.'

The experienced warden of the Ullapool youth hostel pulled a face. 'We're full all week with school kids and wouldn't you know it'. The sounds of pop music and girlish giggles wafted from the sparse lounge. 'There're plenty of B&Bs here though.' She paused and looked into our weather-beaten faces. 'Where are you from and where are you going to?'

We told her and she nodded approvingly. After all, these hostels were originally intended for walkers. There was a short pause and then she asked, 'Do you know the path from here to Achiltibuie?'

We said we had done it in 1995 on our coastal walk.

'Good,' she replied. 'It's just that a lot of people don't realize how hard it is and come unstuck. The rescue services are really stretched at times. I'll ring the warden at the Achininver and book you in.'

Our landlady, Louise McKenzie, put our filthy boots in her greenhouse and told us there was a launderette at the campsite. We had just filled up the machine with smelly clothes when I realized we had no change for soap powder. I asked two tough-looking young men, busy erecting a small tent they had obviously carried, if they had some change. They dug into their pockets, changed my pound and asked me where we were going. When I told them we were on the Cape Wrath Trail they looked at me in disbelief.

'You're not really, are you? *The* Cape Wrath Trail?' and their eyeballs nearly hit the grass. We're doing it too.'

We chatted about rivers and wilderness and arranged to meet later. When they rang from a noisy pub at 9 p.m. that evening, we had already hit the bed and were suddenly feeling like grandparents. We wished each other well and hoped we'd meet up before we got to the Cape.

At breakfast Louise, an energetic lady nearer sixty than fifty, told us that she had run a care home in Strathpeffer for many years. This meant a fifty-mile (eighty-kilometre) drive every day of the year over remote roads in all weathers which was part of life in the Highlands. She had also raised £125,000 for the hospice in Inverness after many years of taking part in the

Great Highland Challenge Walk, and there was a battery of medals on her wall to prove it. This annual walk of thirteen or twenty-five miles (twenty-one or forty kilometres) was a route over the testing terrain of the Fisherfield and Letterewe Forests, and we knew exactly how testing that could be.

For the first time since we had left the West Highland Way, the sun shone from a cloudless sky and we set off in T-shirts and shorts with clean socks and almost dry boots. As we walked north out of Ullapool on the A835 we saw the ruined crofts along the shores of Loch Broom. For thousands of years people have settled on these fertile patches of land. Many of the early settlements date from the Bronze Age and by the end of the eighth-century, when northern Scotland came under Viking control, Loch Broom was an important route giving access to the interior and providing a short overland crossing to the east coast. The loch attracted Viking settlers because of the abundance of fish: cod, ling and shoals of herring. The town of Ullapool itself was established by the British Fishing Society in 1788 and still has a fishing fleet of twelve boats.

The demise of crofting started in the eighteenth-century when the estate owners rented their land for sheep grazing and many of the crofters were evicted from their smallholdings. The new owners invested money in the area, built lodges and developed the sporting interests of the estates. Today, deer forests, along with hill farming, crofting and conservation, are a major part of the land usage along Loch Broom.

The blue waters of Kanaird Bay sparkled beside an arc of bleached sand and the line of white cottages on the strand looked out to Loch Broom and Isle Martin. It took us three hours of brisk walking to reach the Falls of Blughasery, a good spot for lunch; we sat in the sun watching pied wagtails on the warm rocks beside the frothing waters of a mini gorge. It was a moment to relax before we started the arduous scramble across the notorious 'Postie Path'. On our coastal walk in 1995, my father had supported us in this part of Scotland and had taken our packs for us. Now we would have to manage this tortuous path, at the rocky base of Beinn Mor Coigach, with camping gear and provisions for the next few nights. As we started climbing we saw a notice which read: TO ACHILTIBUIE. DANGEROUS PATH.

The first few miles were exhilarating, with good views south to the bulky silhouettes of An Teallach and west to the rocky Summer Isles, lying in the calm water like a group of basking whales. We managed the undulating rocky terrain without much trouble until mid-afternoon, when heat and fatigue began to take their toll. While we paused for a breather, Richard told me to check that my rucksack was strapped firmly to my back; from now on the path took us up the mountain over rock faces, down into gullies, and along tiny tracks of friable peat which hugged the steep slopes; one slip and we would have plunged hundreds of feet down to the sea. A solitary seal in the cove far below waved an encouraging flipper; I waved back and just hoped the postman didn't have to carry too many parcels.

The youth hostel at Achininver, a mile from the string of cottages that made up Achiltibuie, was well off the little road. It was an enlarged croft, white under an orange tin roof. From here we had a close up view of the Summer Isles and beyond them the headlands north of Gairloch; to the south east the silhouettes of An Teallach and the Fisherfield Mountains rose across the clear water. Towering above us at the back was the massive bulk of Beinn Mor Coigach. A group of young people were enjoying a meal on the little terrace, tucking into great plates of pasta washed down with red wine. We found the warden, sharing his little room with a large black labrador, and checked in. I asked if meals were provided.

'I'm afraid not,' he said, handing me a youth hostel sheet. 'You have to cook your own here. If you're short of milk I can let you have some.'

We had left Ullapool at 10.30 a.m. and it was now 7.30 p.m. The effort was over, the warden was kind, and suddenly I felt near to tears.

As I sat on the seat outside, removing gaiters and boots, a cloud of midges appeared from nowhere and drove us all inside. The living room with kitchen annexe was furnished with wooden tables, benches and a cosy stove. There were warnings on the wall about the severity of the Postie Path. Among the walking magazines were leaflets on the Highland midge which made gruesome reading: there are thirty-seven species of these little monsters, six of which attack humans, and, as Richard was quick to point out, only the female bites. It is, of course, survival tactics as the female needs blood to lay her eggs. She is equipped with a well-developed mouth and a fine tooth, which cuts, scissor-like, into the skin of the victim. When the cut is deep enough, the female rolls her mouth into a tube to suck up the flowing blood, and pumps in saliva to prevent it from clotting. If left undisturbed, she will happily gorge for up to four minutes, and will continue her vampire-like activity until, at one ten millionth of a litre, she has had her fill. A swarm of midges could, it seemed, leave their victim in need of a blood transfusion.

No one has yet been able to rid the Highlands of these well-adapted creatures, which form an integral part of the eco-system and food chain, although many different remedies have been tried. Perhaps this is just as well; Scotland is one of the most underpopulated areas in Europe and this is part of its charm. The midges, along with the harsh terrain and the unpredictable weather, help to keep it that way.

Everything in Scotland is a bit tougher: unlike the English youth hostel which now provides family rooms, delicious three-course meals, comfortable lounges and even e-mail facilities, the Scottish ones are run more on the old lines, offering only basic warmth and shelter; if the hosteller needs food, they have to bring their own.

This little hostel was nearly full, but most of the residents had come in cars and several groups were in this part of Scotland hoping to see the annular eclipse of the sun on 31 May. It was an exciting prospect; the last annular eclipse was on 8 April 1921 and the next one would not be until 23 July 2093. This eclipse, in three days' time, would be visible in the Scottish Highlands, Orkney, Shetland and Lewis starting at 3.45 a.m. and ending at 5.45. We decided it was well worth rising early in order to see it.

Sleep in our crowded dorm under the skylights, was impossible; I think my body was walking on to Cape Wrath. In the morning some kind person brought me a cup of tea and I dosed my aches and pains with paracetamol. After a bowl of porridge and two cups of tea, I felt ready to go.

It was an easy day's walk on the same road we had used in 1995. At that time Achiltibuie was throbbing to the sound of pipe and drum as the locals enjoyed their annual Highland Games. We had downed a can of McEwans and watched a group of children with swinging kilts and little tartan hats dancing on the green strand as the sun set over the mountains. This time it was damp and grey and our spirits echoed the weather. At the hamlet of Polglass, we met a herd of Highland cattle beside a low white farmhouse, peering inquisitively at us through curtained eyes; down on the shoreline were neat strips of croft land, and the stone shells of the old buildings, all that remained after the Highland Clearances.

We were cheered to find an unexpected pub open on our way to the Brae of Achnahaird. After soup, chips and beer Richard suggested I rang Scot Rail and booked our sleepers home. We had tried to do this before we left, but were told it was too early and to try again in May. I had been hoping to get a reduction on an advance booking, but it was too late for that now. I managed to get a signal outside the ladies' loo and booked a sleeper on Friday 6 June from Inverness to Euston, a day earlier than anticipated. Due to cutting down on our wilderness walking, we still had a day to spare, and Richard had decided we would treat ourselves to a day off at Scourie and a visit to Handa Island, for it was the very best time to see the nesting seabirds there. Back on the road Richard asked me what date I had booked our rail tickets for. I got the date right but the day wrong; we were in our usual 'tomorrow is tomorrow' mode. An interrogation followed.

'Are you sure you booked that sleeper for Friday, June the sixth? You just said Thursday was the sixth.'

'I'm sure I booked it for the Friday. I had the itinerary in front of me. It's allright. Don't panic.'

He wasn't convinced, and when we reached the campsite at the Brae of Achnahaird I double-checked and found I had been correct. In his anxiety to ensure that everything ran smoothly, Richard now doubted everything I did. If we were in a hotel he would ask, 'Have you locked the door?'

'Yes.'

'Have you got the key?'

'Yes.'

'Are you sure you've got the key?'

The only way to stop the interrogation was to produce the evidence. The trouble with this was that I began to lose confidence in myself and I found it difficult to shrug off these doubts.

The wind was gusting over the bay at Achnahaird and the familiar silhouettes of the mountains of Assynt, Cul Mor, Cul Beag, Stac Pollaidh, and Suilven, rose up from the brown moorland in front of us; a line of primeval monsters, just names to those who don't know them, silhouettes to those who do, and soulmates to those who have been lucky enough to climb them. Beyond lay the rocks and lochans of Sutherland and the wilderness of Cape Wrath.

We tucked our little tent under a stout hedge at the Brae of Achnahaird campsite, ate our pasta on a bench table, and slept well. We were amused to see a gentleman drive his car from his caravan two hundred yards away to the toilet block and it wasn't even raining.

As our boots hammered along the twisting little road towards Lochinver, we discussed our plans for Europe, and decided to take a three-week break at home. This would mean we could be with Richard's mother to celebrate her ninety-fourth birthday, and we would be really rested before tackling our next marathon walk to Nice. In order to catch our window of weather we would have to miss out the GR5 long-distance path in Holland and northern Belgium, and start walking further south from Spa in the Ardennes.

'That will mean no long mileages on the flat,' Richard said comfortingly. 'We'll be in the Ardennes straight away and then you'll have plenty of hills to climb.' It sounded like a good plan, although I wouldn't really believe any of it until we reached the Cape.

At Inverpolly we came across a salmon hatchery, long green sheds like aircraft hangars under the rocky hillside. We learned that the North Assynt Estate of 21,500 acres (about 9,000 hectares) was purchased by the inhabitants from a foreign landowner in 1993. It was the first transaction of its kind in the history of crofting in the Scottish Highlands and it gave the local Scots control over a small part of the territory lost after the collapse of the clan system and the subsequent policy of land clearance practised by the Duke of Sutherland. The crofters now own the land, together with the mineral, fishing and shooting rights. The purchase price was raised by local and world-wide donation, together with grant and loan assistance from the regional council and public agencies. We wished them luck and wondered what the Duke of Sutherland would have thought.

The metronomic call of the cuckoo pursued us through the Highlands and rang out along the rise and fall of the lonely road. We rested briefly on the green sward beside the River Kirkaig, our feet cooling in the swirling waters while we watched hundreds of little elvers darting round our toes. Richard recalled a holiday in Scotland when he and his family had picnicked under the shade of a rowan tree on that very spot, and cooled their hot feet in the river. 'That,' he said, examining his white appendages through the clear water, 'was fifty years ago.'

We reached the fishing port of Lochinver in good time to find a B&B; any fears about the village's being full of eclipse seekers had been unfounded. We were almost alone in the grand dining room of a baronial hotel near the harbour. The barmaid told us that the fishermen were now mainly Spanish, Portuguese or Faroese.

'The inshore fishin' boats can still make a livin' but there're no' many larger boats now. Those great sheds out there are beerly used,' she told us as she served two Spanish trawlermen with only a few words of English between them.

After our meal we walked past the empty reception sheds where a dozen or so boats, bristling with masts, antennae and spools of green netting, were tied up. Orange and white plastic boxes sat on the quayside, and the air was thick with the stench of rotting fish. The shiny black heads of a few hopeful seals bobbed up and down in the water, and gulls screeched at each other and everything else they could see.

Lochinver, another long village, lies under the great cone of Suilven, one of the Assynt group of mountains which are the remnants of the Torridonian sandstone topped with younger harder white quartzite; the erosion of the sandstone has exposed a thousand-million-year-old fossil landscape. Perhaps it is their incomprehensible age that gives these individually shaped mountains their mystique.

We scrutinized the war memorial in Lochinver while we waited for the Tourist Office to open; there were fifteen names from the Second World War, thirteen from the surrounding villages and only two from Lochinver itself. Clashnessie, where we were going that day, is a tiny hamlet, and the two Macleads who died must have represented about half the adult male population. Three times as many men were listed as having lost their lives during the Great War and again as many as four men came from places that were no more than a few farms and cottages. The only war we had been concerned with on this walk was the war with Iraq, and hostilities had ceased on 1 May, but the two world wars were to play a large part on our route in Europe. Then we would be walking along France's boundaries with Belgium, Luxembourg, Switzerland and Italy, past the sites of many twentieth-century battles. We were to become increasingly aware of the privilege of belonging to an island race.

Summer had arrived at last and we reached the empty white sands of Clashnessie in warm sunshine. We found a good spot on the hillside near a ruined croft to pitch the tent, and indulged in a little sunbathing before the midges arrived and drove us down onto the beach where we had our first swim of the summer.

Back at the tent I prepared our staple camping diet of savoury rice, ham, banana and chocolate. We turned in early, but were so anxious to wake at 4 a.m. to see the solar eclipse that neither of us slept much. I seemed to have just nodded off when Richard was shaking me awake; we pulled on our clothes, and unzipped the tent, crawled out into a dimly lit world of grass, heather and rocks. The little burn beside the tent chuckled noisily in the silence. Below us a monochrome sea idled beside the pale beach; there was a chill wind in the damp air. We put on our boots and set off up the inky hillside towards the lighter sky in the east. On the crest of the hill we stood on a big black rock and watched the aurora. The sky was blushed with pink and we could see that the rising sun was veiled in thin cloud. We waited and watched as minute by minute the blush deepened and a hazy crescent of sun became visible. Then the clouds parted to expose a circle within a circle, the moon perfectly centred within a halo of brilliant light. This fireball, suspended over the dark outlines of Ben Stack and Arkle, was framed by thick bands of grey cloud; very slowly, the moon moved across the sun, until once more it was a blazing crescent and then a familiar red ball which turned the sea pink and sharpened the outlines of distant hills. We stood in awed silence, pin silhouettes on some of the oldest rocks in the world against a sunrise that wouldn't recur for more than three generations.

The little road wound round and over the bare Sutherland landscape, clothed only by coarse grass, occasional drifts of stunted trees, and clumps of yellow gorse. Down by the tree-clad lochs, there was a softer look: fishing boats and yachts were moored on the water or rested on the brown seaweed; dog roses bloomed along the roadside by Loch Drumbeg and drifts of buttercups and orchids could be found in the more sheltered places. From time to time we could see stags on the green hillside, their antlered heads silhouetted against the sky. In this part of Scotland there was a welcome absence of conifer plantations, which meant the natural species of mountain ash, hazel and birch could flourish, and views were not obscured by vast tracts of dense firs.

The rising temperatures and hilly terrain gave us a good thirst but we resisted the temptation to have a drink at the Drumbeg Hotel where their Seafood Platter on the lunch menu cost £59 for two! Instead we quenched our thirst at the nearest burn. We bought some lunch at the Drumbeg post office and shop, which was for sale, and then investigated a small stone barn advertising fruit and vegetables; it was run by a man in a designer sweatshirt and immaculate jeans who came from Five Ashes in East Sussex and had moved up to the Highlands in 1971. This greengrocery business was a new venture, he told us, and he had to buy his stock from the delivery vans travelling north, catching them when they stopped to unload in the larger towns. It all sounded a rather precarious venture and his petrol bills didn't seem to be reflected in the prices of his fruit and vegetables. He had a tempting display of fresh oranges, kiwi fruit, melon, fresh leeks, broccoli and tomatoes, so unlike the rubbery carrots and shrunken cabbages of the local shops. We couldn't resist a melon, the heaviest fruit on the market, and sat by the burn cutting it up with a minute penknife and scooping the juicy flesh using our teeth like spoons, enjoying every succulent mouthful.

On our way to Kylesku we could see the long ridge of Foinaven, a reminder that if we had stuck to our original plan we would be striking off the road from Kylesku round the back of Arkle, and along the ridged back of Foinaven to Kinlochbervie, Sandwood Bay and the Cape. Looking at the distant monster I was glad Richard had opted out.

Our accommodation that night was a luxurious A-frame bunkhouse at Kylesku with a clear view of the great buttresses and corries of Quinag across the still waters of the loch – all for £10 each.

June 1, and Richard pulled the last OS map we would need in the UK from his rucksack. We were on the A894, twenty-five miles (forty kilometres) from Durness; Durness was significant as it would be our re-entry point into the real world after two nights camping on the Parbh wilderness near Cape Wrath.

Scourie campsite had everything: washing machines, tumble dryers, clean showers, hairdryers, a café, and a magnificent view across the bay to Handa Island. Road walking was taking its toll of my leg muscles, and I was excited at the prospect of a tourist day on the island. A Scottish footpath took us from Scourie village over the knobbly terrain of bare rock between pools of peaty water. The three miles (five kilometres) with only a day pack was a pleasure and we arrived at the hamlet of Tarbet to see the little ferry, loaded with passengers, about to leave. Since it was Scotland, they waited for us to race down the last slopes and join them, before the ferry chugged across the Sound of Handa, past the grey-green Sutherland rockscape to the island nature reserve. It was the breeding season, and on our four-mile (six-kilometre) circuit we were dive-bombed by great skuas near a line of ruined crofts whose inhabitants had emigrated to Nova Scotia to face equal hardships in a foreign land. Sea pinks carpeted the edges of the cliffs and turned the natural path into a rock garden where puffins had their burrows. Guillemots, razorbills and fulmar were nesting on the rock ledges, iced white with guano. The air was filled with the screech of seabirds. To the south we could see the distant mountains of Assynt, the sands at Clashnessie and the lone sandstone stack at the Point of Stoer. The grey silhouettes of Arkle and Foinaven smudged the horizon to the east. Looking north, a grey-blue Atlantic frothed against the last few miles of rock and cliff to Cape Wrath on the north-western tip of mainland Britain.

Back on the footpath from Tarbet to Scourie we came up behind a middle-aged couple; the wife was bringing up the rear and having difficulty in keeping up with her fleet-footed husband. She had my sympathy for a while, but I lost patience when she refused to let us pass; we must have been on her heels for nearly a mile when she joined her waiting husband. She looked hot and in no mood even to wish us the time of day. As we walked past them I heard myself say brightly, 'Lovely day. This path's a doddle, isn't it?' Two pairs of eyes bored through me like rapiers; it was easy to forget that everything is relative, and my remark kept Richard sniggering all the way back to the tent.

A sunset with sea and mountains has to be the nearest thing to heaven on earth; that evening we walked a mile or so up the hillside, past the gently curving bay where a line of oystercatchers was feeding at the tide-line, over white carpets of delicate bog cotton, skirting reedy lochans, to watch the sun sinking behind the ancient rocks leaving a fiery path across the water. On our return, thick cumulus clouds were suspended above the dark still water; low black rocks stretched into the sea like crocodiles, and the silence was only broken by the piping call of a redshank.

Our last day of road walking to Rhiconich took us along the main road where a geological time map had been blasted through the ancient rocks exposing grey gneiss, black dolerite and pink granite. This stripy effect is due to the molten dolerite and pink granite entering the solid gneiss and forcing open cracks which eventually harden; then the earth's movement over the years brought these rocks to the surface. All this happened millions of years ago and the recent blasting of the high rocks gave us an excellent geology lesson.

Near Loch Laxford we watched a man cutting rectangles of peat and leaning them against each other to dry off. Peat is the accumulated remains of plants which grow in waterlogged places, where it has been forming for several thousand years.

Most residents have traditional rights to cut peat on particular pieces of ground. It is normally cut in the spring and left to dry over the summer.

'They certainly earn their free fuel,' I said to Richard as we watched the man's back-breaking endeavours. 'For hundreds of years it was their only means of keeping warm, poor sods,' I added. The pun fell on deaf ears.

Tramp, tramp, tramp along the road among the endless scoured rocks, reedy lochans and strange round stones scattered over the hills. These were erratics, formed 20,000 years ago when the land was covered in a thick sheet of slowly moving ice. When the temperature rose and the ice melted, these boulders (which had been carried along by the glaciers) were left; it was as though a giant had been playing marbles on the bony hills and had forgotten to put them away.

The third of June was our wedding anniversary and the Rhiconich Hotel had given us the attic/penthouse suite with marbled bathroom and Jacuzzi bath with ample room for two. The Velux windows looked over Loch Inchard and our last stretch of road to Kinlochbervie before we set off for Sandwood Bay and Cape Wrath. In the 1950s-style dining room, among the clatter of cutlery and the hushed voices, we raised our glasses of Colombard Chardonnay. Our conversation ran something like this.

Shally: 'Cheers. Happy anniversary.'

Richard: 'How many years is it?'

Shally after short pause: 'Thirty-six.'

Richard after long pause: 'How many years since we met?'

Shally: 'Thirty-eight years since I received your appointment card in illegible handwriting.' (Physiotherapy students had their dentistry free if they let a dental student do the work.)

Richard (affecting Maurice Chevalier accent): 'Oh yes. I remember it well.'

Shally: 'What was I wearing?'

Long pause. Richard: 'Something green?'

Shally: 'You were all in white.'

Richard after very long pause: 'Well, whatever you were wearing I did give you your first crown.'

The croft houses and red-roofed farm buildings of Rhiconich were strung out above the long shores of Loch Inchard like a necklace of orange and white beads. Each dwelling had a green rectangle of croft land sloping down to the water's edge, delineated with dry stone walls. Neat lines of green floats marked salmon nets in the loch, and flocks of sheep and lambs grazed the coarse grass. I guessed that many of the crofts were now second homes or holiday lets, and the farms owned by incomer 'gentlemen' farmers. Fishing at Kinlochbervie was once a thriving industry, but today there are only a handful of local boats.

Aware that we needed to stock up with provisions for the next two days, we were pleased to find the London Stores in Badcall Inchard open. The minute shop was so full there was barely room to move, even when you'd lost a stone in weight and left the rucksack outside. We squeezed our way past the Thai seaweed crackers, knitting needles, OS maps, fishing lines, tins of soup, packets of pasta, fruit and veg, chocolate bars, Mills and Boon and post cards and staggered outside with enough food for at least forty-eight hours. Richard nobly took the extra weight.

At the top of the hill above the little hamlet of Oldshoremore, we said goodbye to the mountains of Assynt until the next time. The cloud cover lifted enough to allow patches of sun to light fields of buttercups which ran down to sandy coves and a sea that had turned from steel to turquoise. At Blairmore we left the road and went through a little gate which said *No dogs. Walkers welcome. Sandwood Bay 4.5 miles* and up the familiar sandy track where we met a trickle of other walkers; it seemed the world wasn't entirely ours after all.

Sandwood Bay is one of Scotland's most beautiful beaches, unspoiled because it is so remote, approachable only on foot. To the north it is bound by the rocky headland of the cape, and to the south the towering stack of Am Buachaille (the herdsman) stands as an icon of the power of the sea and the glory of the brutal cliffs. The rock-strewn girth of pink sand softens the bay and shelves up to form great dunes fringed with coarse marram grass.

A thin white band of surf stroked the sand as we walked among the great lumps of sandstone and dolerite rocks and absorbed the spirit of this ancient and humbling stretch of coast. The sheer cliffs and lone stack at the southern end were dark silhouettes against a pale blue sea. We sat on an ancient lump of rock and stilled ourselves: our bodies, our thoughts, our focus. It was as if some powerful presence was holding us in the hollow of a hand; at any moment we could be tossed away or put down gently. We were trespassing in this implacable landscape, south-land of the ancient Norse, and our arrogance was being tolerated. We had been on this very beach on a wild September day in 1992 when the wind played with us like spume on the beach and it was a fight to stand up. We had struggled back to Blairmore, and when we finally arrived it took two hands to close the car door.

'I think it's time to move on and find a place to camp. If we walk another mile that will mean one less tomorrow.' Richard had returned to reality.

We picked our way across the shallows of Sandwood River, which scours deep into the sand, and scrambled up onto the next headland. Once the edge of the known world, the last few miles of north-west coast stretched before us like a three-dimensional map: naked cliffs thinly covered in coarse vegetation plunging into the calm sea. Somewhere up there was the lighthouse. Cape Wrath does not mean anger, but turning point, so called by the Vikings; and for us too it would mean turning for home.

We pitched our little tent by a noisy river which tumbled down the hillside and emptied itself into the sea far below.

The sun shone for us on our penultimate day as we set off over the heather, peat, rocks and rollercoaster hills for the Cape. A brisk wind kept the midges at bay, and we walked as near the sea as we could and watched the white surf crash onto the sparkling sandstone cliffs. Everything was clear and clean, the blue sky, the indigo sea, the cliffs, the hills, the flowers. There was no litter and no one. The wild cliffs of Cape Wrath grew nearer, but between them and us were ranks of steeply shelving hills, deep gullies, and rivers to cross. At times the ground beneath our feet was covered with golden guineas, sundew, butterwort and bog cotton and sprang under our tread. A skylark trilled as it rocketed into the great blue space above us. We dropped down into little coves and then scrambled up the other side, and discovered a stone bothy, (a shelter for walkers in remote places) in the lee of a hill. Inside there were a few wooden boxes, some polystyrene to sleep on, plastic water bottles and a heap of firelighter blocks. Part of the heather and turf ceiling was propped up with a box; basic but possibly life-saving in really bad weather.

Then we saw the thin metallic road that led to the lighthouse; we still had hills to puff up and race down but, warmed by the sun and fanned by the breeze, we revelled in our fitness and arrived on the road with a minibus full of tourists who had come from Durness on a day's outing. We walked the half-mile to Stevenson's lighthouse in silence.

How did it feel? For me there was a sense of bathos, disbelief possibly, or the knowledge that this was not journey's end but the halfway mark. I used up the last two exposures of my film as we made sure we had proof of our arrival, and cursed at not having bought another one at the London Stores. We ate bread and sardines washed down with burn water while looking at kittiwake and fulmar on the sandstone cliffs and watching the sea frothing round the dark rocks far below. Suddenly there was a roar followed by a muffled explosion, and as we watched smoke and spume far below grew into a giant fountain.

'They're bombing the cliffs. Just target practice', came the answer to my unasked question. Repeated muffled explosions in this wild place, gave the scene a sense of virtual reality; kittiwakes and fulmars squawked latent disapproval.

As we walked a further five miles along the lighthouse road, we were overtaken by the tourist-laden minibus. The driver stopped and asked if we would like a lift. We refused politely and told him we were going to camp.

'You'd better watch out,' he said darkly. 'The wind's rising and the ferries don't always run in bad weather.'

We watched the bus drive off and disappear into dead ground; later we saw it moving slowly up the tortuous road, a white ant among the barren hills of the Parbh. That night I dreamt that our efforts to cross the Kyle of Durness were thwarted by huge waves which threatened to drown me and my rucksack. All I could think about was keeping my camera dry.

Kearvaig is a remote bay at the end of a mile of rough track leading off the lighthouse service road to the Kyle of Durness. Here the weary traveller finds a simple Victorian shepherd's hut, now a bothy. Below the green fields and hidden from the outside world, a golden beach stretches between high cliffs. As we paddled in the surf kittiwake, fulmar, razorbill and puffin shrieked alarm from their rocky ledges and a flock of gulls flew up from the water's edge. We were intruders, but like all those who find this haven, we had worked hard for this moment in paradise. I caught Richard's arm, kissed him and murmured, 'Thanks for taking me along with you.'

'Thanks for putting up with me.'

We pitched our tent outside the bothy, and while I cooked supper Richard went down to the beach to gather driftwood. We ate our savoury rice and ham and Mars bars in front of a blazing fire, sitting on rickety armchairs, enjoying the last dram of whisky and watching the shadows dance, while outside a full moon rose above the beach. On the wall was a newspaper cutting about Margaret Davies, a 30-year-old experienced trekker who was found dying of starvation and hypothermia by some shepherds in December 2002. Her photo showed a good-looking woman, with long fair hair and an open honest face. In spite of the lighthouse track, this is a remote and unforgiving place, especially in winter. Margaret, weak from lack of food and water, could not have summoned enough strength to walk the thirteen miles to safety. She left a note in the window asking for food; we were pleased to see that there was a pan full of tins and packets, suspended from the ceiling to prevent its being eaten by mice. No one who passed this way would be allowed to starve to death in future. On the wall someone had written a poem which perfectly captured her spirit:

> Golden girl I will cut peat for your fire
> And rushes for your bed.
> Plenty food and drink for you.
> May you be happy in your wanderings
> Soft rain on your face, light wind in your back
> Hear the surf on the shore, lark song in the air
> Flowers at your feet, eagles above you.
> See sunlight glisten in the dragonfly's wing
> Moonrise over mountains.
> Peace to you always in your wanderings.

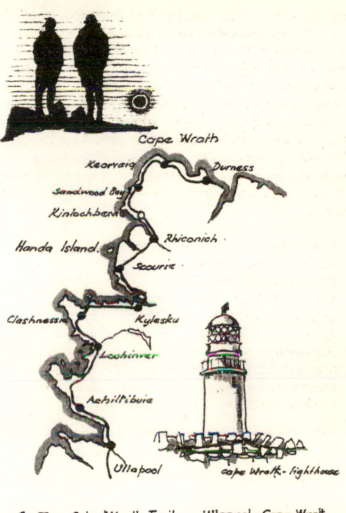

Cape Wrath

Keorvaig   Durness

Sandwood Bay

Kinlochbervie

Handa Island.   Rhiconich

Scourie

Clashnessie   Kylesku

Lochinver

Achiltibuie

Ullapool   cape Wrath - lighthouse

9. The Cape Wrath Trail — Ullapool - Cape Wrath.

0   10   20   30 m

0   10   20   30   40   km

PART TWO

HOLLAND
Bruges
Antwerp
BELGIUM
Liège
Spa
Luxembourg
GERMANY
Paris
Metz
Nancy
Strasbourg
Belfort
Besançon
L.Neuchâtel
Pontarlier
SWITZERLAND
Myon
Lake Geneva
Samoëns
Lyon
Chamonix
Mt. Blanc
Grenoble
Modane
Briançon
Larche
Walle
Nice
Marseille
FRANCE
Mediterranean Sea.

Route through France.

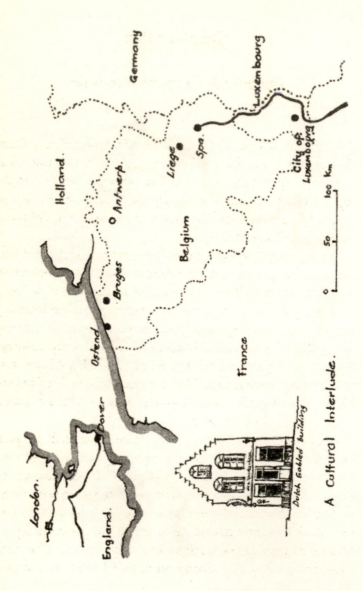

A Cultural Interlude.

Chapter Nine

Europe: A Cultural Interlude

The flat green fields and brick and tile villages of East Kent flew past the window of our empty carriage; the train slowed, hugging the base of Shakespeare Cliff. It was 30 June, exactly 104 days since we had stood at the top of these cliffs and squinted across the Channel at the blurred coastline of Europe.

During our three-week interlude, we had recharged our batteries, caught up with the family and put our affairs in order (in case we fell off a mountain or were eaten by wolves). Exercise was limited to a few cycle rides round the Romney Marsh and one three-mile (five kilometre) walk that nearly finished me. The unrest in Iraq rumbled on, Granny's ninety-fourth birthday had been duly celebrated and Wimbledon was in full swing. Richard and I had a restless sense of unfinished business during this period; we were walkers with a mission, anxious to achieve our goal.

Both Bruges and Antwerp were on the long-distance path known as the Grande Randonnée Cinq (GR5/E2) which we would be following all the way to Nice. We decided to prolong our break and treat ourselves to two tourist days in both cities.

The Sea Cat from Dover took us swiftly across the Channel to Calais; for some reason there are no longer crossings to Ostend so we were taken there in a courtesy bus. The front rows of the upstairs seating were filled with overweight middle-aged men who wheezed and coughed their way across the polders on the tobacco run to Zeebrugge.

Ostend welcomed us with a closed railway station; we walked round and round the booking halls and platforms looking for signs of life, and assumed that they had adopted the Mediterranean habit of siesta time. Eventually we found a notice informing customers that there were no trains due to a one day strike. It was comforting to know that we are not the only nation whose railway service is unpredictable.

The Bruges youth hostel, only £9 a night for B&B, was a mile from the city centre. Crossing a wide canal we watched a bridge rising skywards while opening its jaws to allow a laden working barge to pass through; the bridge descended, a loud bell rang, and torrents of cyclists and cars streamed across.

The city of Bruges has gift-wrapped its heritage: canals, cobbles and campaniles, pitched roofs, step gables, and elegant spires. White-haired ladies, Vermeer vignettes, sit in doorways manipulating a bewildering array of bobbins as they weave a spider's web of cotton into a delicate froth of lace. The imposing squares are origami stage sets from the time when economic, political and social life took place in them. The little streets smell of chocolates, *pommes frites* and horse dung.

Between the heavy showers we stood watching motor boats phut-phutting along the River Dijver, laden with tourists sheltering under a carapace of black and red umbrellas. Tour guides locked into microphones gave booming sound bites of information; at one boat a minute it was like planes landing at Heathrow airport. Our meandering progress was accompanied by the mechanical sound of carillon bells and clip-clop of horse-drawn carriages.

The warm interior of the Church of Our Lady radiated soft light from stained glass windows and candles, and the great triptych by Hans Memling glowed above the altar. In a side chapel we found Michelangelo's *Our Lady and the Infant*; the pale pensive face of the Madonna seemed more flesh and blood than marble and the folds of her garments fell round her seated figure with the softness of real cloth; the unique tenderness of a mother and child shone from the little statue. We gazed in awe, lit a candle and departed.

Having spent much of our working lives in hospitals, it was interesting to see the fifteenth-century Hospital of St John, now a museum and art gallery housing some of Hans Memling's greatest works. Many of the original artefacts were also on display: primitive surgical instruments, sedan chairs, and silver cups with a special lip for easier administration, each cup inscribed with a nun's name. A painting of the original interior showed three lines of beds, one for men, one for women and one for the dying. The relics of the appropriate saint would be hanging near each patient's bed; a few teeth from St Apollonia, the patron saint of dentists, would, it was thought, have a beneficial effect on any patient with jaw disease.

The ethos was of a stoical acceptance of death; great importance was attached to the art of dying, in the certain knowledge that, with sins confessed and forgiven, a peaceful release into the spiritual world awaited the sufferer. Memling's exquisite triptychs and reliquaries helped give the beautifully restored building an atmosphere of calm acceptance.

We spent a pleasant hour looking the paintings in the Groeninge Museum. When we came to leave it was pouring with rain and a small cluster of tourists waited patiently for the cloudburst to pass. Warm and dry, we looked out from the entrance hall onto the little path where a trickle of colourful people hurried along the watery cobbles in search of shelter. It was a scene that might have come off one of the canvases: a bald man with wispy beard and Jesus sandals, two ladies with patent leather shoes, roll-brimmed straw hats and leopard skin umbrellas, a young woman with pre-Raphaelite hair with two little boys in tow. The ingress of dripping, panting, and sodden humanity shook themselves and their umbrellas over us and exchanged frustrated pleasantries in American, Japanese, English, Australian and Italian. We stood hypnotized for a long time watching this *tableau vivant*; the once thriving Hanseatic city had now become a tourist port.

Antwerp station was a cross between mausoleum and palace: black marble gold-embossed pillars, a marble staircase with balustrade, graceful arches and a gold clock like the sun's rays. The Belle Epoch opulence was matched by twenty-first-century technology, a seamless transport system in four tiers: the new high-speed rail link was being constructed at the bottom, trams were on the next tier, then ran the underground and finally, at ground level, the trains. We caught a tram to our youth hostel on the city outskirts. It was closed till 4.30 p.m. so we left our packs and headed back to the city centre.

Antwerp is a big bustling city wrapped around the old town. The great sixteenth-century city hall and guild halls dominate the Frankish Grote Markt, enduring symbols of the unashamed wealth of the burghers of the time. The Gothic cathedral has a delicate 123-metre spire, the highest in the city, and a sparkling white interior the size of a football pitch, with forty-eight slim pillars like silent worshippers on each side. The intricate stone tracery on the forty-metre ceiling is a web of lacework. During Antwerp's Golden Age in the sixteenth-century, Emperor Charles V laid the first stone of a substantial extension which would have made the cathedral the largest building on earth at that time. A fire in 1533 destroyed the nave, preventing the construction of the proposed extension; perhaps God was trying to tell them something.

A *rondwandeling* (circular walk) took us down the old streets to the River Schelde, once teeming with working boats and now a 500-metre-wide conveyor of emptiness. The spidery cranes of the busy port of Antwerp were visible on the grey horizon; all shipping traffic has been moved to large new docks to the north. However, the ghosts remain: the Steen pontoon runs along the river here beside lines of old sheds held up with elegant wrought-iron work. These pontoons once swarmed with hundreds of immigrants who took the Red Star boats to America, and later the Congo boats were moored here. We passed the fairy-story twelfth-century Steen Castle, renovated by Charles V, which still bears his coat of arms. Searching the internet for more information about Steen (first a castle then a prison and now a maritime museum), I found the following which I have reproduced word for word:

Het Steen was the first building in Antwerp to be erected. It served for a big time of its history as a prison. No mercy for the prisoners who where kept in the basement when the tight of the river came up and they were about literary in big trouble up to their neck.

On our way back to the city centre, we passed a long line of plate glass windows in a dingy back street. In each window, a scantily-clad mannequin was perched on a pink bar stool; one of these was holding a mobile phone. I was surprised that this store sold nothing but lingerie, and it wasn't until one of the mannequins gave Richard an inviting smile that I realized that these charming ladies were there to satisfy the voracious appetites of the maritime trade. Considering the paucity of boats I felt they must have been very bored.

Belgium seems to lack identity. Their language is incomprehensible to any foreigner so they have adopted cosmopolitan-speak, enough English, French, and German to get by with. I found this rather disconcerting, as I like to have a few words of the vernacular for starters anyway. We went into an optician to replace the cord for Richard's glasses, and I asked the well-groomed lady behind her shiny counter if she spoke English.

'Of course I do,' she replied stiffly. 'Everybody asks me that. I studied English at university and have visited England on several occasions.'

I apologized profusely, realizing that I had somehow implied that she wasn't an educated professional woman.

Then there was the question of Belgian food; it seemed to us as footslogging tourists, that all they offered was an eclectic mix of imported junk foods, gourmand rather than gourmet. You could start with a tasty Belgian beer and end with a delicious Belgian chocolate but in between it was unremitting fish and chips, hamburger and chips, chicken and chips, pizza and chips, pasta and chips. Belgium gave us our first introduction to the euro, useful if you just want to pop across to Germany, France, or Italy, but very inflationary as we were to discover.

Exhausted from dodging traffic and people on miles of hard pavement, we slept well on the truckle beds of our 1960s youth hostel cell. John Calvin's words, 'For it too often happens that riches bring self-indulgence, and superfluity of pleasures produces flabbiness as we can see in wealthy regions and cities,' seemed applicable at that moment. Richard and I had had enough of cities and were ready shake the gold dust of Flanders off our boots and move on to the muddy hills of the Ardennes, the start of our long walk to Nice.

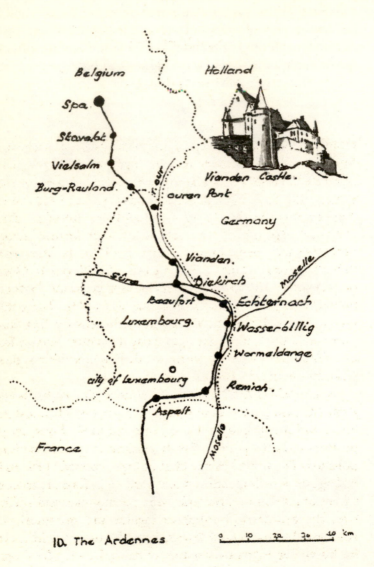

Belgium

Holland

Spa

Stavot

Vielsalm

Burg-Rauland

r. Our

Vianden Castle.

ouran Pont

Germany

Vianden.

Diekirch

r. Sûre

Moselle

Beaufort

Echternach

Luxembourg.

Wasserbillig

Wormaldange

city of Luxembourg

Remich.

Aspelt

France

Moselle

10. The Ardennes

0   10   20   30   40 km

Chapter Ten

The Ardennes

Coming from the spa town of Tunbridge Wells, we felt that Spa, near Liège in the Ardennes, seemed a good place to start our walk to Nice. This Belgian town was once known as the Pearl of the Ardennes. It is the original spa and the name comes from espa, the old Walloon word for a fountain. The chalybeate springs of iron salts with their health-giving properties have been known about since Roman times, and in the fourteenth-century Spa became a health resort. Over the centuries, the town has been visited by some famous names: Margaret of Valois, Kristina of Sweden, Peter the Great, Victor Hugo. In the eighteenth-century Spa was nicknamed the Café of Europe; today it is better known for the annual Grand Prix de Formule I de Belgique which takes place on the nearby Francorchamps circuit.

In the 1970's, John Hillaby mentioned Spa in his book *Journey through Europe*, describing it as a pearl that had lost its lustre and mentioning peeling paint and junk shops, fried potatoes and petrol fumes. Thirty years on the pearl has been polished. The town lies in a cleft of high wooded cliffs, and its large *fin de siècle* casino and baths are set in formal gardens where umbrellas of pink and white geraniums stand stiffly over the geometric borders of tagetes and marguerites; amongst the manicured lawns, large fountains spill their health-giving waters over statues of naked ladies. The shops sell smart clothes, perfume, expensive knick-knacks, and delicious-looking breads and patisserie. There are hair salons, good hotels, and a plethora of banks.

We found a café, filled our stomachs with walker-size baguettes and set off, cursing a heavy downpour which meant pulling on anoracks as we sweated up the steep hill out of Spa. We had intended to camp in the town and then walk the twenty-one miles (thirty-three kilometres) to Vielsalm next day, but were so eager to be off that we decided to have two half-day walks instead of one long one. By camping at Stavelot, we would only have an afternoon's walk of eleven miles (eighteen kilometres). Soon we met our first GR5 waymarks, a painted white over red band, with arrows indicating left or right. There was even a failsafe device: if you overshot the turn, the white and red band would appear on the next tree with a line through it. I began to think it was so easy even I could follow it, but the euphoria was short-lived; when we reached Luxembourg, the waymarks changed shape and colour and were confusing even for an experienced orienteer. These waymarks, or *balisage*, were to become as comforting for us as a dummy is to a baby, for the familiar stripes were reassurance that we were on the correct path. If they disappeared, we were on the wrong path, and that meant expending valuable time and energy in correcting the mistake.

Great stands of beech clothed the hills and our well-marked path took us through the leafy forests across many of the streams that give Spa its healing waters. There was no question of fording them, as stout rustic bridges were always provided. After nearly an hour's climb, we were over 576 metres up and emerged onto a large expanse of moor and heathland at Fagne de Malchamps. These *fagnes* are barren places with a fragile and specialized habitat. They rank among the tundras of Western Europe, a relic of the days when the Ardennes was the outermost wall of the ice-sheets that crept down from Scandinavia.

'Look where you're walking.' Richard's head was down as he scrutinized the vegetation on either side of the protective boardwalk we were on. 'Can you see the sundew?'

Among the bilberries and sphagnum moss we found the carnivorous sundew, the very plant we had been walking over on the Parbh in the hinterland of Cape Wrath. That, however, was where the analogy ended, for this well-marked dry path was the antithesis of a Scottish one. It was a month since we reached the Cape and already our UK walk belonged to another world.

The boardwalk paths over the fragile habitat led from north, south, east and west to an RAF war memorial at the highest point of the *fagne*. A simple erect stone commemorates the loss of airmen in Squadron 550 on 23 April 1944. This was our first brush with the two world wars of the twentieth-century. During the Second World War, the Battle of the Bulge, as the Battle of the Ardennes was called, lasted from December 1944 to January 1945 and was the largest land battle of the war in which the Americans participated. More than a million men, including Germans, British and Americans, fought in this last-ditch attempt by Hitler to delay inevitable defeat. Hitler hoped the offensive would succeed in retaking Antwerp, divide the Allies and hold them long enough to buy some time to work on secret weapons and build up his troops. Casualties on both sides were enormous; thousands died and many towns and villages were reduced to rubble. However, the Allied advance on Berlin was delayed for a month and the Russian army was the first to arrive in that capital. If the Allies had not been delayed the course of the next fifty years might have been very different.

Although it was only half a day's walk, the eighteen kilometres seemed more like eighteen miles. Our three-week interlude had had its effect on my thigh muscles, and they were complaining about our renewed exertion. If Richard was also suffering, he was doing it in silence. A surprise attack by a mass of black clouds soaked us before we had time to get our waterproofs on. Compared to the rigours of the Cape Wrath Trail, it was easy going on a well-marked track; corn marigolds, oxeye daisies, clover and yarrow were flowering in the verges as we crossed fields of grazing cows, passing the traditional black and white farm buildings, large white squares under slate roofs. We were often in dense woodland, a mix of firs and hardwoods, where the only track became a narrow green tunnel between the trees. It was easy to see how tanks could have become bogged down, or reached an impasse if they met a tank coming the other way. The weather in December and January 1944–45 had been bitterly cold, with heavy snow falls which must have added to the general misery and chaos.

Deep in a beech wood we were surprised to see woodcutters pulling the felled tree trunks using Clydesdale horse power in the traditional way. Manoeuvring horses is possibly easier in these dense woods than using modern machinery. The ground was wet and muddy as we slipped and slithered down the steep descent into Stavelot.

We found a campsite two kilometres out of the town with no shop. It was 6.30 p.m and we needed to find food. I set off for the town centre while Richard pitched the tent, and on my way down the campsite drive I checked my pockets for my purse which contained £75 in euros, my debit and credit cards, my driving licence and YHA card. However hard I dug into my pockets, it simply wasn't there. In the calm state before shock sets in, oblivious of the cars that nearly ran me down, I searched methodically. Good walking trousers have pockets for all necessities, and I had a special place for each of my most precious possessions: glasses, purse, mobile, camera, Lipsyl and handkerchief. No sign of my purse. Then I returned to the tent and checked that it wasn't there. Nothing.

It must have fallen out of my pocket that afternoon, or I must have left it in a shop. Then, hardest of all, I had to break the news to Richard, a man who doesn't panic over anything except money and phones. He took the news surprisingly calmly, although I knew he would worry until we had retrieved our purchasing power. What made things worse was that we share a current account, and Richard is the primary card holder. As my ability to find anything is almost as bad as my sense of direction, Richard checked my pockets, my rucksack and the tent, discovering a comb, a few grubby tissues, and a bus ticket, but no purse. He said nothing, but gave me enough money to buy bread and ham for supper, and offered to rise early and go and search for the missing purse in the morning as we thought it might have dropped out on the Fagne de Malchamps. As I walked the two kilometres into the town to buy food, the clouds and my mood grew blacker. This was an inauspicious start. Richard would be very stressed, and it was my fault.

A damp grey mist had descended over the river, and the occupants of the few caravans and tents had an end-of-a-wet-week look about them. We turned in early. Sleep was difficult on my polystyrene bed roll and I cursed having left my Therma Rest inflatable mattress behind in an attempt to reduce the weight of my pack. I had also lost my natural padding, and my hip bones didn't enjoy their acquaintance with the hard ground. As the weather became hotter and drier and the ground harder, I would spend the night revolving like a spin drier in the cramped confines of the minute tent. Neither of us slept much and Richard rose at 6 a.m. on a hopeless quest for my purse. The owner of the campsite was very sympathetic and rang the police in Spa for us.

'People in Belgium are very honest,' she told me. 'It will probably be found and returned to you.' I had less faith in her countrymen.

We were so preoccupied with money and cards that the splendour of Stavelot's Romanesque tower (all that remains of the abbey church) was lost on us. We fed plastic cards frenetically into cash machines but no euros were forthcoming. Richard, normally unflappable, turned pale under his tan when the machine temporarily swallowed his card; we imagined a cashless scenario and Richard didn't 'do' begging. I felt guilty. Convinced that someone had access to my missing card and had spent all our money, we feared the rest of our walk might have to be aborted. Steadying myself, I rang our bank who reassured us that our balance was healthy and we were just asking for too much money at one go. They also suggested we rang the Lost Card Centre. Standing by the hole in the wall on our third attempt to draw cash felt like landing an aircraft with one engine. We held our breath as we punched in our pin number. The few seconds' wait seemed like hours; then there was a promising clunk, and 400 euros' worth of crisp notes appeared as if by magic. Richard looked a little less unhappy.

The GR5 took us over rolling tree-clad hills and through large dairy farms. Plump cows with dripping udders grazed the wide meadows and it was ironic that a café in Vielsalm was unable to serve us with milk for our coffee. The kind warden of the town's busy campsite managed to squeeze our tent in beside a static caravan. The town of Vielsalm was the Comte de Salm's ancient capital, best known today for witches and bilberries. There is an annual Witches' Sabbath on 20 July followed by a bilberry festival. We ate in the candlelit cellars of the count's old house, tripping over broomsticks and twigs on our way to find a vacant seat on one of the bench tables. We avoided frog's legs and casseroled rat but enjoyed a fish dish with myrtille (bilberry) tart and cream for dessert. The old building had bars at the windows of the upper storeys, and a life-sized statue of the Witch of Vielsalm stood on a pile of stones near the entrance, broomstick at the ready. We managed the return trip to our campsite without turning into pumpkins.

It was Sunday and our first sunny day in Europe. There was a mountain bike rally in progress, and from time to time bright strings of cyclists would race past, flattening us into the undergrowth. Men and women were out in the fields haymaking, and the verges were full of harebells and vetch. The air smelt of new-mown hay.

The names of villages were sounding much more Germanic as we walked over the rolling countryside towards Burg-Reuland. Richard seemed to have appropriated the gifts of Doctor Dolittle; he reckoned the large white cows with ridge backs and bullish buttocks had a sex crisis and when we reached a small village called Braunlauf near Schirm he was sure the chickens were German. It was the first German-speaking village we had come across, and indicated our proximity to the border. We noticed that some of the nineteenth-century gravestones had German names on them, and schoolchildren greeted us with 'Guten Tag.' The shiny brick houses had polished roofs and immaculate set-square gardens, neat explosions of petunias and geraniums burst from newly-painted window boxes and Alsatian dogs barked their disapproval as we walked past.

The thirteenth-century truncated ruins of Burg-Reuland castle stood among the buttercups and yarrow above the white houses and onion-domed church of the seemingly deserted village. At a café down by the river, a few people were sitting under walnut trees drinking *pression* beer. There should have been a campsite but it no longer existed, and the big hotel we had passed on our way in was closed for a further two weeks. From now on we had to appreciate that the holiday season in this part of the world is a mere two months, and if you were visiting either before the middle of July, or after the end of August, *tant pis*. After a refreshing beer in the café/patisserie I asked Madame if there was anywhere we could camp. She looked at me and smiled.

'*Bien sûr, Madame*. You are welcome to camp in the garden here.'

As there was no shop in the village, we dined on baguettes and *milles feuilles* and slept well until 7 a.m. when the jangle of the church bell summoned the faithful to Mass.

It seemed that religion was still in vogue in southern Belgium and Luxembourg; at frequent intervals along the road and in the scattered villages we found beautifully tended shrines, and one path even took us past the Stations of the Cross. Seats were plentiful – every kilometre or so we would find a shiny new bench, with or without rain covers, and there were also picnic tables, litter bins, information boards, directions, and signs. Everything the walker might need for his or her comfort and convenience was there by the roadside, sometimes beside a shrine, but often for no reason at all. Once or twice our path took us through a *parcours d'exercice*, so in case you didn't feel fit enough, you could do press ups, pull ups, jump ups, squat downs, reach downs, or up and downs, on beams and bars and logs all carefully placed for your personal use every few metres of a kilometre course. In short, the walker could exercise everything from his abdominals to his biceps, eat, rest, pray, orientate himself, and learn all about the region he was in; the only missing element was *les marcheurs* (walkers).

Our route rose and fell over the gently undulating countryside; dark pine woods dressed the valley walls and the wide expanse of flat land on the tops was used for arable farming: glossy green fields of maize bordered with flowering arnica; deep yellow sunflowers lifting their great heads to the light; delicate barley, ripening oats and large hay meadows. The sun had summer warmth in it, and for the first time we donned sun hats and dark glasses and, like the sunflowers, raised our faces to worship the warmth. We had the path to ourselves, and the only signs of life were a few brand new John Deere tractors harvesting the corn with farmers at the wheel behind wraparound glass shields.

We descended into the valley of the Our, described in the Topo Guide as 'paradise for campers and fishermen'. The chuckling waters of the river, at times as much as twenty metres wide, ran through thick woods and lush hay fields, hugging the German border. We had the little path to ourselves as it climbed steeply up the hillside and then plunged down towards the river. We were glad of the cool shade of the pine woods and dipped our hot feet in the water when we stopped for a bite of bread and cheese and a much-needed drink.

'Good name for a river,' Richard said between mouthfuls.

'The Our?' I queried. 'Why?'

'Ours or yours,' Richard replied with a grin. 'You see, we are just at the no-man's-land between Belgium, Luxembourg and Germany.'

Our campsite by the River Our at Ouren Pont was run by a Dutchman called Walt with spiky platinum hair and a black T-shirt. The Lost Card Centre had asked us to call again and there was no signal on my mobile. I explained the situation to Walt in French and he let us use his land line providing we spoke English. As primary card holder Richard had to make the call, and the phone was handed to him across the reception desk. A frantic half-hour followed while Richard gave his bank details, his name, his mother's maiden name, his post code, his address, his phone number, and his life history to a bank clerk somewhere in Europe. There was a long pause and then he was connected to a Chinese voice somewhere in the world. A tripartite conversation followed, frequently interrupted by

Walt who was longing to practise his English, and by happier campers coming to reception with questions or to book in. Richard was in hell. He kept his cool, but I could see the tension rising from the top of his head. Eventually the Chinese gentleman was edged out and the bank clerk told Richard to ring again when they had looked into it. Sweating profusely, he put the phone down and headed for the loo, leaving our only remaining credit card on the reception desk. Walt was highly amused; plastic cards, it seems, do not go well with the nomadic lifestyle.

At Ouren Pont we came across the European monument (*Europadenkmal or Le monument pour Europe*), inaugurated in 1977 to commemorate the signing of the Treaty of Rome in 1957. The idea of the European Union grew out of the Second World War, when co-operation through economic and political intergration by the six founding member states of the European Economic Community, France, Germany, Italy and the Benelux countries, was thought to be the way forward to ensure a peaceful and secure future. We stood silently by the flags of those six countries forty-six years on, wondering what General de Gaulle and Konrad Adenauer (two of the six Fathers of Europe), would have thought about the 1992 Maastricht Treaty, the continuing enlargement of this European supra-state and the euro now lining our pockets. This controversial but enabling coin meant we could cross the River Our into Germany, buy a beer, and walk back again.

Standing at the Trois-Frontières, more than ten years after the implementation of the European Union, the ethos felt less 'ours or yours' and more a melt-down of identities. However, as we walked down the frontiers between Luxembourg and Germany, France and Germany, France and Switzerland and France and Italy, we felt that regional identities are alive and well in spite of all bureaucratic endeavours to make a United States of Europe. *Vive la différence!*

Buzzards mewed above the pine forests where once wolves, bears and wild boar roamed. We were in the Grand Duchy of Luxembourg, a country heralded, appropriately enough, by a gold ball instead of our familiar white and red stripes. Already we were lost. (Sorry, Richard, not lost, we had just temporarily mislaid the route.) We found ourselves on an unmarked path down by the river which quickly petered out. Our only option was to ford the river and join a path on the other side. A lady was leaning out of her window in a house on the German bank and she directed us to the nearest bridge, where we crossed back into Luxembourg and headed straight for a café called Le Pont, beside a garage on the main road. Sadly it was *Dienstag geschlossen*. We had to make do with a little water and half an apple while we gazed at a cardboard cut out of a Swiss-made ice cream cone.

It was 7 July and the temperature had climbed into the 30s centigrade. The GR5 was taking perverse pleasure in keeping us off the road by climbing up the steep hillsides and then, almost as soon as we had puffed up to the ridge, taking us back down onto the road, only a couple of kilometres from where we left it. In the end we toiled along the tarmac to Untereisenbach and our campsite by the river, frequently caught in the slipstream of furiously pedalling cyclists. They made us feel very unfit as we plodded along the melting tarmac in the afternoon heat.

At the top of the hill a kilometre above Untereisenbach, a man with grey hair and beard and a jolly plump lady were clutching two overloaded bikes and gasping for breath. We watched them clamber back onto the saddles and freewheel gratefully downhill. When we reached the campsite some ten minutes later, Madame was still on her bike, so exhausted she couldn't dismount, and gallant Monsieur was in the process of separating the woman from her wheels. We saw them some time later, having pitched a good-sized tent and set out chairs, a table, a fishing rod and a large umbrella.

For some unknown reason the ladies' washrooms were locked and I was so desperate for a shower that I went into the Gents. The only intruder on my ablutions was the large Belgian lady who had had such trouble dis-entangling her overweight form from her overweight bike. We showered in adjacent cubicles shouting pleasantries in phrase book English and German about heat exhaustion and tired muscles over the sounds of splashing water. I don't know what the gentleman who came in next thought about the falsetto chorus emanating from the showers.

The campsite café was not open for evening meals so we walked the 600 metres to the little village of Untereisenbach, just off the main road. We discovered a spotless white church with dunce's hat spire, and a few old houses behind a barricade of road works. There were several hotels but only one was open. Three locals lolled round the bar and Madame, a German-speaking lady whose shrunken figure was encased in a floral tabard, spoke neither English nor French. She delegated us to one of the 'fixtures', a weathered-looking stick insect who was obviously the local jester.

'The village is deserted because of the road works. Nobody wants to come here anyway.' He glanced at Madame with a twinkle in his eye. 'After all, we are a backwater where the people are peasants who don't even speak French!'

We sat on a terrace among geranium pots and oleanders, with views across to the lush Our valley and dark wooded hills, drinking beer and tucking into goujons of turkey, *pommes frites*, green salad and ice cream. It was perfection, as these things are on balmy summer evenings when body and soul reap rewards for the day's exertions.

Next morning, on our way to breakfast we found a dead kingfisher. It had flown into the plate glass window of the café and broken its neck. These brilliant birds thrill the eye as they streak across the river in a flash of electric blue, or precision dive into the water for food; to see this dazzling corpse with its turquoise back and orange breast, limp and motionless on the dark tarmac was both disconcerting and surreal.

It was a beautiful summer day and we only had twenty-two hilly kilometres to walk. Our path was often overgrown and it was hard work up the hills without shade. Grazing on wild raspberries and cherries along the way was a good thirst-quencher, and the warm sun made short work of drying the socks and pants which hung insouciantly from our packs. However, as the day progressed and our socks got sweatier and sweatier, blisters appeared on my heels. I stuck sheep's wool on them, my favoured remedy, before we climbed the 485-metre Mont Saint-Nicolas. The hamlet of Stolzembourg at the top of the hill had a well-sited bar, and we refuelled on Diekirch beer and coke. Once again the place was almost deserted and poor Madame was having a bad hair day. She scowled as we entered; glared at us when we requested drinks, and could hardly lift her great frame off her stool to serve us. I addressed her in French, but that too was wrong and she replied sulkily in English. The only other customer was an inebriate whose incomprehensible mumblings were unstoppable.

We spent the afternoon plodding along a wooded path which pushed insistently against the contours of the Ardennes. We were, it seemed, travelling in the footsteps of Victor Hugo who had stayed at the little town of Vianden as a tourist in exile in the mid-nineteenth-century. In 1871, as a political refugee, he occupied a house in the town which is now a museum displaying some of his drawings and letters. A frowning bronze bust of the great bard by Rodin sits on the bridge opposite this *Maison de Victor Hugo*.

Vianden could have come straight out of a J. K. Rowling novel. The renovated fourteenth-century Kafkaesque castle, with steeply pitched roofs and turrets, each topped with a witch's hat, is perched on a wooded cliff brooding over the town. It would be easy to imagine Harry Potter and friends on their broomsticks playing quidditch round the turrets. Old houses and tiny squares tumbled down the cobbled streets to the trout-filled river and wherever we looked the castle towered above us. Many of the eighteenth-century tradesmen's houses have the mark of their trade over the porticos: loaves of bread for the baker, tongs for the blacksmith. One *auberge* had iron grilles in front of the windows and a long-haired man in a straw hat sat, like Papageno, next to a bird cage. There were smart hotels, draped in swags of ivy and dripping colourful window boxes.

We stayed in a modest *chambre d'hôte* (the French equivalent of our bed and breakfast), as the youth hostel was filled to overflowing with teenage girls. After four nights with only a centimetre of polystyrene between us and the ground, a mattress was real luxury. I sat on it, lay on it, and patted it like a small child with a favourite teddy. Hot water, towels, pillows, loo paper all gave the same childish joy; we showered slowly, hung our Gore-tex anoraks on hangers, and washed dirty clothes with glee. It seems that doing without is the only way to make us appreciate the twenty-first-century luxuries we all take for granted. Later, among the geraniums and honeysuckle of a hotel courtyard, we dined on *truites aux amandes* and *tarte aux pommes*, washed down with a bottle of local white wine. We wandered back to our room, hypnotized by the floodlit castle, and then collapsed into seven hours of dreamless sleep, woken only by the church bells and a dawn chorus.

Harvesting was well under way as we walked through rich farmland on our way to Diekirch; combine harvesters plied through hectares of wheat leaving a golden wake and some fields were already reduced to rich brown soil. Sitting at the edge of a cool wood at the top of a hill, we could see beyond the harvested fields to the wide vista of Lorraine. Below us lay the valley of the River Sûre (pronounced sewer), into which the River Our we had been following drains. The River Sûre drains into the Moselle which then joins the Rhine which eventually meets the sea at Rotterdam.

The landscape of Lorraine was less hilly than the Ardennes and, as we were to discover, very different in character. The sleepy villages we passed through all the way to Lake Geneva had farm buildings in their main streets and large arches with stout doors wide enough for carts to pass through; some were still used as farms, some lay empty, and a few were converted for domestic use. All were nearly deserted. The only time we met other walkers was near car parks or on designated short walks round well-known beauty spots. In this multilingual national meltdown, it was difficult to know how to hail a passing walker. I tried *'Bonjour'*, but got some very old-fashioned looks. Neither 'Hello', 'Hi' nor even *'Guten Tag'*, produced the hoped-for response. In the end I went for a sort of multilingual jovial 'Morng' which produced a reply that sounded like *'Moien'* with or without an accompanying smile.

In Diekirch we met two friends from Wiesbaden. Richard's Rotary Club in Tunbridge Wells is twinned with the Wiesbaden Rotary Club in Germany, and over years of exchange visits friendships have been formed. Gustav and Gudrun, on hearing of our planned walk, asked if they could join us for two days in Luxembourg. Like most of us, their exercise is limited to a constitutional whenever time permits, so the prospect of walking sixteen kilometres for two days in high temperatures must have seemed daunting. They were brave souls. We met them in the hotel as arranged, and regardless of our sweaty bodies they gave us a welcoming hug.

Our German friends had come prepared. They were attired in pristine gear which included enviable walking trousers with zips up the side to allow the legs to breathe without the sun's harmful rays affecting the skin, and some anti-fly spray. Like us, Gustav had two sticks. The temperature rose steadily as we walked the sixteen kilometres of farmland and forest across undulating hills. The few deserted villages we passed through offered no hospitality. We had insufficient water for all four of us so we shared half a cucumber to quench our thirst while sitting on a pile of spruce logs. Just when we really needed them, we had lost all those lovely seats and litter bins. My walking trousers were a dark blue colour which didn't show the dirt, helpful when you have to sit on the ground much of the time, so when Gudrun and I got up off the logs we had a good dollop of resin imprinted on our bums. While mine just merged with the trousers, Gudrun's smart khaki ones were less discreet. We arrived in Beaufort in the early afternoon and had to wait outside our modest hotel while *monsieur le propriétaire* was sorting out the plumbing. Finally installed, and grateful to find running water, Gustav and Gudrun then had the unenviable task of sallying forth once again into the heat and finding their way back to Diekirch on public transport to collect their car. The hotel owner told them that there was a bus in the village that would take them there. The hottest time of day is 3 to 6 p.m.; they had been told to catch the school bus which was no longer running as the school holidays had started. They had to stand on their overworked feet for twenty minutes until a bus arrived to take them to the next town of Echternach. From there they were eventually able to catch a bus back to the hotel in Diekirch and flop thankfully into the air conditioned comfort of their own car. Gudrun confessed afterwards that they hadn't travelled on a bus for fifteen years and that the smell was overpowering. The round trip took them over two hours and I think it will be another fifteen years before they catch a bus again. To their great credit they didn't complain and appeared in time for dinner looking wonderfully fresh.

Beaufort is a small village with the romantic ruins of a twelfth-century sandstone castle which was enlarged in 1380. The towering keep stands beside a Renaissance castle built in 1649 which is currently lived in. As we were walked along the road beneath it, an old lady in a small Peugeot car passed us, hooting.

'That,' said Gustav, waving his stick in the direction of the car, 'is the owner of the castle and aunt of one of the members of our Wiesbaden Rotary Club. She is well over ninety and still going strong.' We waved at the vanishing car boot, as if to royalty, and were rewarded by a clash of gears.

Our path took us past a lake surrounded by copper beech and cypress trees. The vegetation was green and lush and the castle ruins were reflected in the still waters of the lake. With its quota of white swans it could have made a perfect opening scene for Tchaikovsky's ballet. As we walked into the cool woods beside the little Halerbaach River, we were in what is known as Little Switzerland. It seemed an inappropriate description for a monstrous rock garden, densely packed with weathered sandstone cliffs topped with precarious rocks shaped like dragons and great toads. Many of the cliffs were sliced as if some giant had slashed them through with his sword; water not blood seeped from the wound. As we walked through these labyrinths, rocky gargoyles stared down at us, strange creatures from a mythological world. We were Lilliputians beneath those great defiles, winding our way between the slim tree trunks under a canopy of beech leaves, submerged among the ferns that bordered the streams, pools and waterfalls.

Gustav and Gudrun are opera buffs and worship at the shrine of Bayreuth. One particularly cavernous group of rocks was called the Wolves Gorge because it had been used as a trap; wolves were driven into this natural corral and slaughtered. The last wolf to be killed was in 1871. Gustav looked round him with amazement. 'This,' he exclaimed 'is like the wolf glen in Weber's *Der Freischütz*. The setting is perfect for Weber or Wagner,' and with that he raised his stick like a conductor's baton and the couple burst into song with a duet from that haunting scene. We applauded this spontaneous outburst and the rocks echoed approval.

On a more prosaic note we learned that a beech tree gives off 1.7 kilograms of oxygen in one hour, and absorbs 2.3 kilograms of carbon dioxide in the same time. In addition

400 litres of water pass through the tree and are evaporated from the leaves in one day. This reminded me of the saturated fly sheet we found in our tent every morning, the moisture collected having come from just two pairs of lungs.

The fortified medieval town of Echternach was one of the few tourist towns we passed through. It owes its fame to a seventh-century Anglo-Saxon called St Willibrord who is said to have cured St Vitus's dance. In honour of this achievement there is an annual *Springprozession* when 'dancers cross the town in leaps and bounds, swaying to the strains of a polka march and tied to each other by white handkerchiefs'.

The cobbled main square is a stage set of Renaissance and eighteenth-century buildings round a central market cross. The tall thin towers of the Basilica dominate a town which was severely damaged during the Battle of the Bulge in 1944. Most of the old buildings, including the basilica, have been beautifully restored and we admired the light uncluttered interior of the church founded by St Willibrord spanning a period 'from the dark days of arrowheads, through the illuminated manuscripts of early Christendom, to today's electronic components from Japan'. We assumed that meant the taped liturgical music we were hearing. The sounds of a rather different music emanated from the eleventh-century crypt; intrigued, we descended the steps and were surprised to see a group of singers giving an impromptu but faultless rendering of the *Ave Maria* with handbags still on their shoulders. We listened as the clear notes resonated among the low arches of the ancient crypt and quietly applauded this celestial outburst.

Eating on the terrace outside our hotel in the main square we watched a group of young men performing a series of flag dances on the cobbles. Except for aspiring Billy Elliots, I can't imagine twelve to eighteen-year-old boys in England gyrating gracefully as they wheeled large flags in all directions in time to the music. In Luxembourg, however, flag dancing is an important part of Flemish culture. A crowd gathered to applaud the boys' efforts, and silhouetted figures watched from the backlit balconies of a Renaissance building on the opposite side of the square.

After breakfast next day we bid *auf wiedersehen* to Gustav and Gudrun, and waved as their four wheels sped away across the cobbles. No sooner had they left than Sally and Martin arrived. Richard and I knew Sally from our student days at King's College Hospital where she was two years ahead of me. By the time I was let loose on patients she was a qualified physiotherapist. I remember being greatly in awe of her as she showed me round the wards and the Intensive Care Unit in the days when life support machines were little more than iron lungs. We hadn't seen each other since then and yet she had offered to give us hospitality for no fewer than four nights in Luxembourg. We embraced warmly with a chorus of 'You haven't changed a bit, I'd have recognized you anywhere!' as the intervening forty years fell away.

Her lean fit husband Martin, ready to share our day's walk in floppy sun hat and daypack, taught me how to kiss: left, right, left. Or was it right, left, right? The nuances of European greetings are always hard to grasp; perhaps I should improve with practice.

Martin set off like a firecracker; when he reached a hill he slowed for a second, as if changing gear, and then roared up it leaving us hard pressed to keep up. With a rucksack on my back I wouldn't have stood a chance, but Sally had taken our packs with her and was meeting us at Wasserbillig that evening. He'll slow down soon enough, I thought. It's early in the day. I made a bet with myself that he would be crawling along when the hot sun was high in the sky. I was wrong. His pace never wavered and they were some of the quickest twenty-four kilometres of the entire walk.

Not only was Martin a formidable walker, but he was wonderfully knowledgeable about wildlife, landscape and culture. We were finding walnut trees in almost every field. 'They attract insects so farmers plant them to keep the flies off the livestock,' he said in a rare moment when I had caught up with him. When we entered the first of many woods he told us that there were still a few lynx left and that the population of wild boar was on the increase. We had noticed signs warning of swine fever and Martin told us it was endemic. 'The farmers are planting more maize these days and the wild boars love it so their population is increasing.' We walked on quietly and then heard a faint tapping sound. 'It'll be a black woodpecker. Keep your eyes open and you should see one. There are also red kites, peregrine falcons and pine martens here, and those,' he pointed to a Wendy house on stilts on the edge of the wood, 'are for huntsmen. Hunting in Luxembourg is a very elitist sport.'

A little further on we were out of the wood and looking at the viaduct of an auto route over the River Sûre. 'When that was built,' Martin told us, 'they made a special platform in the hope that peregrine falcons would nest here. The miracle is it worked and the falcons use it and continue to breed.'

It was a hot Sunday afternoon and families were fishing, picnicking, swimming, and cycling along the banks of the River Sûre. One man with a round cap on his head and dark robes was smoking a long-stemmed pipe, while the lady in purdah beside him was eating a slice of juicy water melon. They were speaking Luxemborgian, a strange mix of German and French. Martin told us that ten per cent of the population of Luxembourg are Portuguese. As we approached Wasserbillig, the sound of accordion music and singing wafted down the hot afternoon and soon we were caught up in the town's annual summer river festival known as the *Sûre Fest*. Tables, benches and makeshift bars were lined up under canvas along the river bank. An Amazonian female was cradling an accordion and belting out folk songs in front of a microphone. Crowds of men, women and children were eating, drinking, jumping onto bouncy castles or just singing along with the toe-tapping, hand-clapping folk tunes. A few couples began to polka and quickstep, whirling around the tarmac path like spinning tops, singing the familiar words with infectious enthusiasm. We downed a beer and applauded loudly.

Swans were preening themselves on the muddy banks of the Sûre as it passed under the road and rail bridges and drained into its big sister, the Moselle. As we looked up at the electric railway bridge, Martin told us that the voltage on the French and German sides was different; this meant the train driver had to rev up and then disconnect the overhead electric supply so that the train could float over the bridge under its own momentum. The driver would then reconnect to the new supply: a quirky anomaly that had not yet been standardized.

Sally met us in Wasserbillig as arranged and drove us back to their home in Junglinster, apologizing for the two kilometres of petrol stations and supermarkets on the outskirts.

'The Germans come across the border for petrol, beer and wine, as it's cheaper here,' she told us.

Luxembourg was, it seemed, a land flowing with petrol and wine, euros and diplomats, wealthy farms and satellite systems. All the well-surfaced empty roads lead to Luxembourg City. The indefatigable Martin drove us in to see the capital after our day's walk. It was a city where you got two for the price of one, with the old buildings in a gorge beside the gently curving river looked down on by the new. Much of the Duchy's wealth comes from the diplomatic service, or the *grosses légumes* as the legal beagles are flippantly referred to. If there is poverty it is well hidden, and expectations were as high as the radio mast outside the Cardews' home town. This red and white iron alien was used from the early 1930s to broadcast popular music from the station known as Radio Luxembourg, reaching a peak of popularity in the late 1950s and early 1960s and giving the teenagers of the day a frisson of pleasure. Now it was owned by Astra, the European Satellite System, for more orthodox uses. Sally told us cheerfully that it also made an excellent firework display during thunderstorms.

'My daughter Melanie and I sit on the stairs and watch when we can't sleep,' she told us. 'When both children lived here they used to go out onto the mast hill and find thunderbolts the day after the storm.'

Not really what I wanted to hear as lightning is yet another of my fears. When I was young I used to hide under the bedclothes during thunderstorms and now I'm not really much braver. I knew that we couldn't expect to walk through the mountains of Europe for three months without storms and I just hoped they'd come at night. The air already had that humid feel and during our stay with the Cardews we were all happier to eat our delicious evening meals on the terrace watching the hose playing over the vegetables and flowers.

'It hasn't rained properly since January. Just a few storms which cool the air for a day or two and then the temperature rises again. These really are drought conditions' Sally and Martin had every reason to complain; from now on the *canicule* or heat wave was really on us with tragic results to man and beast. In a few days time we were in Lorraine and saw proof of the drought; herds of cattle were eating straw, and a horse we passed was gnawing the bark of a tree. Later in the Jura, farmers were very anxious for the welfare of their livestock as the springs themselves were drying up.

Due to the heat we rose at six o'clock next morning and set off from Wasserbillig to Wormeldange, a distance of twenty-four kilometres. We had at least intermittent shade in the woods, but when we reached the vineyards of the Moselle the heat swamped us like a sauna. We looked down on the wide blue river snaking between serried ranks of vines which stretched endlessly in all directions. The steeply pitched roofs and onion-domed church tower of Grevenmacher, nestled in a bend in the river. This little town is the centre of the wine industry *luxembourgeois*. Germany was a mirror image on the opposite bank. Concrete paths stretched like white rulers between the green corrugations and reflected the heat upwards. It was like walking on hot coals. Richard, like most men, sweats freely, but I rarely do. Beads of sweat poured from my head, dripping off my hair like raindrops from a twig. My nose ran and moisture trickled steadily down my back and settled round my waist. It was a sensation I was to get used to. A strange chemical smell hung in the hot air and put a metallic taste in our parched mouths. We began to know the meaning of real thirst for, although we were carrying a litre of water each, we needed to ration our dwindling supply as we still had several hours to go before we reached Wormeldange. I found an apple, and spent a memorable twenty minutes slowly extracting every drop of juice in each little mouthful and swallowing it slowly, savouring the way it momentarily lubricated my mouth and throat. Unripe Bacchanalian grapes hung temptingly among the shading vine leaves and little channels of water flowed between each group of vines. Desperate to cool off I plunged my hands and wrists into the water.

'Don't!' Richard yelled. 'It'll have chemicals in it. And for heaven's sake don't drink it.'

I rapidly removed my hands and wiped them on my handkerchief, imagining they were itching already. It was ironic that these chemical-sprayed vines produced delicate

white wines with delicious bouquets such as the Riesling, Silvaner, Pinot blanc, Pinot gris and Gewürztraminer. When we reached the crest of the hill, we saw the helicopter that sprayed the vines and left such a pungent smell in the air. I made a mental note to wash all fruit in future and to carry more water with us in these high temperatures.

Having seen the monument celebrating the birth of the Common Market at the Trois Frontières, we were interested to see the one commemorating the Schengen Accord on the Moselle embankment at Remich the following day. Three monumental slabs of polished granite decorated with outsize gold stars marked the spot where, in 1985, on board a river boat called *The Marie-Astride*, representatives of the Benelux countries, the Federal Republic of Germany and the Republic of France signed the agreement to abolish controls at their common borders.

Perhaps we take the abolition of these trade barriers for granted now as we move seamlessly from country to country.

It was certainly a courageous Accord and will hopefully ensure the peace and stability of Europe in the twenty-first-century. I took a photo of Richard and Martin, leaning nonchalantly on either side of the central slab, to endorse our approval.

In the cool of the evening we sat in the Cardews' garden sipping a Pinot gris with their neighbours, an English judge working for the European Parliament, and his wife, who took Girl Guides on outward bound expeditions. They were also walking some of the GR5 in short bursts as holidays permitted, and kindly gave us some tips on accommodation and books to read when we returned. The conversation turned to the subject of ticks. I had always associated these little insects with animals, and was surprised to learn that they could latch onto humans and possibly cause a nasty illness called Lime's disease. We joked light-heartedly about it but the Cardews' daughter, Melanie, was seriously concerned. Ticks had apparently affected all the members of the Cardew family and we were told that doctors took them very seriously, often prescribing strong antibiotics if they thought the creature had not been completely removed. Martin showed us a picture of the little insect with a black carapace which embedded itself somewhere on the body and could excrete the disease-giving substance.

'They are quite hard to get out,' Sally told us. 'You need tweezers and you must twist them anticlockwise. It is extremely important that every bit is removed. Doctors at the local hospital spent twenty minutes removing one from Martin's eyelid last summer.'

The story got worse. If the offending insect was not removed completely, or if you treated it by putting vinegar on it, the little thing would panic and excrete every nasty substance it knew how. Sally's friend added the corollary that if you left them in, you could lose the use of not only your legs and your eyes but also your brain. She obviously felt we were not taking any of this seriously enough. 'You could even end up in a wheelchair,' she said after a suitably dramatic pause. As my eyes are not good, and my brain cells seem to be leaking away without any help from ticks, I certainly didn't want the little beggars to paralyse my legs.

'What's the best thing to do to prevent them?' I asked, swigging my wine nervously.

'Don't wear shorts and keep your arms covered,' Melanie suggested, adding as an afterthought, 'and if this heat continues you should take salt tablets.'

For the next two sweltering days we followed their advice, but the heat got the better of prophylaxis and soon we were bare-legged and bare-armed again, although we did carry out cursory inspections of our limbs from time to time.

Before we left Luxembourg for France, the Cardew family did us yet one more favour. Accommodation in Lorraine was going to be difficult; since the collapse of the iron industry, the region has been depressed, and the locals haven't yet realized that tourists are economic good news, especially if they are the tired, hungry and thirsty English variety. Melanie, who seemed to speak every European language with equal fluency, spent several hours on the phone and internet trying to find us accommodation for the next week. In the end there was nowhere for us to stay in either Rumelange or Joeuf. The formidable Sally was undeterred. She went straight to the phone and rang the town hall in Rumelange.

'I am looking for accommodation for my two friends,' she said in fluent French. 'They are walking the GR5 and we haven't been able to find anywhere for them to stay. I don't believe you can't find them somewhere in your town. You see, they are professional people, and having nowhere for them to stay wouldn't reflect too well on your town.'

We gaped in astonishment as Sally told us they would see what they could do and would ring her back when they had sorted something out. Once a physio, always a physio, I thought happily. A little later the phone rang and we almost heard the smile on Sally's face.

'Yes. That's better. I'm delighted you can help. They will do as you suggest. *Au revoir, Monsieur.*'

Everything was fixed. We would spend a night in Rumelange at a hotel owned by the council, and the night at Joeuf with a friend of Sally's who was spending the weekend in the Vosges.

It was impossible to thank the Cardew family for their kindness, hospitality and local knowledge. They had gone many extra 'kindness' kilometres for us. All we could do was to give them a big farewell thank you hug and wish them every happiness.

A rainstorm temporarily cooled the air and it was pleasant walking from Aspelt to Rumelange through crewcut wheat fields and shady forests. We also passed grass-covered spoil heaps, tramways and quarries, the healing scars of opencast mines from when Lorraine still had a steel industry. The town of Rumelange boasted a National Mine Museum which we were unable to visit as it was only open in the afternoons.

Our concern about the lack of accommodation in Lorraine made us worry that eating and drinking places might be equally scarce, so we tried the very closed-looking door of a corner pub, in rather dreary village called Tétange. To our surprise it opened, and we were greeted by a tornado of barking fur.

'*Tait-toi Luna,*' a gravelly voice scolded from somewhere behind a row of bottles. Luna took no notice and continued her maelstrom with definite designs on my left ankle. A little Jack Russell behind her wagged its tail in encouragement. Calm was restored when we removed our rucksacks and sat down. We ordered two beers and two *croques monsieur* from the gravelly voice, who broke a glass before she served us. A large grey parrot behind the door had one yellow eye on the television (where streams of brightly coloured figures crouching over their bikes were pedalling furiously in scorching heat somewhere near Toulouse) and one yellow eye on us. Polly had her priorities right, however, and the Tour de France soon claimed both eyes, followed by a series of enthusiastic Luxembourgian screeches. Before leaving I went to the unisex loo which had the word ABORT written in large letters on the door.

Arriving in Rumelange we made our way to the Place Grande Duchess Charlotte. Not feeling at all professional, we pushed open the sparkling glass doors of the *hôtel de ville* and entered a cool marble vestibule, just glad that our boots weren't muddy. A charming young man in an air-conditioned office greeted us like royalty and, flourishing a key, insisted on accompanying us to our hotel, leaving the lady waiting patiently on a seat to be even more patient. As we crossed the square with our escort, he explained that the hotel we would be staying in was now owned by the *commune* as there were insufficient tourists to keep the hotel in business. He showed us a comfortable en suite room, asked us to sign a diminutive piece of paper, and told us we could pay in the morning. We slept so soundly that neither of us heard the church clock in the square chiming every fifteen minutes, and the cost was a mere 20 euros (£14).

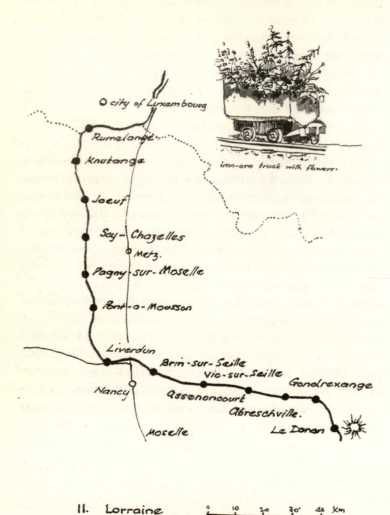

O city of Luxembourg

Rumelange

Knutange

Joeuf

Sey-Chazelles

o Metz.

Pagny-sur-Moselle

Pont-à-Mousson

Liverdun

Brin-sur-Seille

o Nancy

Vic-sur-Seille

Gondrexange

Assenoncourt

Abreschville.

La Donan

Moselle

iron-ore truck with flowers.

II. Lorraine

0   10   20   30'   40 Km

Chapter Eleven

Lorraine

On 18 July we left the Grand Duchy of Luxembourg and entered France. On the edge of a wood an E2 signpost (Holland to the Mediterranean) gave the distance to Nice as 1,656 kilometres (less daunting as 988 miles). We were now reunited with the red and white waymark of the GR5, and pathfinding became an easier task for Richard.

Walking into France was like meeting a kindred spirit; we both love the country, the language, the culture and the cuisine. However, Lorraine is not France's flagship of excellence for the tourist. The days of a booming steel industry are over, and the region showed all the symptoms of recession: rusty steel pipes, cracking concrete on foundry sites, angry graffiti smeared on the walls of empty factories, deserted hotels. The town of Nilvange was suffering a bad dose of decay, with crumbling dance halls, cinemas and factories; the glazed eyes of closed shutters stared out from the peeling paint of the once prosperous homes of the steel barons; the few hotels still in business seemed to be on the edge of bankruptcy.

Melanie, Sally Cardew's daughter, had found us just such a hotel in Knutange, a faded town where the afternoon heat radiated from tarmac, terraced houses and advertisement hoardings. *Madame la propriétaire* was a monosyllabic lady with a blonde rinse and swollen ankles. She stood behind an empty bar amongst scattered tables and chairs and wilting pot plants.

As she handed us the key she warned us that our room was not en suite. We were just glad to get out of the claustrophobic heat and climb thankfully up the staircase to our simple room at the end of a long corridor. It had a washbasin, a rickety table, a double bed with a darned candlewick bedspread, and a chair. Wooden shutters over the large sash window kept the temperature cool enough to be tolerable. For us, the hotel was perfect; we soaked ourselves in tepid water in the cast-iron bath, relaxed on the sagging mattress and didn't have to worry about dirty boots on the lino. That evening Madame cooked us a very simple meal of chicken legs in breadcrumbs (describing the menu, she pointed to her ample thigh, indicating that there would be plenty of meat), boiled rice, salad and ice cream. We were alone in the large dining room with the pink paper tablecloths and the plastic flowers.

The GR5 takes care not to take walkers near roads at all, let alone main roads through the industrial debris of Lorraine. Our accommodation problems meant we had to leave the GR5 in order to stay in Knutange, and much of our route to Joeuf was on roads. The deep valleys trap the heat and walking past steel mills, sidings, flyovers and mountains of steel pipes was a stroll through hell. Hayange, the last gasp of Lorraine's dying steel industry, was still alive with clanging and banging, the belch of smoke from blast furnaces and the rattle of coal-laden trucks scuttling along locally made steel tracks. We hugged the shade of buildings, hurrying across roads and pavements that gave no relief from the burning sun. A few iron ore trucks along the way had been filled with geraniums in a brave attempt to add a little colourful relief to the stone, steel and tarmac. It was heaven when we eventually climbed out of the valley and found ourselves in shady woods.

LORRAINE

We reached Joeuf in the suffocating heat of mid-afternoon and had to wait an hour and a half for Paul, the son of the owner of our lodgings. We sat on a bench under the rows of plane trees that flanked the main square. The leaves hung limply. No birds sang. No dog barked. Nobody moved. Even the fountain had dried up. A clock boomed four times. There was a scrunch of wheels on hot gravel and a car arrived, followed by another and another. Men in suits and women in dresses climbed out and gathered in little knots under the trees on the far side of the square. Another car appeared and parked in a designated spot; a lady in a brown suit with a chiffon scarf stepped out and headed briskly for the town hall. Suddenly there was a stir from the little crowd as a black limousine decked out with ribbons, bows and plastic flowers drew up. A man in a suit opened the rear door and a vision in white with a low-level silk top hat and net veil disengaged herself from the back seat and beamed at the cameras. The wedding party moved slowly towards the town hall and disappeared into the cool interior.

I shut my eyes against the glare; a few minutes later I heard yet another car arrive. A harassed couple jumped out and shouted expletives to each other across the scorching bonnet of their white Peugeot. There was much looking at watches and shrugging of shoulders. The woman opened the rear door of the car and pulled out a reluctant little boy in waistcoat and shiny shoes. They ran towards the town hall, the woman dragging the boy and the man tying his tie. Minutes later the wedding party reappeared. There were more photographs and much kissing. The men in suits and ladies in dresses climbed back into their cars and followed the shiny limousine waving, cheering and hooting. The clock struck the half-hour.

Nothing stirred until another squeal of tyres (shares in Michelin must be doing well) announced the arrival of young Paul, who let us into his dad's house just opposite the square. I found Paul's French very difficult to understand, but he told us to use any rooms we liked and not to worry about him as he would be partying until late. We didn't hear any noises in the night and crept away at 5.30 a.m., bumping into Paul on the doorstep. His car was bulging with *jeunes gens* waiting impatiently for our departure. They were going to enjoy *le weekend* without parents.

The intense heat made our feet sweat so much that I began to get blisters on my heels and toes. Our walk to Moulins-lès-Metz, where we hoped to find a bed for the night, was going to be thirty kilometres and Richard watched me lancing my blisters with a gloomy face.

'If your feet are like that,' he said, 'I don't think you're going to make it.'

Not really what the troops want to hear, but I assured him it was going to take a lot more than a few blisters to stop me walking to Nice. However, he allowed me more stops to take my boots off and cool my feet and I think he was happy to do likewise.

We headed out of Joeuf as the sun, an energy-sapping dragon, was rising over the steep hill out of the town. At our high spot for the day we were able to see the woods and fields of Lorraine stretching away to the Moselle valley where the city of Metz, crowned by its Gothic cathedral, looked like an eighteenth-century print beside the river.

As always the GR5 took us up all the steep hills including the Col de Lessy, and much of the day we were in the full glare of the sun. It was while we were sweating and puffing up the steep incline that we first met Melvin, whom we later nicknamed the Flying Dutchman. He was also walking the E2 and had started from Port Patrick in south-west Scotland on 2 April. Melvin was the only other person we met during the whole six months of our walk who was doing both the UK and the European sections of the E2 route. There wasn't a bead of moisture on his young face, just a friendly smile. We compared notes and felt sure we would soon meet again. The moment he was out of sight, I lay on my back on the twigs and dead leaves (sod the ticks) and rested my lower legs on a fallen tree trunk. Bliss. We ate a slice of quiche and drank as much water as we dared before moving on.

On the lower slopes of the hills, the landscape was changing from large arable and dairy farms to the more intimate landscape of orchards, vegetable gardens and soft fruit fields. There is nothing quite like the French veg patch. The soil is always a fine tilth, rows of burgeoning onions, carrots, lettuces and tomatoes resemble the pictures on the seed packets, weeds daren't raise their heads, and nothing ever seems to wilt in spite of the hot sun. Our path took us through attractive stone villages with ancient fortified churches. Gorze had a famous abbey founded in 749 by the Bishop of Metz. Our proximity to that big city was apparent in this area where the villages seemed prosperous and sophisticated. They also provided walkers with washing troughs and drinking water *gratuit*. We were now so hot that we took off our caps and filled them with water and then poured it, elephant-style, over our heads.

The sensation of that cold water running down our faces and shoulders was excruciatingly pleasurable.

It was early afternoon when we walked through the enchanting village of Scy-Chazelles, known not only for its twelfth-century fortified church and attractive little streets, but also as the place where Robert Schuman (not the composer but the 'Father of Europe') had lived and died. I was busy heading for the village fountain, looking forward to another delicious head-dunking session, when my observant husband pointed up a side street to a sign above a stone terraced house; it was an attractive cockerel on a green background.

'That's the Gîte de France logo,' he announced. 'Let's see if they have a room for us. I'm not sure that Moulins-lès-Metz will have any accommodation as this Topo Guide is ten years old.'

I congratulated my knowledgeable guide and was promptly despatched to knock at the door. There was a moment's hesitation when I noticed a printed sign with *Architect* written on it but Richard nodded encouragement and I rang the bell nervously. The door was opened by an attractive woman with her dark hair tied back in a little red scarf. When I enquired about a room she gave a welcoming smile. '*Mais oui.*' She said brightly. 'You are in luck. I still have one spare room just for tonight,' and she took us up the curved wooden staircase to a refreshingly light room with bright bed throws and contemporary pictures on the white walls. Mathie, and her architect husband Jean Paul, had bought the old mill house three years ago, gutted it, and renovated it to their specification. The main living area was lower than the rest of the ground floor; the roof went up to the rafters with a balcony framing the room and French windows looked out onto a shady terrace and charming walled garden.

We showered and rested and then felt strong enough to go

out and be tourists for what was left of the afternoon. Robert Schuman (1886–1963), was a devout Catholic who began his career in politics after the First World War. He was arrested by the Gestapo during the Second World War and placed under house arrest, but escaped in 1942. Having witnessed at first hand the horrors of two world wars, he worked tirelessly to achieve closer union in Europe. After the establishment of the Common Market in 1957, and the signing of the Treaty of Rome, he was elected president of the European parliamentary assembly. In 1960 he became ill and retired to Scy-Chazelles.

The long low house, typical of the region, was built on the slopes of Mont Saint-Quentin and overlooks the Moselle Valley. It was simply furnished and reflected the asceticism of its owner. Robert Schuman, who never married, gave his life to the vision of uniting Europe as a cultural community. In photos, this 'Father of Europe' looked every bit the sage with domed pate and owl glasses. His house and gardens are a place of pilgrimage for many. We were glad we had made the effort to visit the 'shrine' of this visionary, wondering whether he would be pleased that the original six countries of what is now the European Union were about to become twenty-five.

Back at our comfortable lodgings, Mathie and Jean Paul, asked us if we would like to have supper with them as they were having friends in that night. We felt flattered, but declined. The addition of two English guests would put a strain on the conversation and we also knew how exhausting it would be for us. Mathie looked so disappointed that a compromise was reached: we would eat out and join them for dessert and coffee. We walked another kilometre down the hill to Moulins-lès-Metz and ate pasta and pizza before returning to Scy-Chazelles for raspberry and rhubarb tart on the terrace with Mathie, Jean Paul and two other couples. We conversed in a mixture of English and French and were plied with *vin de pays*.

'The English can always speak French when they have had some wine,' they teased.

The edge of a thunder storm during the night did nothing to relieve the humidity. We ate breakfast on the terrace: Lorraine sausage, croissants, fresh bread, home-made strawberry jam, yogurts and coffee in a bowl of hot milk, perfect for me to dunk my bread in. After the loss of a filling, I was very concerned that the crusty baguette might remove the rest of my decaying dentition.

A recently retired French couple, also staying in the house, joined us for breakfast. We learned that their son had had a serious road traffic accident and was critically ill in hospital in Metz. His accident occurred the day his first baby was born which was also his mother's sixtieth birthday. They had been staying with Mathie and Jean Paul for three weeks. When we expressed sympathy, Madame smiled and said simply, *'C'est la vie'*. In spite of their own considerable expenses and problems, the couple gave us 40 euros for our charity before we left.

We picked up the GR5 again in Moulins-lès-Metz. I was queuing in the *boulangerie* for some quiche for lunch, while Richard waited patiently outside. A straight-backed pensioner, also in the queue, was obviously intrigued by us. When we left the shop, he stood staring at our legionnaire-type caps, our sticks, and finally our boots. When Richard swung his big pack deftly onto his back, the old boy could contain himself no longer and, shouldering his baguettes like a bayonet, he mumbled toothlessly, *'La marche est comme la guerre, n'est-ce pas?'*

Reminders of the war were everywhere: *Café de la Paix, Rue de la Liberté, Avenue Charles de Gaulle*; soon we were to come across First World War trenches and cemeteries.

LORRAINE

At Pagny-sur-Moselle we had to catch a train to Pont-à-Mousson off the GR5, as this was the only place Melanie, our multilingual friend from Luxembourg, had been able to find us a *chambre d'hôte*. The road from the station took us round shunting yards where goods trains laden with coal trucks stretched to a pinpoint on the horizon. It had been a long hot twenty-four-kilometre walk to reach Pagny-sur-Moselle and the short train journey had done little to revive us. By the time we reached our accommodation in a quiet cul-de-sac, the sparkling modern house owned by a successful builder looked the perfect place to stop. However, Monsieur Bernard met us at the gate of *Le Cottage* and announced that we were not expected. There was no room. '*Désolé, Madame.*' This was a real blow as we knew how difficult accommodation was to find. Madame was then consulted, and came to check us over. When I showed her our itinerary with her name and address on it she took pity on us, although why she wasn't expecting us remained a mystery.

'You can stay but I'm afraid you will have to wait while I prepare the room. My daughter has just left,' she said kindly, pouring us a drink of squash. We were asked to wait on reclining chairs on the neatly paved terrace of her immaculate garden. We had a wonderful view of the citadel on a nearby hill, and our bodies enjoyed the reclining chairs. An hour later, Madame reappeared, and led us to a softly carpeted room with a new double bed, a balcony, an all-singing-all-dancing en suite, and the largest, softest burgundy towels I have ever seen. After seeing to our own ablutions, we turned our attention to our grey underwear, T-shirts and shorts which were always drenched in sweat. I usually squeeze the moisture out of my clothes in a towel, and my underpants retained burgundy polka dots to the day I chucked them when we reached Lake Geneva. It was difficult to know where to hang our grubby smalls without lowering the tone of that de luxe establishment; the balcony was certainly out of the question.

At the *guichet* on Pont-à-Mousson railway station I asked the young clerk for two tickets for Pagny-sur-Moselle. As she pulled them out of a machine and handed them to me I enquired, '*A quel plafond, s'il vous plaît?*' Her robotic face creased into a smile and the smile into a giggle. I had asked her where the ceiling was.

We were soon back on the GR5, but had an annoying diversion as a construction company was bulldozing the fields in readiness for laying the track for the new TGV (*train de la grande vitesse*). It was a gentle walk through woods and fields criss-crossed with many paths. Our host, Monsieur Bernard, had insisted on lending us a cool bag and some fresh tomatoes to go with our lunch. Because of our train ride, we were able to spend two nights at Pont-a-Mousson which gave us the joy of a pack-free walk.

The judge and his wife in Luxembourg, who had walked sections of the E2, told us that they had picnicked in a World War One shell hole, and their twelve-year-old son had picked up a hand grenade. That afternoon we walked through *La forêt du Bois le Prêtre*. The original forest would have been destroyed during the fighting in 1915 and replanted after the war. Beneath the beeches and oaks, now over eighty years old, lay the remains of a honeycomb of trenches, rusty barbed wire, gun emplacements and shell holes. Today they are filled with dead leaves, crumbling steel posts, and the ghosts of 7,000 French soldiers killed in January 1915 and a similar number of Germans; 22,000 men were wounded; and this, as Richard reminded me, was nothing compared to the battles of Verdun and the Somme. The front line trenches were sometimes as little as thirty metres apart; men lived like rats and fought like giants. Now the only sounds in the wood were the crackle of twigs under our feet, the startled cry of a jay, and the mew of the buzzard. As we gazed at hundreds of white crosses covering the parched grass of the hillside, I could only think of Siegfried Sassoon's war poem 'Reconciliation' written in November 1918:

When you are standing at your hero's grave,
Or near some homeless village where he died,
Remember, through your heart's rekindling pride,
The German soldiers who were loyal and brave.

Men fought like brutes; and hideous things were done;
And you have nourished hatred, harsh and blind.
But in that Golgotha perhaps you'll find
The mothers of the men who killed your son.

As we walked back to Pont-à-Mousson, Richard and I mused over Britain's ambivalent role in the forging of modern Europe, and the numbers of our men killed during both world wars. We were beginning to understand our politicians' ongoing reluctance to be wholeheartedly a part of Schuman's vision of a closer union in Europe. The British have an island mind-set, very different from other European countries whose foreign neighbours live within firing distance. In a block of countries, frontiers are more easily encroached upon, destroyed, or changed, than on an island. It was only by walking along the frontiers of Belgium, Luxembourg and France for hundreds of miles that we began to appreciate the difficulties these countries had faced over centuries of disputes brought on mainly by the fear of occupation. A united Europe was essential to prevent this ever happening again.

'Take us, for example,' Richard said as we left the cemetery crosses behind us. 'We have been walking for three days with Germans, stayed with English friends who have made their lives in Luxembourg, and enjoyed kindness and hospitality from the French in their country which we love. Perhaps all the carnage has not been in vain.'

Our expectations of Pont-à-Mousson were zero after our dismal walk from the railway station the evening before. Zero is a good place to keep them as there is then no chance of disappointment. We were amazed to find a beautiful cobbled square in the town centre surrounded by houses which included a Palladian town hall, a Renaissance arcade, a handsome bridge over the Moselle, and a sixteenth-century college of medicine, law and theology. Monsieur Bernard took us on a guided tour, and told us that the Nazis had taken over the eighteenth-century building that now houses the cinema as their headquarters during the Second World War.

'It was hard for my parents,' he told us. 'There were many collaborators. It was a nasty business.' These simple words brought home to us the horrors of occupation. We stood silently on the bridge and watched banks of pink cumulus clouds and the twin towers of an old church reflected peacefully in the still water. We were then driven up to the limestone bluff of the citadel to see the ruins of the old château bombed by the Americans when they liberated Lorraine in 1945.

'They thought Nazis might be hiding up here', said our host.

'*Plus ça change*,' I said softly thinking of Iraq.

The American bombs had done their job, and little of the old château remained. It was certainly a strategic spot, with panoramic views over the the rolling countryside of Lorraine. To the west, the Moselle glistened in the twilight as it slid darkly past the old buildings of Pont-à-Mousson. To the north the great sprawl of Metz was freckled with lights. The sun had disappeared over the horizon leaving a fiery red line in the western sky. We walked up a flight of steps to a giant crucifix silhouetted against the sunset and thought of all those wasted lives. 'We will remember them.'

It was 23 July and we had thirty-two kilometres to walk to Liverdun. However, yesterday had been easy enough without packs, and we planned to spend two nights at a campsite in Liverdun. This was not a scheduled rest day, but a pit stop to replace my walking boots. After just under 1,500 miles (2,400 kilometres), the soles had worn paper thin and soon I would be literally on my uppers. Richard's Vibram soles showed little signs of wear and he looked smug.

It was a long day's walking, but the countryside called *la petite Suisse* undulated through woods and fields and along the banks of little rivers and lakes. At times our dusty white track took us onto a high plateau between golden stubble and the cinnamon earth of ploughed fields. Occasionally the top of a church spire would appear over a distant rise, assuming its true proportions as the hill receded, revealing yet another silent village. On the brow of some hills we could see several villages scattered below us and hear the church clocks from each one striking the same hour, one after the other. We stopped for lunch in one such village called Rogeville, and ate our quiche on a convenient bench-table under a walnut tree opposite the village school. General de Gaulle's famous rallying speech, *'La France a perdu la bataille mais la France n'a pas perdu la guerre'*, was written on a white enamel plaque on the school wall. The children of Lorraine must remember too.

It was a pretty village with whitewashed stone cottages with a few geraniums in troughs outside the heavily shuttered windows; hard to believe that people really existed behind those thick walls. I thought I heard a voice coming from one of the cottages and went over to ask for water. A stocky lady in a wraparound apron obliged with a smile, and we were soon gulping back two bottles of chilled drinking water. *Vive la France* indeed, I thought.

Medieval Liverdun, with its imposing gateway complete with classical statue in niche, was a town ripe for conversion. Delightfully crumbling terraced houses, 500-year-old churches, and ancient civic buildings, fell down the steep cobbles towards the river. The precipitous streets were empty and shuttered and we managed to find a shabby bar near the railway station where we could rehydrate. The campsite was busy with incoming caravans, and we queued patiently at the reception desk, a rickety table beside the ice cream freezer. Madame, her rolls of adipose tissue squeezed into a mauve T-shirt dress, was head down in paper work. Without looking up, and thinking that we had a caravan, she asked if we needed plugging in.

Her husband, Michelin Man, ran a café which we were happy to patronize as there was nowhere to eat in town. He did the cooking while 'Manuel', a swarthy individual in jogging pants and hi-top trainers, waited at table. We were the only customers and he was attentive. Menus, wine and water arrived promptly and we both chose a rabbit casserole.

'No rabbit,' he told us apologetically in broken French, the air whistling past one lonely tooth. We chose spaghetti instead, at which command 'Manuel' bowed his way backwards from our table towards the kitchen. After a long pause he reappeared, walking forwards this time.

'We have just found two rabbits. OK?' We nodded, wondering if he had shot them. He bowed his way back to the kitchen door where he turned round and bawled like a lager lout at a football match, *'Deux lapins! Vite!'* Surprisingly enough they were quite edible, although the red wine resembled anti-freeze. It was then I felt a mild itching under my watch strap and on examination discovered my first tick.

Not waiting for *le dessert*, I dashed back to the tent, found a pair of tweezers, returned to the café and removed the little beast with Richard's assistance. Feeling I had somehow been initiated, I finished my melting ice cream.

The bus ride into Nancy took us through kilometres of industrial dross before we reached the heart of the city. Purchasing new boots is always a nightmare, and we had no idea whether Nancy even had such things. Fortunately there was just one shop that sold sports and outdoor gear, and there was just one pair of boots that fitted me for the reasonable sum of 100 euros (£70). After the sweat and tears of 1,500 miles, my boots and I were well bonded, and when I placed them reverently in the campsite bin I felt I was dumping an old friend. Or was it two old friends?

Nancy had a golden heart; Stanislas Square was a mini-Paris without people or traffic. We wandered past the neo-classical façades of an opera house, a theatre, and the *hôtel de ville*, and on under triumphal arches; passed Joan of Arc and General de Gaulle and finally through delicate wrought-iron gates dripping gold, to a park filled with acacia, lime and chestnut trees. We sat in the shade near the Belle Epoch bandstand, all hung about with elaborate gold lanterns and monumental swags. As Nancy boasts to be the gourmet capitol of the region, we had a quick nose in the food market and then indulged in a delicious three-course meal in an elegant Art Deco restaurant. Feeling mellow (so mellow I couldn't even remember what I had eaten), we explored the medieval part of the city, and admired the castellated gate with twin towers topped with dunces' hats. In true Lorraine fashion, there were no tourists, and only one shop sold post cards.

Back at the campsite, we met Melvin again. He had pitched his little peapod tent near the washroom and was expecting two friends to join him that evening. We looked first at him and then at the tent. 'They will not be sharing my tent,' he laughed, adding: 'Anyone who does that has to be a *very* good friend.'

Next morning on my way to the loo, I saw a tall red-headed girl welcoming the sunrise in the lotus position. By the time I returned, the red-headed statue had one leg wrapped round her neck and the other outstretched; a small crowd of male admirers, their boxer shorts slung low beneath tanned beer bellies, had gathered to watch.

We were on our way to Brin-sur-Seille in salt country. In three days' time we would be approaching the Vosges. The prospect of walking through a different landscape was exciting, as the endless harvested plateaux and sleepy villages of Lorraine were beginning to lose their appeal. To our surprise and delight, we found a bar open in one of the little villages we walked through that day, and were unable to resist the urge to have a rest and quench our thirst. At 2 euros (£1.40) for less than half a pint and 2.40 euros for my Orangina and water, they were the costliest drinks yet. We were finding France more expensive than either Luxembourg or Belgium. Since the advent of the euro, inflation in France has risen by 25 per cent to the detriment of the indigenous population as well as unsuspecting tourists. We ended the walk 25 per cent over budget.

Amance, a little flower-decked village on a hill, gave us a wonderful view from its thirteenth-century church. Standing in the shade of a giant cedar tree, we could see across the flat belt of Lorraine to the blue hills of the Vosges mountains and the Col du Donon which we should be climbing in three days' time. The sight lifted our spirits, my new boots were not giving me blisters, and we strode on with renewed vigour to our *chambre d'hôte*.

Brin-sur-Seille was an unremarkable village, shrunk into

its own recession. Madame César, an ample lady with amber beads and enamelled earrings, opened the door of her end-of-terrace house and beamed a welcome. She took us up a polished wood staircase to a simple room with single beds and a table stacked with regional information and coffee table books on Nancy and Metz. The house was a 1940s time warp, and the bathroom was part of the kitchen, only separated from Madame César's chopping board by a head-high partition. Our ablutions were somewhat inhibited as we lay in the bath listening to our hostess whisking eggs and chopping onions. Supper was a delicious five course meal of regional specialities, starting with terrine and melon, followed by coquilles St Jacques, followed by a savoury mince in pastry, followed by a cheese board, followed by mirabelles (pronounced mee-ra-bel). These are very small plums, the colour of a greenfinch, quite inedible raw, but delicious cooked or in jam.

Madame César joined us after the main course and not only gave us some mirabelle liqueur, but her life story and a host of anecdotes. In perfectly articulated French she told us that she had adopted two Algerian boys who had been abandoned by their mother. The elder, and obviously her favourite, was doing well at the Saint-Cyr Military Acadamy in Paris when he was tragically killed in a car crash. There was a catch in her voice as she described in detail how she had gone to the hospital and closed his eyes. She smiled dreamily. 'But I can still see him sometimes.' Noticing our puzzled expressions she added, 'On the other side. You see, I am a medium'. That same year she also lost her husband. 'But now,' she said more cheerfully, 'I have my *marcheurs*.'

She had started her bed and breakfast business after an exhausted walker knocked on her door asking for water, and enquiring if there was any accommodation in the village. She knew there was nowhere and invited him in. Down the years, her pedestrian guests had provided her with plenty of stories too. One of them fell downstairs during the night. 'I knew he would,' she told us proudly. 'I am blessed or cursed with second sight, but I was unable to prevent the accident's happening.' She played nervously with her amber beads. 'When I found him in a heap at the bottom of the stairs, I thought he was dead, and phoned for an ambulance. At that moment he opened his eyes and told me he was fine. Apparently he was a judo expert who knew how to fall.' She looked hard at me and added, 'And you, Madame, will have a torch tonight.' At that moment I spilt a little red wine on her lace tablecloth and worried that it might be a sign or portent. We were sitting round an oval table under a large orange lampshade fringed with silk and I quite expected tarot cards to come with the coffee. Madame César cleared the table, poured us the mirabelle liqueur, sat down centre stage and returned to her *petites histoires*. We heard about the provinciality of the village, the glories of Lorraine, Joan of Arc, General de Gaulle, Nancy, Metz, quiche and coquilles. The area where she lived was famous for salt mines; the river was salty, and in the old days salt was bartered for other goods. Much of the village was destroyed in the First World War.

Her French was becoming less and less comprehensible. Our feet throbbed under the table. Our eyes glazed over. Eventually, Madame paused for breath, and we rose to our feet as quickly as our stiff legs would allow, gave thanks for food, wine and entertainment, and headed off up the lethal staircase.

I knew it would happen. At 1.30 a.m. I just had to have a pee. Armed with Madame César's torch, I crept down the polished stairs hugging the banister. The bulbous grandfather clock at the bottom chimed the half-hour, making me jump. As I approached the loo, Madame César, resplendent in a Chinese silk kimono, opened the door and stared as if she had seen a ghost. Regaining her composure with a *'Bon soir,'* she lumbered back to her room. I mumbled something incomprehensible and paid the speediest visit of my life.

Madame César's stories continued over the breakfast table. There was the one about the GR5 walker who was on his way to Rome for an audience with the Pope and when he got there the Pope was unable to see him. Fancy that after all that effort! And then that poor lady who had just bought new boots; her blisters were so bad she had to stay three days and when she wasn't in bed she was either at the doctor's or at the *pharmacie*. At this point Madame César produced her *livre d'or* (visitors' book) and told us about the Dutch couple who had given her the china clogs, and the Belgian couple who still sent her Christmas cards.

'I keep up with all my *marcheurs*', she said proudly, setting the large book in front of me on the table. It was packed with *bons mots* from grateful walkers. 'Render to Caesar the things which are Caesar's' was one entry. I couldn't compete with that, and spent a long time chewing my biro before I wrote something banal in my poorly spelt French.

After a prolonged farewell on the doorstep, we waved goodbye and set off for Vic-sur-Seille, on the same salty river. We called in at the village shop to buy something for lunch, and were amused to see Madame César's terrine (her en croûte speciality) and the coquilles St Jacques all laid out on the cold marble of the *boucherie*. It seems the traditional quiche has been so successful that the inhabitants of Lorraine wrap everything up in pastry. Our lasting memories of the region will be the paucity of people, the plethora of pastry, mirabelles and manhole covers. Every manhole cover we walked over on our way to Nice, and there were many, was memorably inscribed with the words Pont-à-Mousson and a logo of a bridge.

St Christopher is the patron saint of travellers, and Vic-sur-Seille was celebrating his feast day with a funfair in the village and disco on the campsite. Our routine was to pitch the tent, shower and rest, before setting off to find somewhere to eat. Vic appeared to be a prosperous village with well-preserved old buildings and geraniums splashed liberally below windows. However, in the only available restaurant, we were not even given a menu, but the few dishes on offer were grudgingly reeled off verbatim. Service was slow and the patron and his wife were not a bit interested in their customers. As we were the only tourists they had no excuse. Afterwards we wandered into a *bar tabac* in the main square for coffee and a local liqueur, and were ignored for a long time. Eventually an obese man in T-shirt and braces, a *Gauloises* dangling from cracked lips, asked what we would like.

'*Deux cafés et deux Ricard, s'il vous plaît.*' *Monsieur le patron* nodded at the coffees but couldn't cope with my request for local liqueur. I tried asking for mirabelle but that foxed him even more; he shook his head, nearly losing his fag, and let out a string of incomprehensible patois. We had to be content with a *demi-tasse* of coffee each before we walked the kilometre back to our campsite by the lake.

We were flat on our backs in the tent when the disco began at 9.30 p.m. Disco music in France has to be just as deafening as in the UK, and we were assaulted until the early hours. We could cope with that, but things did not improve when a drunken fisherman who had rented one of the summer huts stumbled round our tent, singing lustily, f'ing and b'ing when he couldn't catch a fish, and throwing up at intervals.

Melvin and his friends had pitched their tents nearby, and when we passed him on a bleary-eyed trip to the shower early next morning we commented on the noisy night. 'All part of the challenge,' he grinned. His friend Simone, the yoga expert, had worn earplugs and slept soundly. We concluded that St Christopher had had the night off.

It was a dull twenty-six kilometres of mainly road walking to our *gîte* on a farm in another dormant village called Assenoncourt. From time to time the blurred hills of the Vosges appeared on the horizon, growing tantalizingly nearer. Salt was still on the menu as we passed through the fortified village of Marsal, which had been the centre of the salt industry since the thirteenth-century. We walked through an imposing eighteenth-century building straddling the road which is now a salt museum. It was Sunday; the museum was shut and the village deserted.

Our *gîte à la ferme* was like the *Marie Celeste*. The iron-roofed barns were full of cows and calves, a black and white mongrel was tethered to a chain, and there was no sign of anyone anywhere. We waited for half an hour and then it began to rain, the first we had had in three weeks. The annexe door was open and, feeling a bit like Goldilocks, I found two sparse bedrooms with basic facilities ready and waiting. After two hours, a car drew up and out spilled the farmer and his wife, daughter, son-in-law, uncle and two granddaughters. We were given a simple meal of home-made pâté and home-grown beef tomatoes, lamb chops *à la ferme*, a large slice of Camembert sagging perfectly, coffee and a pitcher of wine, all for 15 euros each. Their dining room was very much as I remembered the houses where I au paired in France as a student in 1959. There was a large table, a rustic cupboard and sideboard, an iron pot-bellied stove and some dried flowers. With the exception of the plumbing, it seemed that rural France had not changed so very much in forty years. There were spiders in our modern shower, and cobwebs on the window sills, but, compared to our tent, it was a palace.

Now we were in a land of lakes (known as *étangs*), drains and canals. It was cheering just to have a change in scenery and from time to time we could see the wavy blue line of the Vosges getting closer. The little village of Fribourg had more life than most, with children playing in the street, adults chatting in doorways, and a mobile shop ringing its bell. There were three water troughs in the village, one for white clothes, one for colours and one for horses. We had no idea which was which, but the water tasted wonderful. Everything seemed good after a night's sleep, I was getting used to my new boots, my blisters were healing, the weather was cooler and we saw our first stork. The lakes were covered with water lilies and jewelled with dragonflies; frogs croaked, herons flapped and great crested grebes gazed contemptuously across the still water.

Gondrexange campsite was very full, and we had to pitch our tent near the washrooms beside a large caravan with awning extension. After a good meal in a restaurant overlooking the Etang de Gondrexange, we watched the sunset marbling the water of the Marne au Rhin canal in pinks and greys. When we returned to the campsite our 'neighbours from hell' had returned. A German couple had lit a brazier, turned up the stereo, and were entertaining a French couple in phrasebook French. From the inside of our tent, their wall to wall music was background to a raucous exchange of recycled banalities, as the world's insoluble problems were solved with the help of much wine and several packets of cigars. The hours ticked away, the brazier spat and crackled, the arguments grew more heated, the language took on a Babel quality, and tongues of flame danced intermittently across the green nylon of our tent. At 2 a.m. Richard could bear it no longer and walked round the town for an hour. I got up and explored the possibility of moving the tent, but there were no spare places. I then asked our neighbours to shut up as politely as I could, telling them they were keeping everyone awake. They had the goodness to turn down the volume on the radio, but threw more wood on the fire and continued their slurred conversation where they had left off. As day broke, protracted goodbyes were shouted across the campsite and quiet was restored.

The temperature climbed steadily as we plodded eastwards towards the forests of the Vosges. Cocks crowed and dogs barked in shuttered villages until we reached Saint-Quirin and entered a different world. The church spires sprouted onions, we were walking up hill, the old houses were freshly painted with coloured shutters, and there were several hotels and even a tourist office. We sampled a beer at a crowded hotel bar, but Richard's was sour and the barmaid refused to replace it. This did nothing for his humour. When we set off again Richard was unsure which way to go. He checked and rechecked the waymarks and consulted his Topo Guide which had such poor black and white copies of the map that the contour lines were often confusingly merged. After much dithering, we set off up a steep hill in the heat of a late July afternoon. Our lack of sleep the previous night was telling on us and we were finding walking up the hot road surprisingly hard. After three kilometres there was a track off to the left and Richard stopped and deliberated. His Topo Guide began to gyrate, always a bad sign, and then he told me he had taken the wrong turn. As we headed miserably back down the hill he made an announcement.

'I've lost my enthusiasm for this; its hard slog day after day after day.' There was a pause and he continued, 'I'd catch a train home now if I could.' And he meant it.

Strasbourg

La Donon

Mt. Sta - Odile

Schirmeck

La Hohwald

Barr.

Châtenois

Haut-Kroenigsbourg

Ribeauvillé

Le Bonhomme

Germany.

Col de la Schlucht.

La Markstein

Grand Ballon

Rouge - Gazon

St-Amarin

Ballon
d'Alsace

Giromagny

church of St. Quirin.

12. The Vosges.

0   10   20   30

Chapter Twelve

The Vosges

Once upon a time, in a small town at the foot of the Vosges, there lived a baker and his wife called Monsieur and Madame Baguette. It was a very poor town because it was on the boundary of two countries; sometimes it belonged to Germany and sometimes to France. It had once been famous for iron, pottery, sauerkraut, white wine and savoury pancakes covered in cheese and spicy meats. Now the inhabitants had to live on stale bread and cheese with a little sausage meat on saints' days.

Someone left a baby girl called Gretel on the baker's doorstep with a note asking them to adopt her. The baby grew into a beautiful woman with dark hair and milky white skin.

One fine day Gretel went up the hillside to pick bilberries, but she wandered too far into the forest and was soon lost. Tired out, she lay down in the cool shade and slept. She was awakened by terrible squeals and shouts from a hunting party, and saw a handsome young man slaying a wild boar only two metres from her resting place. Their eyes met and they fell in love. He introduced himself as Prince Hansel, lifted her onto his white charger and carried her back to his turreted castle on the crest of the Vosges. They were married in Gretel's little town which quickly became prosperous and filled with visitors from many countries. The tourists spent their money on food, wine and pottery and admired the narrow streets where the crooked buildings leaned towards one another and window boxes blazed with flowers.

Walkers of all nationalities were welcomed, except those from the Low Countries who always had their own supplies of food and rarely stayed in a hostelry.

The handsome prince soon became king and stopped all the wars, demolished trade barriers and forged a coin called the vuro, which was accepted in all the countries that had once been at war with one another. King Hansel ordained that the place names remained German, but allowed his subjects to speak French. The environmentally conscious Queen Gretel only had two children, and insisted that everyone at Court should recycle their wine bottles, parchments and old coins. The young king and queen opened their castle to the public to defray expenses.

As time went by, the beautiful tree-covered mountains became a National Park and this encouraged the growth of pines, oaks and beech trees, and discouraged tourists from dropping litter on the rich flora and fauna, or picking the many wild flowers. Black cows with a white band down their backs grazed the meadows, and wild boars, lynx and deer lived in the woods. Woodpeckers tapped away on the bark of trees and everybody lived happily ever after.

The Vosges is a fairytale region and we fell under its spell as soon as we started climbing the tree-clad slopes of the Petit Donon, a warm-up for Mont Donon itself at 732 metres. Storms had shredded some of the trees, and their decapitated trunks stood out like warning sentinels. Seeing the devastation, I became apprehensive about being caught out in the storms which were inevitable at that time of year.

From the saddle between the two hills it was rewarding to look back at the lakes and rolling farmland of Lorraine. Nice was too far away to even contemplate, but we set ourselves the task of conquering the hills of the Vosges with new found enthusiasm.

It doesn't matter where you go; the Romans and the Dutch always seem to get there first. After a very steep pull up to the top of the Mont Donon, we found our Flying Dutchman and his friends sitting in the nineteenth-century reconstruction of a Roman Temple of Mercury. From here we had an imperial view across ridge upon ridge of blue-green hills to the horizon. In the shade of the great sandstone pillars we exchanged experiences and addresses with Melvin's friends who were returning to Holland next day, ate apples and drained our water bottles. On our way down we came across real live tourists, middle-aged couples, families with children, a student gazing at the copy of a Roman sculpture, and some young men with day packs. A few children were picking bilberries.

That night we treated ourselves to a Logis de France hotel at the Col du Donon, with an empty car park and a wonderful view of the mountains. Half board (*demi pension*), costs about the same as a modest bed and breakfast in the UK (hotels being less affected than almost everything else by the inflationary effect of the euro). We had a very comfortable en suite room, and a delicious meal served by the unshaven owner in a crumpled T-shirt escorted by a large friendly Alsatian. The bill was only 53 euros (£35) each for dinner bed and breakfast including wine and coffee. It was a good start.

The day's walk to le Hohwald, where we planned to camp for the night, was to take more than eight hours; (distances in the mountains are measured in time rather than kilometres), but the temperature was bearable, and we were mainly in the shade of the trees which cover 90 per cent of the Vosges. As we walked downhill to the bustling town of Schirmeck, we rapidly lost all the height we had gained the previous day. A huge supermarket on the outskirts was so stacked with temptation that I had to leave my basket behind and only take what I could hold in my arms. We hydrated with a litre carton of orange juice before we moved off. In the luxury of our hotel I had managed to write some cards to the family and Jiffy bag the Topo Guide we had just finished using. I spent a precious fifteen minutes queuing in the post office, and my thoughts turned to the family; Tunbridge Wells was a lifetime away, but thanks to my Sony Ericsson mobile phone we could catch up with news from home. Richard had taken up his usual stance on the pavement outside the post office, and as soon as my post was in the box we were on our way out of the town, climbing steeply to rejoin our rollercoasting friend the GR5.

At the summit of Mont Donon, we had noticed a tall concrete pillar in the distance. This was the memorial at the Struthof labour camp which claimed 30,000 victims between 1941 and 1944. The GR5 went right past the camp and, although we were hot and tired and had a long way still to go, we felt obliged to visit this terrible place. Richard, bare-chested in the heat, was asked to put his T-shirt on. There was nowhere to leave our rucksacks so we kept them on our backs, a small burden compared to the immense suffering of those who had been through the gates where the words *Arbeit macht frei* were written. The only freedom from work here was death.

The camp had been torched in 1976, and one of the huts had been rebuilt and made into a museum. Skeletal prematurely aged figures and the starving faces of men, women and children stared out at us from the black and white photographs which covered the walls. We were not even spared decapitated and de-limbed bodies which were the victims of Nazi medical experiments. There were photos of pyjama-clad figures crucified on the barbed wire of the camp, lifting impossible loads in the quarries, and herded to the gas chambers. There was nothing here we hadn't already read about or seen on celluloid, but the atmosphere of sorrow and shame was palpable. A small stream of tourists walked round with us. Nobody spoke. The only sound was the tread of feet on the wooden floorboards and a few muffled sobs. As we entered the door the following lines were written on the wall:

Passant, qui que tu sois	Passers-by whoever you are
Français ou étranger	French or foreigner
Toi qui viens te recueillir	You who come to reflect
En ce haut lieu	In this high place
Ou tant d'hommes ont souffert	Where so many men suffered
Dans leur chair	In their flesh
Dans leur âme	In their soul
Dans leur coeur	In their hearts
Ou tant d'hommes ont donné	Where so many men have given
Leur vie pour la liberté.	Their life for liberty
MEDITE	MEDITATE
L'humanité ne devrait	Humanity must never
Plus revoir cela.	Let this happen again.

Outside the perimeter wire, the meadows were full of harebells and butterflies.

It was a good hour before we could face eating our meagre lunch and after this we had a long hard pull up through the woods to reach the crest of the hill. The landscape then opened out into a wide grassy area called the Champ du Feu (Field of Fire) where we saw our first ski lift and our first shepherd. This weather-beaten man was the proud owner of a long stick with a trowel on the end, a straw hat with heather in it, a toothless grin, a flock of scraggy sheep and two mangy dogs. Unusually, Richard was having trouble picking up our red and white waymarks so I asked the shepherd if he could help.

His patois was so incomprehensible that we were none the wiser after he had spent a good five minutes telling us exactly what to do. Meanwhile, his two dogs were beginning to round us up while his sheep were straying all over the place.

The campsite, on the perimeter of le Hohwald, was attractive and peaceful. The little town was tucked in a deep valley surrounded by firs and hardwoods, meadows and streams. Somewhere we heard the discordant clang of a cowbell. There was a faded alpine elegance about the wooden buildings many of which had fretted eaves and elaborately carved balconies; one or two nineteenth-century hotels were in terminal decay. We had a quiet night with well-behaved fellow campers and our first *flambée*, a cross between a pancake and a pizza, covered in cheese and meat in the only *auberge* which was, of course, deserted. Next morning we ate our *petit déjeuner* in bright sunshine on a terrace outside the *boulangerie* beside great banks of geraniums and petunias, which were being watered by an old man in beret and blue overalls using a Vittel bottle. Any thoughts of giving up had evaporated in the magic woods of the Vosges. The village shop provided us with bread and cheese and fruit for lunch, and we set off for Barr with a spring in our step. It was 1 August and although we had only been walking through Europe for a month, it seemed more like a year.

Our route took us up the steep incline to Mont Sainte-Odile, shaded by the conifers and beech and chestnut trees so prevalent in the Vosges. Many paths criss-crossed the hillside and Richard had to have his wits about him to find the waymarks. It was easy to miss them if you were thinking about something else, which I usually was, and even Richard's vigilance let him down occasionally.

We had almost reached the top of the hill, but were still deep in woodland, when we stumbled across an ancient wall; the large beautifully preserved stones enclosed an area of about ten square kilometres. Mont Sainte-Odile rises steeply above the plain of Alsace, making it strategically important and a natural fortification. The great wall at this vantage point was not unlike Hadrian's in Northumberland. It was certainly restored by the Romans but is thought to have been built in the eighth-century BC. Its original function remains a mystery. The megalithic rocks have been formed into strange shapes, some like great pillars and others like piles of giant-sized dinner plates which might have been used as sacrificial altars in prehistoric times. Whatever the reason, the ancient rocks lying on the bracken and dead leaves of the forest floor, with the cool green of the canopy of leaves above, gave a sense of pagan spirituality to the wood reinforced by the pungent smell of resin.

After the pagans came the Christians; the story goes that a Merovingian duke had a daughter Odile, who was born blind but miraculously regained her sight at her baptism. When Odile grew up she moved to Alsace and built an abbey on the present site which grew and flourished. She died in 720 and her abbey went through the usual routine of being destroyed and rebuilt, burned and pillaged. During their revolt in 1521, the peasants did such a good job of burning it down that all the nuns fled, leaving a few novitiate priests to guard St Odile's tomb. After that it became, and still is, a place of pilgrimage. The abbey was restored to its present splendour in the nineteenth-century.

We emerged from the pagan woods into a network of hot tarmac roads and full car parks. The impressive block of abbey, chapel and residential quarters was heaving with French, Japanese, Dutch, German, and English tourists who were spilling out of cars and coaches.

The abbey on Mont Sainte-Odile stands on a sheer outcrop of sandstone more than 600 metres above the plain of Alsace, with Odile herself perched on the domed roof on the tallest turret. Never mind the saint on her turret, even for tourists on the terrace (especially ones who had been walking for days in thick wood) the view was memorable. The Rhine Valley rolled out before our eyes like a smouldering *flambée*. Through the heat haze we could clearly see the Black Forest, and just pick out the smudge of Strasbourg with the Rhine cutting through the plain like shimmering steel. Looking down, I began to appreciate that every day we would be walking down towards the plain (known as the foot of the Vosges) to find accommodation, and climbing all the way up next morning. Thanks to the thick covering of trees, we would be in the shade for most of the day. Without this protection from the increasingly ferocious sun, the intense heat would have got the better of us.

Back in the forest we stumbled on a kiosk perched on the edge of the wood; not the sort that sells ice creams, but a bamboo and wooden hexagonal with an oriental feel. It was built as an elegant shelter in the mid nineteenth-century, and from it we could see the green wooded hills of the Vosges stretching away onto the horizon and a fairytale castle peeping out between the dense trees. Below us lay a scattering of little towns; clusters of red roofs jostling round church spires among the neat lines of vineyards.

We walked down through the woods into the baking sun and on through the vineyards of Barr where Gewürztraminer and Riesling wines were produced. On our search for the local campsite we passed an attractive-looking *gîte,* and I had great difficulty stopping my blistered feet from going up to the door so that their owner could ask for accommodation. My tired body craved a mattress and pillow and dreaded another night on thin polystyrene on the iron- hard ground. However, Richard was blazing a trail and I had to put all these fantasies out of my head and keep pace with him. He was definitely a man who can.

The campsite, in the grounds of the local school, was full. Luckily the *gardienne* was very solicitous towards backpacking walkers.

'I am expecting a group of Italians,' she told us, 'but they haven't arrived yet so I am going to give you their site. However, I would be grateful if you could put your tent as near the neighbours as possible just in case they do turn up.' They hadn't turned up by 7 p.m. so Madame put several other small tents on the same piece of tired grass and we spent a sleepless night tent peg to tent peg with Friar Tuck and Maid Marian, who, when they weren't snoring loudly, were tucking into mountains of sausage and bread washed down with beer. In a brasserie in the town centre, we enjoyed *flambées* and local wine, with a German family on one side and a French couple on the other. We reflected that Robert Schuman would have been pleased to see this entente cordiale sharing the same pavement and using the same currency.

Barr seemed to have almost as many clocks as campers, and they chimed relentlessly throughout the long hot night. We set off at 7 a.m. on an eight-and-a-half-hour walk to Châtenois. One of the few bonuses of staying on a campsite, apart from the price, was the ability to set off early in the morning before the day began to roast.

Barr is a typical Alsace town, the narrow cobbled streets lined with colourful timber-framed houses, their shuttered windows frothing geraniums. Wide stone arches gave peeps into cobbled yards where dilapidated farm buildings invited conversion. It took us an hour to slog up the road to the next town of Andlau where we stopped for breakfast in the back alley of a *patisserie*. The French have a knack of making the best of even a small space, and this tiny slot between high buildings was painted terracotta; the miniature wall-fountain, lush green pot plants and white tables and chairs made it a shady oasis in which to have our croissant and coffee. We then bought a couple of filled baguettes for lunch, before heading up to the crest of the Vosges once again.

It was Saturday, 2 August, and Andlau was preparing for a wine festival. Stalls were set out in the market place and crates of chilled wine were just arriving in vans. Richard was sorely tempted to stay. Instead, we walked resolutely out of the town, past the cool river where colourful gardens were crammed with yellow and purple rudbeckia, squash, sun flowers and petunias, while geraniums fell in cascades from balconies and window boxes.

Although it was still only 9 a.m., the sun was already hot as we climbed the steep hill through beautifully tended vineyards to the welcome shade of the trees. In temperatures that were now approaching 40 degrees, we could not have walked all day without shade.

After an hour of steady climbing through the woods, we reached a viewing platform on the summit of the Ungersberg. At last, at a height of 901 metres, we were finally rewarded with good views of the Vosges and the plain. We even met a few other walkers who had come to see the view and picnic nearby. Shunning company, we moved off to a shady spot and threw our sweaty bodies on the ground for lunch and a twenty-minute snooze. Walking with big packs in these extreme temperatures was physically demanding, and our overworked bodies needed a rest. We would always allow a fifteen to twenty-minute mid-morning break for a drink and an energy bar or banana, and three quarters of an hour to an hour for lunch, and another short break mid-afternoon. Although the heat sapped our energy, the fine weather enabled us to have these 'pit stops'. All the same, the afternoons were hard for us both, when, after a long descent from the mountains we had to face an hour or more in the scorching late afternoon heat in order to find accommodation.

I was in focused mode that afternoon, and barely noticed the ruins of the Bernstein and Ortenbourg castles, destroyed during the Thirty Years War, which were on our route. All I wanted was to arrive, and I braced myself for the rise in temperature as we walked the baking tarmac kilometres into the town of Châtenois. We had trouble locating our *chambre d'hôte* and headed off in the direction of the cemetery which, in our state of dehydrated exhaustion, seemed as good a place as any. We eventually found Monsieur and Madame Bayer's residence behind a frilly wrought-iron gate surrounded by an immaculately paved yard which was bursting with white pergolas, plastic fountains and potted geraniums.

The coolest part of Madame Bayer's house was her enclosed stone staircase. She was a diminutive lady with a face like a walnut, and her limited French vocabulary so Teutonic that communication was difficult. As she opened the door into our simple bedroom, we felt like two buns going into an oven. I just managed to remove my boots before flopping onto the bed like a deflated balloon. Richard, despite the heat and the extra weight he was carrying, always seemed to have more energy at the end of the day than I did. He showered and washed his clothes before settling on his bed with his head in maps and guides. After a deflated half-hour,

I just managed to make the short trip to the bathroom for my ablutions. The large room had a cubicle shower on one side and a loo like a throne in the middle with a coy screen between the two. The one skylight window had a blind over it and the light didn't work. As I was leaving I literally bumped into Monsieur Bayer, a Mr Greedy lookalike, starkers except for an invisible loin cloth. We laughed nervously, exchanged apologies in a variety of languages, and went our separate ways.

My legs told me they would only tolerate a short walk to find an eating place, and, if the nearest hotel hadn't been only 300 metres down the street, I might have gone hungry. The temperature inside the restaurant was almost as warm as it was outside, and as we ordered our food we were aware that we were sweating like a pair of leaky taps. Madame, her hair neatly swept back and tied with a little scarf, looked fresh in her low-cut blouse and well-fitting skirt. The restaurant filled up and she had a busy evening, but looked as cool at the end of it as she had been at the beginning.

Something I had eaten disagreed with me and I was grateful for Madame Bayer's throne on numerous occasions before and after breakfast. We had hoped to buy something for lunch in the town, but it being Sunday everything was *fermé*. However, Madame was happy to let us have some stale bread, pâté and salami-type sausage for ten euros (£7), so we felt the inhabitants of Alsace were not averse to a little tourist milking, especially as our very simple accommodation had been as expensive as a good *demi pension* hotel. Crouching in the woods some time later, I reflected that at least I had had my money's worth of loo paper.

Only eighteen kilometres to the next enchanted town of Ribeauvillé and en route we managed a 600-metre climb to castle of Haut-Koenigsbourg. The château was originally built in the seventh century, and rose through the trees above us in fairytale fashion. Like so many castles it was destroyed and rebuilt at least three times before the present one was completed in 1899.

The sandstone towers and turrets of this magnificent reconstruction would have warmed the heart of Mad Ludwig of Bavaria. As we stood under the great buttresses we were showered with tourists clutching soft drinks and ice creams instead of boiling oil or gunpowder. After puffing up the many steps onto the road, we found every seat on the terrace was taken, so we made do with a nearby wall where we topped up our diminished fluid levels and gazed over the shimmering plain far below.

After the enjoyable morning, the afternoon was less good. The temperature was 38 degrees and I began to feel light-headed and slightly seasick. Or was it walk sick? We passed through a pedestrian's dream of a village called Thannenkirch where every pretty eighteenth-century house advertised itself as a hotel, *gîte*, *chambre d'hôte* or *zimmer frei*. Even better it had no fewer than three drinking fountains, and we dunked our hats and arms and legs in every one of them as well as drinking as much as our stomachs would hold. Richard's plan was to camp in Ribeauvillé still a hard hour's walk away, and it was so tempting to stay here. I loitered through the village, hoping my task master would change his mind, but, as a man with a plan, he kept resolutely on, and I had no choice but to keep up with him.

Three ruined castles rise through the trees above Ribeauvillé, the châteaux of Haut-Ribeaupierre, Saint-Ulrich and Guirsberg and we walked past all three on our way down the stony path into the town. I was no longer up for culture, just concentrating where I put my feet and thankful to have my two metal sticks to help take the strain. Just as we reached the road, I tripped over a potted geranium and stopped.

Richard looked at me and said, 'Well, yes. Why not? Let's go for it.'

I had no idea what he was talking about, until I looked up and realized that the geranium was one of many on the steps of a very pleasant-looking hotel advertising rooms and a restaurant. Richard skulked outside in the heat, while I entered the cool dining room and asked if we could stay. Undeterred by my dishevelled appearance and accompanying odour, the young receptionist smiled assent and we were soon prostrate on a very comfortable bed in a freshly decorated room with brand-new en suite facilities and, praise St Christopher, loads of loo paper.

I lay on the bed and felt as though I had drunk half a bottle of neat whisky: a not entirely unpleasant sensation. After several glasses of water and a shower, I felt able to go down the short flight of stairs for our *demi pension* meal. Sitting on the terrace with my head in an oleander bush and my fork in the *charcuterie*, I soon revived. After a local bottle of Tokay Pinot gris and the obligatory three delicious courses, we had enough strength to wander round this stage-set town which crouches at the foot of the Vosges. It had everything: an old gatehouse tower, crooked colourful houses, steeply pitched roofs, and cobbled streets displaying brilliant window boxes. The town centre was buzzing with people eating and drinking on the warm pavements among shops selling gingerbread, liqueurs, wine and leather goods. We learned that we were now on the Grande Route de Vin (highly recommended), and the local wine growers revelled in the name of Jean and Louis Sipp. The demon sun had finally set, and, at the end of the cobbled main street, the ruined Château Guirsberg rose from the dark bulk of the Vosges, silhouetted against the lemon sky.

After a good night, I was feeling ready to tackle a mere twelve kilometres to Aubure, and hoped my gut would settle without recourse to a *pharmacie*, where you paid well over the odds for anything handed to you by those clinical ladies in white coats.

We were entertained at breakfast by a lady whose legs were poured into pink flowery trousers with matching zipped bag which she placed carefully on the seat beside her. A small portion of the zip was open and a fluffy face with lolling pink tongue and matching ribbons whined pitifully. In France, all dogs great and small are allowed into hotel dining rooms, bedrooms, and restaurants. Richard made the mistake of trying a little French/English accord with it, but his diplomacy was rewarded with a snap of sharp teeth and a growl that might have frightened a French flea.

The heat wave continued mercilessly and, fit though we were, I sweated up the steep hill like a Victorian heroine with a life-threatening fever. I was amazed how quickly my grey handkerchief became sodden as I tried to wipe the perspiration out of my eyes. My unkempt hair, lengthening daily, dripped down the back of my neck like a Japanese torture. Richard looked as though he had come out of a swimming pool. Back in Luxembourg, our English friends had advised us to take salt tablets; we hadn't taken their advice, but compromised by buying anchovies which increased our vicious thirst. Our packs were already so heavy that we only carried a litre of water each, and would drink cautiously hoping to find a fountain or bar to supplement our own supplies. I was also losing moisture from my troubled gut and was glad when we reached the Rocher du Koenigsstuhl at 938 metres in two hours, a little less than suggested in our Topo Guide. The ancient pile of rocks in the deep shade of the forest was shaped like a giant chair; hence the name. We played Kings and Queens and surveyed our kingdom, mostly beech and fir trees, bracken and mossy rocks. It was hard to believe that we were now walking west on the very crest of the Vosges and had to wait for the occasional viewpoint to get our bearings and feel a sense of achievement.

The village of Aubure, at 800 metres, was a *station climatique* and well-known centre for convalescence. This I thought sounded promising, and would certainly have a *pharmacie* where, blow the cost, I could purchase some medicinal concrete. I was also hoping for a hotel with an en suite, rather than a hot campsite with loos a good five minutes' walk from the tent. Aubure was not convalescent: it was dead. There was no sign of a shop, let alone a green cross, a red cross or any other kind of cross; even the *gîte* appeared to be closed. Ever hopeful, I rang the bell and a sexy lady in shorts and mini sun-top leaned her tanned cleavage over the balcony.

'*Désolée, Madame,*' she said firmly. '*En vacances. Je ne fonctionne pas.*' Then she waved her hand imperiously. '*Mais voyons, il y a un site de camping là-bas.*' We stared at her in disbelief. She waited a moment, and then, having decided that we were completely mad, shook her blonde head and departed into the cool of the shuttered house with a parting '*Désolée Monsieur, 'dame.*'

Madame wasn't the only one who was sorry. We had no option but to head for the campsite where we found a shady place for the tent on the edge of a wood. The bad news was that the toilet block was a good three minutes' walk up a very steep incline. It was early afternoon and we had time to rest and catch up on washing and booking accommodation ahead. Richard's worries over where we were going to stay had increased, partly due to my ongoing leaky gut, and mostly because he never likes to be in a position where he has to ask; very Mars. After some deliberation and much guide searching, he gave Venus a list of hotels and *gîtes* with phone numbers to book ahead and save end of day stress. I found it best to remove myself out of earshot while using the phone, as Richard has a habit of cutting in while I was talking, and I am not good at listening to two conversations in two different languages at the same time.

In an empty shelter by the camp gates, I rang the first *auberge* on my list.

'*Bonjour, Madame*.' A polite voice answered. I asked for a room and gave the date.

'*Êtes-vous malade?*' the voice enquired. I certainly wasn't feeling too good, but not strictly ill. Having passed on this bit of information, the voice told me that I had rung a hospital and she didn't think we would really like to stay there.

My bowel kept me trotting to the wood or the toilet block so many times before breakfast that it was becoming obvious that I needed some concreting pills pronto. We sat drinking coffee, no food available, in a seedy *bar tabac* in Aubure, and revised our plans. There was a village called le Bonhomme some fourteen kilometres away which looked large enough to have a pharmacy and a hotel. This was forty-five minutes short of Richard's hoped-for destination at l'Etang du Devin (the Lake of the Soothsayer). Of the two, le Bonhomme sounded more promising, and I assured my anxious husband that I would be able to get there without wilting by the wayside. My greatest worries at that moment were the lack of loo paper, and an increasing difficulty in keeping my shorts in situ; the more weight I lost, the more they resembled a limp washing line.

Scorching heat on a tarmac road, and the loss of my *casquette*, a wonderful cap with sunblind at the back, made a bad start. However, we reached Pierre des Trois Bains, the high point of the day at 1,128 metres, in just over the recommended one hour fifteen minutes. We then collapsed onto the green sward under the trees, and lay for an hour in a comatose state before beginning the descent.

Le Bonhomme was no more than a one-street village deep

in a fold of the hills. It was mid-afternoon when we arrived on a pavement that felt like a frying pan ready to receive a pancake. Our battered feet soon found a Logis de France with a double room. After a shower and a rest, we went out into the oven to search for a *pharmacie*. There were several hotels, a church, a bus stop, a *boulangerie* and a boarded-up café. No chemist. The manageress of the hotel told us the nearest one was down on the plain, a journey which would take us an hour each way on the bus. At this news I took to my bed, and Richard went out again to look up the bus times. I reckoned that our search for medication would take three to four hours out of the anticipated seven hour day to the Col de la Schlucht; it was not good news. I closed my eyes and drifted.

I had no idea how long Richard had been away, but some time later he bounced back into the room like Tigger with a grin on his face.

'Did you find the bus timetable?' I mumbled from somewhere under a sheet.

'Yes. But I found something even better,' he said, waving a small packet under my nose. 'I was at the bus stop when who should appear but Melvin. He was on his way to the phone box to call his girlfriend. We chatted, and when I told him you needed diarrhoea pills he went half-way back up the hill to his tent and gave me his supply.'

I blessed our Flying Dutchman turned Good Samaritan – one of the few young men left who refuses to carry a mobile phone – and spent most of the night downing little green pills to very beneficial effect.

The Col de la Schlucht at 1,139 metres is the highest and most popular pass in the southern Vosges. On our way, the GR5 took us past trenches, dug-outs, tunnels through the mountain, and gun emplacements; a sort of First World War Maginot Line at this strategically important boundary between

France and Germany. Rather feebly I told Richard I didn't want to do the extra climb to the famous Tête des Faux and regretted missing out on some of the most spectacular fortifications of the Western Front.

In spite of the relentless heat, the woods at this height were comparatively cool and this made walking much easier. At a crossroads of paths we came across the Duchesne National Cemetery for soldiers killed during the 1914–18 war. Dappled sunlight illuminated a mass of wooden crosses lined up among the tall pine trees; standing over them, the French tricolour hung limply from its tall white pole, and goldcrests twittered in the resin-scented trees.

Suddenly we were meeting people: ramblers, families, small children, toddlers in push chairs. I concluded we must be near a road. We plodded on steadily, a little concerned about our diminishing water supplies but, at a height of over 1,000, metres happy to have more air. At the halfway mark we came across an oasis in the shape of a rural refuge. White tables and chairs looked tempting under colourful umbrellas and we stepped into the dark wooden hut in search of a drink. Tables were laid for lunch, and at the little bar piles of sparkling bottles, showered by the cold tap, were up to their necks in ice cubes. The sight of those cold bottles and the sound of the water made such an impact on my overheated brain that I could barely remember to ask for two drinks. Feeling the iced fluid soothing our parched throats made the thirsty kilometres worth while. We had just drained our glasses when out of the wood strode a youthful figure in a brown and green T-shirt with a large backpack. It was Melvin, my Good Samaritan. I gave him a motherly kiss of gratitude and Richard bought him two beers. We left him sipping his lager under the shade of an umbrella. He told us later that after this largesse he had had problems getting up the hills.

Stepping out of the forest we found ourselves in a wide

open stretch of meadow called a *gazon*. It felt like the roof of the world as our undulating path traversed the rocky crest of a grassy hillside. The ground dropped sharply away to the east and we could now see a hazy procession of blue waves on the far horizon. Purple heather, rosebay willowherb and yellow ragwort gave relief after the eternal green of the forests. Vosgienne black cows with a broad white stripe down their backs grazed the meadows. From time to time we would walk through clouds of butterflies: swallowtail, fritillary, and orange-tip. A few human butterflies were hang-gliding on the thermals. We now had a chance to look down at a patchwork of parched brown fields and farms and a scattering of shrinking aquamarine lakes. Even this green hilly landscape had not escaped the exceptional drought.

As we neared the Col, we noticed that, when it came to sports, there was something for everyone: mountain biking, rock climbing, walking, downhill skiing, cross country skiing, summer luge. Cow bells clanged as the poor creatures tried to find some goodness in the parched meadows. The wild flowers seemed untroubled by the drought and we came across pale lemon pansies, white pulsatilla, heather, scabious, ragwort, giant plantains, harebells and bilberries. The wild roses were over.

Resting in the shade of a stunted bush, we were overtaken by two obese Germans carrying enormous ill-fitting rucksacks. They puffed their way up the hill ahead and then stopped at the top. When we caught them up I asked if they had walked far.

'No,' they answered cheerfully, 'we're flying.' With that they unrolled their great silk parachutes and hang-glided off into the thermals.

Good though it was to have a view, it was even better to be back in the cool of the woods. In a few days' time we would be down on the sizzling plain between the Vosges and the Jura, with no shade, and the prospect was worrying.

The Col de la Schlucht was the first of many ski resorts we were to encounter; the metal roads, car parks, lifeless chairlifts and hotchpotch of hotels were like the stretch marks on a child-bearing stomach. In spite of this lack of aesthetics, we found a nearly empty hotel which gave us a comfortable night and had a good self-service restaurant. The bare walls were covered in black and white photographs of French soldiers, guns at the ready, standing beside iron gates, sentry posts and an electric railway. What had been a very busy border post before the First World War was now an insignificant holiday resort with bouncy castles, souvenir shops, cafés, cable cars and car parks. Lorries on the D417 thundered past our window all night.

At Markstein we stayed in our first *gîte d'étape* (basic accommodation for walkers or those with slim wallets). The large dormitory was empty except for one small boy who came to bed long after us and rose at first light. The bill for supper, bed and breakfast was only 55 euros (£36) for us both. We set off after a good night's sleep ready to tackle the Grand Ballon; at 1,424 metres this is the highest point in the Vosges, from where we should have been able to see Mont Blanc and the Jungfrau had the heat haze not blotted them out.

We had rung the girls the night before and learned that they too were in the throes of a heat wave with temperatures of 98 degrees Fahrenheit in Kent. Great-granny was not enjoying the humidity and even my publisher told me it was so hot in Chichester that he had sent his workforce home. Electric fans had sold out and life was grinding to a halt. I suggested he poured cold water over his head. We thought of the thousands of people working in stuffy offices, or sweating on the underground, and felt sorry for them. It was hard for us, but at least we were outside and, at that altitude, there was usually a breath of air.

Le Grand Ballon is a smooth round hill with a giant 'golf ball' of a satellite station on the top. We managed to leave our rucksacks in a farmhouse restaurant which made the climb a lot easier. There was not a breath of wind and the air was sticky even at this height. From the summit we had a good view of the Vosges we had already walked through, and the hills waiting for us ahead. A delicious quiche and salad in the cool farmhouse at the Col du Haag set us up for the two-hour descent to Saint-Amarin. We arrived in the middle of the afternoon, thinking only of water, and headed straight for the nearest drinking trough with whoops of joy. We then found an empty bar and treated ourselves to another drink, just to get out of the heat. The amount of money we were spending on cold drinks must have given quite a boost to the French economy. *Madame la propriétaire*, with cerise hair and a print dress, was a fund of information.

'Things are bad here,' she said. 'Two of the three big textile factories have closed and the third is struggling.' She paused and filled our glasses up with ice cubes. 'It's all thanks to cheap labour from the Far East.'

We enquired about the effects of the euro.

'*Abominable*,' was the curt reply. 'It makes so much inflation.' What, we then asked, did she think of Monsieur Chirac?

'*Mon Dieu!* I would not kill him but I would put him in prison for all the crimes he has committed. Politicians do what is good for them and tell us it is for our own good.' She crunched an ice cube loudly.

It was wonderful just sitting in the cool room and listening to Madame's views on the world and all its ills. We lent a detached and sympathetic ear. Having dealt with politics she turned her diatribe on our own royal family.

'Ah, Princess Diana.' She sighed, turning her eyes to heaven. 'She was *un ange*.'

After a long sip of the orange juice we had just bought her, she asked what we thought of Prince Charles, mimicking big ears as she spoke. Before we could reply she said, shaking her head in disbelief, 'And why does he like that ugly woman Camilla Parker Bowles?' I came to the conclusion that *Hello* magazine must be selling well in France.

Before we left, she recommended a local hotel, gave us four freebie biros, and asked to be mentioned in my book.

Our hotel room looked across to a garage with an electronic display showing time, temperature and date. It was 1600 hours on 8 August and the temperature was 39 degrees. The streets of the town were deserted. All was quiet on the Western Front until just gone midnight when it was 'play time' for the young and energetic. A vociferous young lady sounded as though she was being raped outside our window, feet and irate voices went up and down the stairs and into a room marked *privée* next door to us all night, and then a bunch of young bloods decided it was time to get on their *vélos* and GO! The motor *vélo*, invented in Pont-à-Mousson, is an abomination to all except the rider. These underpowered, oversexed bikes are heaven for all those testosterone-laden teenagers too young to be allowed on anything more powerful; however, what the *vélo* lacks in cc's it makes up for in noise. With the silencer removed, this angry insect can pack a punch. First it is revved up at full pitch to impress one's less fortunate friends, then it departs on full throttle, the two-stroke engine hammering against the flimsy casing as the noise increases in pitch to screaming point when the gear is eventually changed down and the noise, now receding slightly, starts at a lower pitch again. This sliding up and down the noise nerve scale continues until the diminishing decibels no longer batter the ear drums.

Richard was anxious to purchase a map. Using Saint-Amarin for our overnight stay he had taken us on a cunning *variante* to avoid losing too much height. It also meant we only had sixteen kilometres to walk to our next accommodation at Rouge-Gazon. We waited patiently for the Tourist Office to open at 10 a.m. only to find they didn't sell maps. Madame suggested we tried the newsagent which had been open since first light; they had just what we wanted for ten euros (£7). Tourist Offices in France were not scoring highly.

The temperature had only fallen to 20 degrees during the night, and it was well on its way back into the high thirties on the long climb into the mountains. Conveniently, we arrived at the *ferme-auberge* Belacker (979 metres) at midday. These simple mountain farms provide basic accommodation and food for walkers and are extremely popular. We were early enough to avoid the crowds and enjoyed sitting at a rough table under some plane trees surrounded by cows, goats, and a mangy farm cat with undernourished kittens. A few cartwheels were propped against the farmhouse wall, and nasturtiums and geraniums bloomed carelessly from old barrels and troughs. A noisy cockerel with his harem of hens scratched the ground under the windows. A very large very slow-moving lady served us a plate of sausage and potato salad which we shared. The bread did its best to remove several more of my fillings. By the time we left, the *auberge* was filling up, and I wondered how Madame would manage to serve all her customers before dark.

Outside, the sky was clouding over, and we were aware of a few drops of unfamiliar rain. By the time we were back in the woods, sheet lightning illuminated the tree trunks accompanied by rumbles of thunder. We stopped and searched for our lightweight anoraks at the bottom of our packs as the raindrops quickened pace. The storm was short-lived, and I felt protected in the shelter of the trees, although I know walkers shouldn't shelter under trees in a severe storm. The woods were a mixture of firs and hardwoods, frequently interspersed with elemental rocky outcrops; a scene from a Claude Lorraine painting. From time to time we would reach a clearing and have a welcome view of wooded hills and still blue lakes. The short downpour did nothing to ameliorate the dryness; the leaves of ash and plane were parchment on the trees, twigs snapped and crackled under our boots and even the moss was anaemic and friable. A strange warm wind got up and tugged ferociously at the dry leaves, pulling them off the branches and swirling them through the air like whirling dervishes before they joined those already on the ground. We seemed to be far from civilization and the time was out of joint. Then, suddenly, we emerged onto a small road leading to a hotel. The trees had been replaced by rolling hills and flower-filled meadows grazed by cows, goats and horses.

Chaume du Rouge-Gazon was a bustling alpine-type hotel, extremely well run by a family who had owned it since 1932. We had been under the impression that it was a *gîte d'étape* and were surprised to find it was a comfortable Logis de France hotel, with a dormitory in the attic for those who wanted cheaper accommodation. I was pleased to learn that this was full, and we were again luxuriating in the privacy of our own room. For once the hotel was humming with people, and we had a drink, overlooking the wooded hills, on a terrace edged with red umbrellas and geraniums. We ate a delicious meal of *cruditées*, boiled ham with a mustard sauce, sauté potatoes with onions, a green salad, strawberry tart with a coulis, Munster cheese, wine and coffee in a large dining room filled with people and live accordion music. It was Saturday night and we were having a party. The accordion player came round asking for requests and soon we were singing Edith Piaf's '*Je ne regrette rien*'. We had our coffee on the balcony where one or two couples danced and the youngsters from the dormitory sang lustily.

It was a good moment to celebrate as the next day we would have walked over 800 kilometres. This meant that we were halfway along our European section of the walk. The next day we only had to climb the Ballon d'Alsace, the most southerly of the Vosges summits, before we left the Vosges and crossed the Belfort gap and then climbed up into the Jura mountains. Richard looked happy, itinerary-wise we were on track; we had had several easier days and were reaping the benefit. I had had a positive response to my suggestion that we might even take a day's rest in order to visit Le Corbusier's chapel at Ronchamp in the Belfort gap, the flat plain between the Vosges and the Jura. It was peaceful in the mountains, and we slept better than we had for many nights.

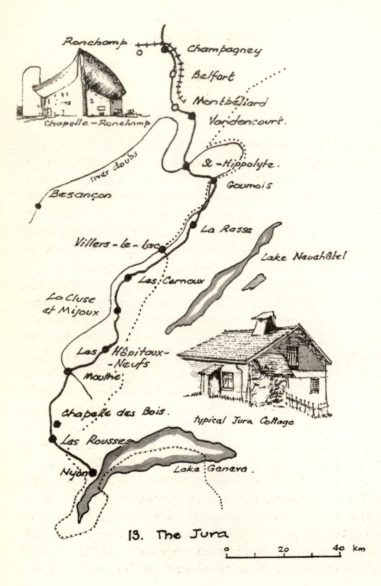

Ronchamp

Champagney

Belfort

Montbéliard

Chapelle - Ronchamp

Vandoncourt.

river doubs

St - Hippolyte.

Goumois

Besançon

La Rassa

Villers - le - Lac

Lake Neuchâtel

Les Cernaux

La Cluse
et Mijoux

Les Hôpitaux-
-Neufs

typical Jura Cottage

Mouthe

Chapelle des Bois.

Las Rousses

Lake Geneva.

Nyòn

13. The Jura

0   20   40 km

Chapter Thirteen

The Jura

After a slightly cooler night, the weather resumed sauna mode and the heat wave was set to continue for at least four more days. A few kilometres short of Giromagny, where Richard had planned to camp, we came across another *ferme-auberge*. It was mid-afternoon, the hottest time of the day, and I went in to ask if we might spend the night there. We were getting used to the luxury of hotels, and I dreaded a sleepless night on the hard ground. I was obviously becoming soft.

We found the extended family under a B&Q-type gazebo in the throes of a meltdown christening party. They were unable to accommodate us as the house was full of family, but they did give us a refreshing drink in the cool of the farm basement, while we watched them bringing in plateloads of perspiring meats, limp slices of quiche and wilting tarts. It was too hot to eat. They were not a traditional farming family, but middle-class intellectuals going for the 'good life', rearing goats and rabbits and making cheese. The owner was very concerned about the drought and feared that the springs were now drying up with dire consequences for his livestock.

As if to bear this out, Giromagny's beautiful hanging baskets and tubs of flowers were not being watered. Beef tomatoes and beans were wilting in those legendary veg patches and even the sunflowers drooped. We were given a hard hot pitch on the campsite, but the showers were good and I spent about fifteen minutes in mine, much of it on all fours letting the water play along my spine – it seemed to lower the body temperature more quickly that way.

It was a Sunday, and it was hard to find anywhere to eat, but there was just one pizzeria run by an overworked and overheated Italian family. Signora seemed to do almost everything (what's new!), while her 'boys' lolled on yellow plastic chairs on what was more lay-by than terrace, chatting and smoking. The temperature in the kitchen must have rivalled Naples in August, but somehow we were served with pizza, chips and ice cream for which we were truly grateful.

The main excitement in the town that evening was *concours de boules* in the shady square; the last few contestants were battling it out as we passed on our way back to the campsite. An enormous lady with an equally large partner seemed to be winning in spite of not being able to bend down. She probably hadn't seen her feet for years, let alone been able to touch them. With a game like boules, this is a distinct disadvantage. Madame Grosse had her own method: she produced a string with a magnet on the end, dangled it over the boule, made contact and deftly flicked it up into her waiting hand. Full marks for ingenuity.

Richard had full marks for ingenuity in planning our next few days, especially as the Tourist Office was closed on Sundays and Mondays. He suggested we walk down to a village on the plain called Bas-Evette, catch a train from there to Champagney and stay at the campsite for two nights. This would mean a free day to visit Le Corbusier's chapel at Ronchamp.

Bas-Evette had a large and tempting lake with cafés and boats for hire and bathing places. It also had a pink hotel with a terrace overlooking the water and a cool garden where willows wept.

'Let's stay here,' I suggested. 'This looks perfect.'

To my surprise, Richard agreed, perhaps because he had

seen the 'Closed on Mondays' notice on the door. A little bar nearby was also closed. Although the station itself looked deserted, we located a chain-smoking station master in shorts and T-shirt who told us the next train to Champagney would be at 5.30 p.m. This gave us two hours to enjoy a rest in the shady park. My observant husband noticed that the railway lines were made in Hayange. Along with manhole covers, and *vélos*, it seemed that Lorraine, like the poor, was always with us.

We know from our camping experiences in Brittany that the French are nothing if not predictable. *En vacances* they rise late, and after breakfast spend a long time grooming either themselves, their children, their pets or all three. With what is left of the morning, they prepare lunch, which is a seriously big meal. Appetizing smells waft across the campsite and then the eating and drinking starts in earnest and carries on well into the afternoon. At about 4 p.m. they are ready to go to the beach. That day the French were running true to form; by mid-afternoon the quiet park was filled with holidaymakers off for a swim. A line of toddlers, with large sun hats and small rucksacks, appeared from the trees holding hands; I thought of our two granddaughters and wondered whether they would recognize us when we got home. Then, while Richard had a swim, I shut my eyes and tried to imagine what it would be like living a normal life again.

The deserted station was like a scene from *High Noon*. A blazing sun beat fiercely on the peeling paint of the nineteenth-century building. The concrete platforms were like burning sand. Not a breath of air stirred the silence. The large hands on the station clock clicked loudly, minute by minute. Two pairs of shimmering rails stretched to the horizon. Click! Two minutes to half past. Click! One minute to half past. Two Lowry-like figures on the platform craned their necks and saw the bright glare of the train lights approaching. A shiny blue bullet, with just one carriage, pulled up. We left the nineteenth-century and entered the twenty-first: an air-conditioned train that looked as if it had just come off the assembly line. Imperceptibly, it pulled away and we had ten minutes in heaven before we had to descend to another equally hot platform at Champagney. This time the station was two shadeless kilometres from the town centre, and even when we got there there was no sign of a campsite. At that moment we passed an elegant three star Logis de France, acacia trees in the grounds and cool comfortable rooms and en suite facilities and… My feet just refused to walk any further on the hot pavement, and I found myself in the foyer of the hotel asking for *demi pension* for two nights. I didn't even think about asking the cost. A cool young lady in a chiffon blouse and a black skirt handed me the room key. It was then I noticed a furious man at my elbow. When we reached our room Richard exploded.

'Why did you do this? You know we had planned to camp. Why do you always have it your way?'

At 60 euros each, the hotel was above budget, but the heat must have turned my head and I didn't apologize. Richard is never mean, but he was concerned that the money we had put aside to pay off the MasterCard was running low. I suggested we rang our daughter (who had received my lost purse and cards) and she could get a balance from the hole in the wall with my Maestro card which we hadn't stopped. That was the extent to which we trust our offspring. Once we knew this, we could write to the bank to transfer funds from our current account to our MasterCard account. Our rest day would be an ideal moment. Banking for long-distance walkers can be a problem and Richard had not recovered from the ordeal of stopping our MasterCard. However, after a delicious haute-cuisine meal on the terrace, wine waiters, sweet trolleys, gentian liqueur, and coffee, he was a new man. Just the thought of having a whole day off made me feel a new woman.

Notre Dame du Haut at Ronchamp was a nine-kilometre walk in the usual searing heat. As we plodded up the hill to the chapel we were once again scuffing through carpets of dead leaves. There had been a place of worship on this hill for many centuries; the penultimate building was struck by lightning in 1913 and replaced in the 1930s by a very conventional church. This was destroyed by artillery fire in 1944 during a battle for the hill. Le Corbusier started work on the chapel in 1953 and it was finished two years later.

Neither Richard nor I had any idea what to expect. We had been recommended to visit the chapel by an architect friend, and it was of course a wonderful excuse for a day off. It was the most daringly different church I have ever seen: a chunky minimalist building with a roof like a tricorne hat, and a Roman candle tower. Concrete is not a material I like, yet here its smooth whiteness emanated light, a receptacle for prayer, both giving and receiving. Its simplicity was the very antithesis of most Roman Catholic churches. Inside, the floor sloped down to the altar and the small windows set deep and high in the thick walls gave the feel of a spiritual dovecot; at midday, the three great bells hanging between concrete posts among the trees swung to and fro in discordant cacophony.

Ending his address to the local bishop in 1955, Le Corbusier said:

I hand over to your lordship this chapel, built of staunch concrete, treated perhaps over-boldly, but certainly with courage. What all of us have recorded here will, I hope, find an echo in you and in those who climb this hill.

It was I think the hottest of all those hot days. This was possibly because we were now down on the baking plain. Our daughter told us it was still impossibly hot in the UK and an all-time record high of 101 degrees Fahrenheit had been recorded at Gravesend in Kent. We didn't yet know about the thousands of old people dying of heat in Paris during this exceptional heat wave.

On the way back to our hotel, we had a swim in the local lake and walked through the parched, treeless, run-down campsite where we had planned to stay. Richard readily admitted that he was glad my extravagance and intuition had won the day. Back at our luxurious hotel we wrote to the bank, sent post cards to family and friends, washed our few garments, cleaned our packs (which had a salt tide line on the straps) and then indulged in a little self-grooming: trimming beards and toe nails, shaving legs, washing hair (the luxury of a hairdryer made this a real pleasure). After these chores we savoured another three star meal on the balmy terrace.

Champagney is a small one-street town with a curious history. In 1789 King Louis XVI ordered every town to have a book of complaints. Jacques-Antoine Priqueler, an officer of the King's Guard with an evangelizing social conscience, lived in Champagney. He persuaded the villagers to complain about the appalling conditions of African slaves. The only black person they knew about was Caspar in their church painting of *The Adoration of the Magi*, and the enlightened Priqueler used him to illustrate the point that black people were Christian beings with feelings and rights just like the whites. He managed to persuade them to sign his complaint. In 1971, the House of Negritude museum was created and expresses the ongoing concerns of Justice, Dignity and Brotherhood amongst all people.

We satisfied our cultural appetite with a visit to both church and museum, and then found an air-conditioned supermarket to satisfy our bodily needs. After my gut problems, we even found a pharmacy and purchased painkillers and salt tablets. The bill came to a staggering 11 euros or £7.50. Champagney had scored highly.

Montbéliard was memorable for Peugeot cars; we ate our lunch on scorched grass beneath the great walls of the ducal palace and watched the real world going about its business. Cars, mostly Peugeots, some gas driven, streamed round the busy roads; businessmen in shirt sleeves hailed taxis, office girls sat on benches eating sandwiches. Trains roared in and out of the station, and the unremitting sun did its best to melt everything.

We had a two-and-a-half-hour walk to Vandoncourt where we had booked ourselves into a *gîte d'étape*. Richard skilfully navigated us away from the fumes of the big city and along the Rhône–Rhin canal where a few working barges lay like nineteenth-century dinosaurs. There was little shade and, having lost my *casquette*, I had to turn my peaked cap round to shield my neck. I thought my six-year-old granddaughter would have thought it really 'cool'. It was strange walking on the flat after hundreds of kilometres of hilly landscape and I hated every minute. It was a relief to pick up our friend the GR5 which took us back into the shady woods.

Vandoncourt was a sleepy little village and we had no trouble finding the timber-framed *gîte*. A tall gentleman with very blue eyes and his short companion greeted us at the door like long-lost friends. 'Richard and Shally, I presume,' the tall man said in perfect English with a broad grin. 'Welcome to Vandoncourt.'

Bart and Anneka were on an extended holiday attempting to walk from Holland to Lake Geneva. They were folk musicians and had met Melvin on their travels so knew all about us. Bush telegraph works well on the GR5. We had a wonderful evening in the simple *gîte,* swapping stories and experiences. Like all the Dutch they spoke excellent idiomatic English and we chatted far into the night.

Bart told me his grandfather had lived on the Dutch–German border during the First World War and was made to fight for Germany against the Russians. During the Second World War he was again made to take the German side and was treated like a slave. After the war he was allowed to return to Holland where he found his home had been destroyed. Even worse, he was now persona non grata. This anecdote seemed to us to be a microcosm of the difficulties of living on the border of two countries.

Anneka also had a sobering story. Some years ago she found a tick embedded behind her knee. She thought she had removed it, but weeks later her knee became very painful and soon she lost the strength in both her legs. The head of the little beast was still there, and she had contracted Lime's disease. It took a long course of very strong antibiotics and months of convalescence to make a complete recovery. We admired her courage at setting out on this long walk, but she confessed to finding her pack very heavy (they were camping) and was currently suffering from blisters. I empathized, and we discussed blister remedies with shared enthusiasm before ascending the ladder steps to our dormitory. In spite of mattresses that were a cross between a hammock and a trampoline, we slept well. For the first and only time we shared our beds with some over-friendly mosquitoes.

As we strode towards the gentle hills of the Jura, the sun vanished, and we felt a few spots of rain; then forked lightning split the sky as we were walking past a line of electric pylons. My heart raced: this is it, I thought, and rapidly telescoped my walking sticks, turned off my mobile phone and removed my watch. Fortunately it was only the edge of a thunderstorm and I chided myself for being such a wimp.

The Jura form a high limestone plateau between the Vosges and the Alps; 59 per cent is thickly wooded with beeches, oaks and firs. The River Doubs has carved out a dramatic gorge which loops through the plateau like an anaconda. The long lines of hills looked deceptively easy, but as they run north-east to south-west, we would be meeting the contours head on, and somehow would have to cross the steep sides of the Doubs gorge as well. It was going to be something of an obstacle course. As I left all the map reading to Richard, I spent most of my time in total ignorance of any impending problems, which meant I didn't have any preconceived anxieties. We met our first limestone 'bridge', an arch deep in the woods, on our way to Saint-Hippolyte. It was a very steep scramble up to the top of the escarpment and a warning of what lay ahead.

Bart and Anneka had set off at 6 a.m. but we caught them up at a *ferme-auberge* on the Swiss border and joined them for a second breakfast. Anneka regaled us with more horror stories about ticks. 'They find their way into the most intimate places,' she told us, indicating her groin. 'Bart and I try to remember to have a thorough search every evening.' We laughed, and Richard told the assembled company he wouldn't let me near his privates with a pair of tweezers. On a more serious note (if there can be a note more serious than a chap's manhood), she warned me that the ticks are most likely to fall off oak trees, not onto the person who walks under them first, but onto the person behind. This made sense as my score of ticks was two to Richard's nil. I wondered how many oak trees there were in the Jura and could see paranoia setting in. Since leaving Lorraine, we had forgotten all about these tiresome insects. Before we parted company, they told us they were not going to walk the twenty-six kilometres to Saint-Hippolyte but invited us to join them for Bart's birthday concert at the campsite in Villers-le-Lac in three days' time.

It was 14 August, my father's ninetieth birthday. We sat in a field beside a 1727 boundary stone on the French-Swiss border and felt that, having left the German boundary behind, we were really making progress south. After a meagre lunch of stale bread and sardines (the supermarket in Vandoncourt was closed for annual holidays until 18 August) we rang my father. I was feeling distinctly guilty about not being with him on this big day.

After wishing him a happy birthday the conversation ran something like this:

'It must be like the desert out there in this heat.'

'A camel might come in handy. How are you celebrating your birthday?'

'I'm having a party. Forty guests are coming this Saturday.'

'How will you manage?'

'I've got caterers. They're bringing tables and chairs and we'll eat in the garden.'

'What if it rains?'

'It won't.'

I wondered what he had planned for his hundredth birthday.

I handed Richard the phone. It was his turn to ring his

mum. It was a low time for her: her only son wouldn't be back for two more months, her youngest daughter was on holiday in Spitzbergen, Wimbledon and the Tour de France were over, and the heat was oppressive. Richard diverted her with our news and she was glad to know we were on schedule and doing some respectable mileages. A rumble of thunder and some large drops of rain brought the conversation to an abrupt end.

Saint-Hippolyte was a peaceful little town with a long pedigree, or, as the guide book put it, 'a rich historical past'. The saint of the same name arrived in the middle of the tenth century, the Turin Shroud had been held in the church at one time and, in the seventeenth century, some forward-thinking Ursuline nuns dedicated themselves to the education of girls and young men. Their convent still stands today. The town lies in the deep valley at the confluence of the rivers Doubs and Dessoubre which the guide book describes as 'clasping the historical centre of the town'. For me, the steep wooded hills and bare limestone escarpments gave the place a claustrophobic feel, but it had an excellent campsite and we ate a good meal overlooking the still waters of the River Doubs. Once again we were alone in the restaurant and decided the French must all be either in the mountains or by the sea.

I had noticed Richard limping that day, and after our meal he rose from his chair like an old man. He was having referred pain from his back, probably exacerbated by our saggy beds the night before. He refused to take anything and seemed better after a night on the hard ground.

Next morning the air had a muggy pre-storm feel about it. Everything in the Jura seemed greener than the Vosges and there were streams and rivers everywhere. At midday it became very dark and began to rain, large drops accompanied by distant thunder and occasional flashes of lightning. Then someone in the sky emptied a lake on top of us; it was useless to shelter so we just kept going while the Gore-tex busting rain saturated every garment and filled our boots. After several torrential kilometres, we found a barn on the outskirts of a village and were able to change our clothes, decant water from our boots and eat some lunch. After two hours the rain eased a little, and we collected our garments from various parts of a combine harvester and set off to find the village pub where a noisy table of French farmers were just finishing a protracted lunch. We were both extremely cold, an unusual sensation, so we ordered hot chocolate and a glass of brandy. The modest bar had some local papers scattered on a window sill and I was interested to see that the Minister for the Environment had written an article warning holidaymakers to beware of severe storms. She advised people not to walk in the mountains, not to shelter under trees, and to ensure that their mobile phones were turned off. An orange alert (whatever that meant) was being put out. I took a large swig of brandy and hoped that the storms of recent days were the ones she was talking about.

We had spent so long in the barn that there was no hope of reaching our planned destination of Goumois, but the barman told us we could stay in the village hall in a little place called Fessevillers which was only two hours' walk away. I rang them and left a message to say we needed a bed, and we set off into the dripping landscape. Richard was concerned that the hall might be shut as I hadn't been able to speak to the warden. However, the barman and his wife assured us that it was open every day of the year. Fortunately for us, they were right.

The French often have accommodation in their village halls and we were amazed to have a comfortable dormitory and good shower and loo just off the main room, which had a baronial-style fireplace and a long trestle table. The warden, immaculate in trouser suit and gold shoes, charged us the modest sum of 12 euros and told us there was a pub in the village but it might be closed today. The little terraced house did indeed look closed, but when I rang the bell a cheery face appeared at the upstairs window and took pity on us.

'I am not open today, *Madame*, but if you come back in one hour I can give you something to eat.' How wonderful to have a lady who wasn't *désolée*. Although she had had a houseful of family in for lunch, she gave us a delicious meal of *crudites*, omlettes, ham, salad, cheese, two beers and a *pichet* of wine. After that I won't have a word said against the French.

It was going to be a long day as we had to make up the two hours that we had lost the day before. The landscape was more open than the Vosges, with large clearings between the wooded slopes where the sturdy Montbéliard cows grazed and the rivers reflected the farmhouses with their broad red roofs. The scattered villages had churches with wooden towers capped by a four-sided bell–shaped structure on which the cross was fixed. The chimneys of farms and cottages were often surmounted by a miniature roof to ensure that the snow or rain was kept well away. Everywhere we noticed neat piles of logs, a reminder of the harsh winters here.

Above the town of Goumois, banks of cotton wool hid the narrow valley below. As we started our steep descent, the clouds gradually thinned and shafts of muted light swirled through the fir trees. By the time we reached the gorge and emerged from the trees, the clouds had lifted from the valley leaving the hilltops drifting like green islands above thin veils of cloud.

Goumois is a frontier town with Switzerland and still retains a customs house. We stopped there for breakfast in a café that was bursting with customs officers being entertained by a blonde lady with a cleavage like the Doubs gorge and a voice to match. We were there for twenty minutes, and the good lady's ceaseless monologue was like a tide race with no perceptible intake of breath, just an occasional heave of the bosom. Meanwhile, anyone wishing to take any illegal substances over the border would not have been detained.

The storm had not really cleared the air and, from Goumois on, our rough path either clung to the edge of the thick woods down by the River Doubs, or climbed steeply upwards like a vertical switchback. It was hard work but the glassy blue-green river reflected the poplars and beeches and was freckled with golden leaves. It looked cool and inviting and Richard joined the fishes for a quick dip when we stopped for lunch. The fierce sun returned as we headed for the notorious *Echelles de la Mort*. This is a series of three long ladders which are attached to vertical cliffs of limestone. If you suffered from vertigo, *tant pis*; it was the only way to get down into the Doubs valley again. It was perhaps comforting that they were made from British steel. I tried not to look down the plunging uprights and thought of the smugglers who originally used them, with a sack of contraband over one shoulder and only one hand to hold on with. I counted each rung, and my knuckles were quite white by the time I reached the bottom. It is amazing what you can do when you have no choice.

As always the afternoon was hard and the path along the Doubs gorge rough with stones and roots. The only signs of life were shoals of fat trout just below the surface of the water and a few fishermen in flat-bottomed boats among the water lilies.

We had left our village hall at 8 a.m. and we arrived at the hotel, La Rasse at 6.30 p.m. The hard day's walk had seemed endless, and there was no sign of habitation of any sort. Eventually, we reached a small bridge at the Swiss frontier where the river turned into a ferocious tide race. Looking up, I saw a simple *auberge* frowning down on us with the words

La Rasse painted on the side. Standing alone in the gorge, it looked as if it had been transported from a nineteenth-century novel. Our spacious room had two large sash windows and I lay in a pulp on the bed looking at the sky and wondering what was in store for the morrow. That night another thunderstorm gave us a superb firework display and very little sleep.

Our path along the gorge was either a scramble through woods under great walls of visceral limestone or on a minute track by the green river where reflections mirrored the height of wooded cliffs and barefaced rock. Occasionally we would come up against a limestone precipice and had to ascend a wobbly ladder to rejoin the path. In the afternoon we reached a fault in the gorge where a 'jetty' of rock on each bank narrowed the river to stream size, and our path tunnelled through the limestone to rejoin the river bank.

The climax of this dramatic gorge was the Saut du Doubs, a nationally famous twenty-seven-metre waterfall; we were now on a wide track through hardwoods, and as it was Sunday, and this was a *site touristique*, mums, dads, children, uncles, aunts and grandparents were all out for an afternoon's sightseeing. There was a feeling of expectation in the air: everyone was listening for the thunder of the mighty falls, waiting to feel spray on their faces and looking forward to seeing the accompanying rainbow. When we arrived at the viewing platform we were confronted by a twenty-seven-metre slab of dry black rock, dampened by less water than you would get out of your bath tap. The dried-up waterfall was an even sadder sight than the stony carcasses of empty rivers we had already passed. Hard by the famous waterfall was a *bateau mouche* waiting to transport any takers the five kilometres downstream to the town of Villers-le-Lac, our destination for the night. We resisted the temptation, and contented ourselves with an ice cream at one of the many cafés. Two kilometres further on we saw the boat discharging its cargo of tourists onto a bus; the river had dwindled to a channel of water only large enough for toy boats. This was no ordinary summer.

In the centre of Villers-le-Lac we met our Dutch friends, Bart and Anneke, in mellow mood having eaten a birthday lunch at an excellent restaurant. They were continuing the celebrations with Melvin at an adjoining café. We joined them for a drink and agreed to come to their concert on the campsite later that evening. This municipal site was situated in a disused football stadium and it was 7.30 p.m. before we had pitched the tent and sorted ourselves out. The toilet block was unisex, and I was trying to find somewhere to pee when the warden's son, six going on sixty, asked if I needed help. When I enquired if there was such a thing as a lady's toilet, he gave me a withering look and pointed to a smelly urinal.

'*Ceci est pour les hommes*,' he said firmly, enunciating each syllable carefully, and then pointed to the WC. '*Ceci, Madame, est pour les femmes*.' Somewhat humiliated by this anatomy lesson, I went where I was bid.

We had just pitched the tent before dark clouds overhead precipitated another cloudburst, and we ran down the steep hill into a convenient and very crowded Italian restaurant. Luckily there was one small table free and the steam from our wet clothes joined forces with our spaghetti bolognese. It seemed that at last we had found out where the French come for their holidays. Service in the busy restaurant was slow, the Chianti was good and we didn't want to get soaked on the way back. When we reached the campsite just before 10 p.m. we saw some balloons outside the changing rooms and heard the sound of folk music. Sadly a mixture of Chianti and exhaustion meant we fell into our sleeping bags and lost consciousness long before the party was over.

The Dutch are very forgiving, and Bart and Anneke insisted that we joined them and Melvin for a *petit déjeuner sur l'herbe* before tackling le Grand-Mont at 1,034 metres. Fresh bread, Munster cheese, and some of the tough sausage that Melvin seemed to live on made a welcome start to the day. We then had to walk a kilometre into the town to buy some food thinking we might have to cater for ourselves that evening either in a *gîte* or possibly wild camp. Uncertain accommodation always worried Richard, and our own personal entente was becoming distinctly less *cordiale*. We had coped well up to now, and survived the searing heat of the Vosges with unified resilience. He had been very good about the loss of my purse, but perhaps it was that incident which lessened his trust in my ability to look after myself. The weather was cooler, the path easier and yet it was at this moment that we seemed unable to agree about anything; everything I said was wrong, and Richard's patronizing attitude was beginning to exasperate me.

'Have you got your purse?'

'Have you hung your towel up?'

'Did you remember to buy milk?'

'Are you sure you got the day right when you booked that *gîte*?'

I knew he felt responsible for me, but I wasn't a child. I fully appreciated that he had the unenviable task of route planning, finding the way, deciding how many kilometres we could manage each day and if we could find suitable accommodation. Had he been on his own, he would not have worried. The irony was that, had I been on my own, even though I would have frequently lost my way, unlike Richard, I could speak the language, was never afraid to ask, and would have survived if only by man's humanity to man.

After some stupid argument about the effectiveness of our anoraks, Richard told me that if we had to wild camp that night I would make a fuss about the hard ground or not having water.

'I never make a fuss', I fumed. 'I always make the best of every situation. If we have to camp we have to camp. I'll cook the meal and go and ask for water if we need it.'

I then reminded him of my morale boosting efforts on the several occasions when he was ready to give up and go home.

Richard found the way to another *ferme-auberge* where, although fully booked that night, the owners were happy to let us pitch our tent on their land; we shared our field with a St Bernard puppy, a herd of cows, and some anorexic turkeys. Hoping to ease the domestic tension, I bought a bottle of what I thought was *vin ordinaire*, but when we paid the bill next day they had sold us a bottle of local Jura wine at 14 euros (£10). Meanwhile, we observed carloads of hungry guests arriving to eat in the busy *auberge* restaurant and departing, well fed and mellow. Richard and I let the sun go down on our anger.

Breakfast on the terrace among the alpine hills did something to restore morale, and we threaded our way along the border with Switzerland, through meadows filled with scabious, cranesbill and tall yellow gentians from which the French make their delicious liqueur. Drifts of white stems beneath the delicate mauve flowers of the autumn crocus stood like Venus nudist colonies. We passed wooden farmhouses tucked into the rolling landscape, where chickens scratched round rabbit hutches and cats slept beside pots of geraniums. The tracks were well marked and easy underfoot, and by mid-afternoon French families were again out in force. At the end of one of the tracks we came across Fort Malher, built in the nineteenth-century and now in ruins. Perched dramatically on the edge of a sheer limestone cliff, it eyeballed the Château de Joux, only a cannon shot away on the other side of the precipitous gorge. Far below, there was just room for the river and a major road where shimmering steel beetles were queuing nose to tail to get to Pontarlier and Lausanne. Our route took us down 360 steps into a world of traffic fumes and revving engines.

The next day we skirted the ski town of Métabief, in summer an empty man-made landscape of roads, railways, ski lifts and apartments. The next ski resort of les Hôpitaux-Neufs was little better; we ate at the Edelweiss and stayed on the municipal campsite. In spite of the aesthetic shortcomings the town was full of tourists and we had almost the last pitch on the site. In summer it is a centre for luge, and a Mecca for the mountain cyclists; we noticed many signs with VTT on them (*vélo tous terrains*) and the steep slopes of le Mont d'Or are used for national VTT championships. As we climbed up the mountain we were parallel to the cycle pistes, and watched a couple of Day-Glo figures about to break the sound barrier as they hurtled down the mountain. At the top, a dozen or so young cyclists were nervously contemplating this black run. Some were without helmets. After a lot of deliberation, the group set off bunched together, but before they had covered 100 metres several of the bikes had collided and one member of the party had injured his knee. I wondered whether I should put my physio hat on, but we had a long day's walk to Mouthe and at least the injured cyclist had plenty of helpers.

It was damp and misty after thundery showers during the night, and, although we were over 1,000 metres high we could only see a blur of distant hills and bald paths snaking down through clearings in the trees.

Our Topo Guide not only gave maps, directions, and accommodation, but occasional titbits of local information. Mouthe, we learned, was not only the source of the River Doubs, but on record as the village where the coldest temperatures in France have been recorded. Winter temperatures regularly fall to minus 30 degrees and, one night in 1888, the mercury fell to minus 48 degrees, earning the nickname Little Siberia. In spite of this, the Hant-Doubs is considered one of the healthiest places to live in Europe; the region is snowed up for five months every year yet the inhabitants have a reputation for longevity. I couldn't help reflecting on our inability to cope with even minor snowfalls in the UK, and on our generally soft lifestyles which do nothing to toughen us up. On the other hand, I would have great difficulty being virtually house bound for five months every year.

The eighteenth-century philosopher Jean Jacques Rousseau, a champion of the natural world, extolled this region where men lived with the rhythm of the seasons, worked their butts off on the land in the summer and survived the winter indoors with their animals, making clocks and wooden knick-knacks for the new breed of eighteenth-century tourist. This simple life appealed to the romantic philosopher, who believed that man should be free and not chained to the self-imposed strictures of society. I think Rousseau would have approved of our walk.

It was 22 August, our penultimate day in the Jura. The mist and cloud had dispersed leaving the green woods and hills in bright warm sunshine with a little breeze; the best walking weather we had had since 7 July. It had been a tough six weeks, climbing three to six hundred metres daily, often over switchbacks in tremendous heat, with only time for eating and walking, interspersed with unrewarding efforts to sleep. As is so often the way, the effect was latent; we were both tired and spent much of the day in silence. Richard still had intermittent sciatica and we were both anxious about tackling the Alps, the biggest test of the entire walk.

However, the little village of Chapelle-des-Bois cheered us up. We stayed at a lively *gîte,* sharing a four-bedded dormitory with one quiet young lady. We had time to enjoy the luxury of a pancake for tea and then wander through the village. We heard singing coming from the church and, on investigation, discovered a local choir celebrating their twentieth anniversary with a lively concert. The celebrations continued in the dining room of our *gîte,* which was overflowing with fifty choristers, a professional entertainer, and four residents other than ourselves. We were given a feast of home-made soup, followed by enormous quantities of a cheese, potato and sausage pie, green salad, cheese board and fresh fruit salad. With this came baskets of bread and *pichet* after *pichet* of wine. We shared this with four VTT cyclists who were having a boys' weekend away from their families. The wine flowed without being requested which we thought was rather strange, especially as we were having free entertainment from the choir who were singing every folk song and French pop tune ever written. We left at 10.30 when we imagined the show was coming to an end. Not a bit of it. The tables were cleared to allow the exuberant choristers to let their hair down: jiving, dancing, singing, laughing and bumpsy-daisy went on far into the night. Upstairs our bunks shook to vibrating sounds of 'Incy wincy teeny weeny yellow polka dot bikini'. No wonder we were plied with wine. I spent most of the night closing the window to reduce the sound level, then regretting it because it was so hot, and opening it again. Then our female dormitory companion would close it and so on. The pale light of dawn was a welcome sight. We compared notes with our cycling friends over breakfast and even they admitted to having had a sleepless night. On the upside, we were amazed that our total bill only came to 53 euros (£37) including litres of wine. It was a memorable night and I shall never think of choristers in quite the same way again.

We set off in bright sunshine and the pleasant temperatures of an English summer. A long steep climb through fir woods to the top of an almost sheer limestone ridge soon had the sweat pouring. Halfway up I was recording and taking photographs and for once fell well behind Richard. Lost in thought, I almost immediately took the wrong path, and didn't notice for some time. As soon as I realized my mistake I retraced my steps, but failed to pick up the red and white waymarks of the GR5. I shouted. No reply. I shouted louder; nothing but the screech of a jay. Minutes passed and I wondered when Richard would notice I wasn't on his tail. Then I remembered my whistle, buried deep in the recesses of my rucksack. I blew shrilly three or four times, frightening any wildlife within half a mile. I listened and thought I heard something crashing in the distance.

'Hello!' I bellowed. 'I'm here!' The crashing was getting nearer; it was either a wild boar or my speechless husband. When Richard eventually appeared he was highly amused.

'There was a great tree trunk over the path to stop anyone going that way. Didn't you see it?'

'Sure. But there are often felled trees around,' I answered, shrugging my shoulders and wondering just how many kilometres I would be able to manage on my own.

At the crest of the ridge we stood by a giant cross and looked over a green blanket of fir woods, farms, and pastures unravelling into the distance. Soon we would reach les Rousses where Alan, Richard's best man, and his wife Julia would take us to their Swiss apartment for two nights. We discussed our plan for the following day, when we hoped to reach Lake Geneva and have our first view of the Alps. The wide white face of a Montbéliard cow shook her head in disbelief.

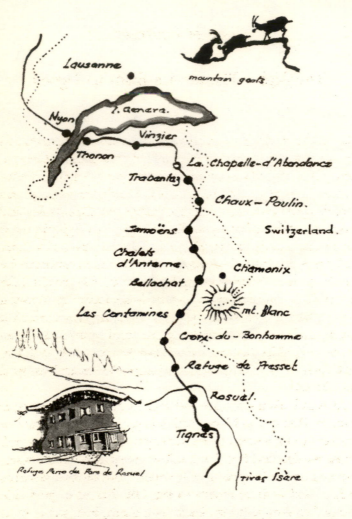

mountain goats

Lausanne

l. Geneva

Nyon

Vinzier

Thonon

La. Chapelle-d'Abondance

Trabentaz

Chaux – Poulin.

Samoëns

Switzerland.

Chalets d'Anterne.

Chamonix

Bellachat

mt. Blanc

Les Contamines

Croix – du – Bonhomme

Refuge de Presset

Rosuel.

Tignes

river Isère

Refuge Perre du Pare de Rosuel

14. The Alps, Thonon-Les-Bains to Tignes.

0   20   40 Km

Chapter Fourteen

The Alps – Thonon-les-Bains to Tignes

I lay in the shade of an oak tree on the immaculate grass of a leisure complex on the gold-plated shores of Lake Geneva. Across the still blue water the jagged peaks of the Haute-Savoie blurred in the heat. It was Sunday afternoon and parents, grandparents, children, babies, young couples and boisterous teenagers were all enjoying an Olympic sized swimming pool, a children's pool, the warm lake, a café and a playground. Julia, like many of those unencumbered by children, was stretched out in the sun. The Swiss take everything seriously including their sunbathing: a young woman near me spent a good hour massaging her man with a variety of sweet-smelling body oils until he looked like an oven-ready chip. At four o'clock two sweaty men with day packs arrived, threw off most of their clothes and jumped into the lake.

Alan had taken my place and walked the thirty kilometres from les Rousses to Nyon, which had given me a chance to wash dirty clothes and check out essentials ready for our trek across the Alps to Nice. I was able to give diaries, films, tapes, Topo guides and anything now superfluous to requirements to Alan and Julia to return to the UK. I tried to persuade Richard to send our tent back with them, but, rather than lose his metaphorical belt and braces, he preferred to carry it and put up with the extra weight. It also gave me the sheer luxury of a day off. That evening the four of us sat on Alan's apartment balcony popping champagne corks and catching up on news from another life.

It was Monday, 25 August. Bright red geraniums flowed from wrought-iron railings on the quay at Nyon where Alan saw us onto a beautifully restored paddle steamer circa 1930. We plied our way effortlessly across the sparkling waters of Lake Geneva (le Léman to the French). With us on the deck of this elegant craft was a group of middle-aged middle England walkers with sun hats, dark glasses and large rucksacks. With the sun on our faces and the wind in our hair, we each felt relieved and exhilarated. Ahead lay the most testing part of the GR5. From Thonon-les-Bains, we would be heading up to the Oche range of mountains: Col des Portes d'Oche, la Dent d'Oche, le Col de Planchamp d'Oche and le Château d'Oche, the great incisors of the Haute-Savoie that had beckoned us from across the other side of the lake. In a week's time we should have reached the Mont Blanc massif; an exciting prospect.

In Thonon, we had planned to meet up with Fred again, this time without the Jack Russells. Having taken Richard on the Tour de Mont Blanc fifteen years ago and loving the Alps, he wanted to spend a few days walking with us and was kindly bringing a 'Red Cross' parcel of shorts, a sun hat, moisturizing cream, Lipsyl, and best of all a new bra and pants to replace my moribund smalls. Whatever the Alps had in store, I was going to face it with clean undies, which would no doubt have pleased my grandmother.

Thonon, strangely, is known as 'the most athletic town in France', probably due to its situation on the steep hillside above le Léman. The old fishing port down by the lake still has real fishermen with traditional open boats, and a thriving twenty-first-century marina where lines of white fibreglass bristle with high-tech antennae. The main town is up a precipitous slope, and there is a funicular railway for those not wishing to tackle the many steps to the centre of this sophisticated spa.

We had time to book a hotel and eat a sandwich under the tired shade of plane trees before meeting Fred off the paddle steamer from Geneva via Nyon. He was so laden with our gear that, like real tourists, we eschewed the steps and took the funicular. That evening, splodges of warm rain and growls of thunder forced a retreat from the hotel terrace. Was it an omen, I wondered?

It was too humid to sleep, and I lay in bed pondering the history of the Alps. Apart from a handful of traders scuttling nervously across the ancient passes, the results of the tectonic collision which welded Italy onto mainland Europe had lain dormant since Roman times, feared for their height and cold, and thought to be inhabited by demons and dragons. Nobody had the least inclination to visit them, let alone walk up them. It was eighteenth-century artists, writers and philosophers who discovered the spiritual qualities of the Alps and started a craving for the rugged outdoors. In just over two hundred years this craving to climb, ski and walk in the Alps has reached such proportions that the spiritual dimension of this great natural barrier is in danger of being lost. I tossed and turned under the thin sheet and finally fell into fitful oblivion.

We had an easy twenty-four-kilometre day from Thonon to the little village of Vinzier, 900 metres above sea level, where we had booked a hotel for the night. The storm had barely touched the shores of le Léman and the air was fresher. We set off in high spirits, chatting away the kilometres until Richard stopped and announced that we were walking in the wrong direction. Consternation set in. Fred, another good map reader, gave his opinion, which differed from Richard's. Maps were spread along the roadside, compasses were produced, fingers were pointed, and sweaty foreheads were wiped. I watched in helpless amusement as the two men endeavoured to find out where we were, so that they could then correct the mistake. It was the first and last time that we were several kilometres off the GR5 and it took an hour of extra walking to put things right. Unused to company and on an easy path, we had all lost our vigilance.

We spent the afternoon climbing through trees, alpine villages, dairy pastures and farms towards the craggy grey peaks, with glimpses through to the blue waters of le Léman. We arrived in Vinzier soon after 4 p.m. and found our hotel deserted, apart from a man in a grubby T-shirt with a battered hat above a black moustache who was mowing the grass.

'Please wait on the terrace,' he said curtly. 'Someone will attend to you shortly' and with this he shouted *'Viens! Ils sont arrivés!'* at one of the bedroom windows.

A dishevelled but attractive young lady soon appeared and asked us to follow her up the stairs. Richard and Fred's eyes riveted themselves on a pair of red lace panties peeking boldly from her half-zipped black duty skirt, rather more exciting than my new bog standard M&S ones. After a shower and a rest we reclined on chaises longues under the apple trees and Fred treated us to a kir before we ate a delicious meal prepared by the gardener, now wearing check trousers, white apron and crisp white hat. His wife, all scent and cleavage, waited on us at table. There were only three other guests.

Through the open sash windows of our room, bright stars shone from the velvety sky and the mountain air was pleasantly cool. We were woken at dawn by the furious crowing of cocks, dissonant church bells, and the village clock, which in that part of the world strikes the hour and then repeats itself at five minutes past just in case you hadn't heard it the first time. This little quirk guarantees that sleep will be intermittent. Then came a deafening clang of cow bells and from our window we saw a herd of the large brown and white cows known as *lunettes*, so called as they have rings like spectacles round their eyes. They were lolloping down the road swinging huge bronze bells and swollen udders in unison. Many of the bells are at least a hundred years old, heirlooms engraved with the name of the founder and the cross of the Virgin Mary. The herd's route, past petrol stations and supermarkets along the main highway to Evian-les-Bains, was however far from traditional.

It was another twenty-four-kilometre, eight-hour day, to our first refuge at the Chalets de Bise. Refuges vary between the very basic, with one large dormitory, an outside cold tap, and a loo that is a hole in the ground, to ones with dormitories and double rooms, hot showers, and flush loos. The joy is that they provide mattresses, food and wine; after self-catering in a tent and sleeping on the hard ground, these modest luxuries were for us the equivalent of a five star hotel. I must confess I was a little concerned about sleeping in a large dormitory literally cheek to cheek with a snoring stranger.

The thrill of being in the mountains made the long ascent easier and Fred managed the steep inclines with no problems especially after I had lent him one of my sticks. After this he was converted to the stick culture. At the Lac de la Case we paused in a vast amphitheatre surrounded by giant rocky teeth; at 1,750 metres we were above the tree line and grey streams of scree and rocks poured down the hillside beside patches of coarse grass. Just below the col we saw our first bouquetins (ibex or mountain goats), sleek brown animals with magnificent backward-curving horns which can weigh as much as five kilos each in a mature male. The herd was sitting nonchalantly on a sheet of scree and the animals were quite unperturbed by our presence and clicking cameras.

Our refuge at 1,502 metres was a working farm as well as giving accommodation and refreshment to walkers and tourists. A road led down from the little group of buildings, which rather spoiled the feeling that we were alone on top of the world. However, the refuge was of the basic variety with generated electricity, a loo and one washbasin, cold water only. There was a queue for this so we were told we could wash in the *cascade* just up the valley. This must have dried up, for we never found it, and contented ourselves with a quick splash in what was left of the stream. The simple meal was plentiful and good, I was able to recharge my mobile and there were only seven bodies in our dormitory so some sleep was possible. Richard, who never misses anything, managed to open his eyes at 2 a.m. in time to see Mars at its nearest point ever to earth. My nearest point to earth was the loo.

We were getting used to the idea that climbing cols would become part of our daily routine. After a modest breakfast of tough French bread and coffee, we puffed up the Col de la Bosse at 1,816 metres, and began our descent into the lush pastoral valley d'Abondance. The steep mountain track led to a tarmac road beside a well-filled river splashing and gurgling through a green sward on the edge of a fir wood; a welcome sight after the desiccated river carcasses of the Jura. The little town of la Chapelle-d'Abondance had an abundance of everything the tourist could wish for: souvenir shops, hotels, sports shops, banks, and an onion-domed church. The buildings were Christmas card alpine and the prices for those with big wallets. We stopped for a drink in one hotel and I rang the *gîte* we planned to use for accommodation that night, which was a gruelling 800metre climb up the mountain.

In our experience, when you start any strenuous walking, the body can manage surprisingly well for the first couple of days, but, by the third day of ongoing masochism, muscles begin to ache and general fatigue sets in. Fred was having the third day blues, and drink in hand he was looking anxiously at our rigorous itinerary for the next few days. He was experienced enough to know what was involved and his forehead creased into a frown. We then decided to find somewhere for a morale-boosting lunch on the outskirts of the town on our way to pick up the GR5. Sadly the restaurant we aimed for was closed, and after enquiries and searching, we realized that a civilized lunch was off the menu. Morale nosedived; the weather was hot and thundery, Fred's pack was uncomfortable and he was getting blisters. When we suggested a *déjeuner sur l'herbe* of iron rations, Fred decided he would leave us to it, and meet us again at les Houches in a few days' time. Knowing how fit and focused we now were, he did not want to jeopardize our itinerary in any way. It was another example of unfulfilled expectations, with resulting low morale. We knew the symptoms well and bade him a fond *au revoir*.

The GR5 took us out of the Abondance valley along a stony track to the river where we stopped for a bite to eat. Our own morale had sunk to the valley floor, and it was a silent little meal. Just as we were about to leave it began to rain and we had to unearth our little-used anoraks from the depths of our packs. At least Richard unearthed his, but I couldn't find mine. These costly Gore-tex lightweight garments folded down to a tiny bundle which gave us valuable extra space in our packs. To lose one was unthinkable. I searched and cursed, and cursed and searched. Richard, knowing how bad I am at finding things, methodically looked through my pack. No anorak. It was now after two o'clock, and we had a two-and-a-half-hour steep climb ahead. The next few days we would be crossing mountain passes, far from shops of any kind. There was nothing to do but return the three kilometres into the town, buy something to keep the weather out, and start all over again.

We left our packs by the bridge and belted along the tarmac road to the nearest sports shop. It was closed until 4 p.m. I then shot into the Tourist Office which fortunately was open, and asked if there was anywhere else in town where I could buy an anorak. The helpful assistant assured me that there was an outdoor gear shop further on, but it also closed at midday. My face hit the floor and I explained our predicament. Unfazed, she rang the owner. Moments later she turned to me, smiling triumphantly.

'Just go to the shop on the right beyond the hotel and you will see the owner watering her geraniums on the balcony above the store. She will open the shop for you. *Allez vite!*'

I have never made a purchase so swiftly in my life. The sun had returned after our shower and we were hot, tired and very cross. Richard loathes shopping, and waited in the blazing heat outside while I pulled something that was the right price off a hanger, tried it on briefly and paid for it. I was in and out in less than five minutes. We then slogged back along the hot road and up the track back to the bridge, collected our packs and set off up the mountain.

We eventually left the forest track and emerged where the path became rocky and steep. I found myself in the lead and kept looking back. Something had happened to Richard; he was labouring up the steep incline unusually slowly, and what was more worrying was that he kept stopping and sitting down. I fed him glucose tablets and asked him anxiously whether he had chest pain. I hoped the problem was just low morale. We were beginning to learn how much the mind affects the body, and had both experienced moments of inexplicable weariness, often when expectations had not been met. We made halting progress and wondered how Fred would have coped with it. A storm was brewing, it was very humid and the path seemed endless.

At last, high above us, we saw two huts perched on the flat top of a grassy bump; this was our Gîte d'Alpage de Trebentaz, a family-owned goat farm just below the great bulk of the Mont de Grange. We hauled ourselves up onto the terrace at just after 6 p.m. and found a group of newly arrived walkers all chatting cheerfully as if it was a family party. Richard, now fully recovered, entered into the party spirit, while I just wanted to wash and lie down. Finally the owners, Monsieur and Madame Thoule, a hospitable couple in their early forties, showed us the dormitory for twenty-four persons, reached by a ladder staircase from the living room, and we thankfully found a bunk bed each and had a wash; no showers or electricity but the luxury of hot water and a flush loo.

Supper was memorable: a salad with fried goat's cheese, home-made sausages and *boulangère* potatoes, a home-made bilberry tart with one millimetre of pastry to six millimetres of bilberries, and a cheese board that would have graced any table in the world and included *fromages du maison*. After this feast, washed down with a *pichet* of wine, my French improved enough to have a very animated conversation with a party of six walkers who go on an expedition together every year. One member had both feet swathed in bandages as she was suffering from blisters on the soles. We had seen her limping up the mountain ahead of us and felt very empathetic.

The view from this eyrie was spectacular. Storm clouds were gathering over the grey buttresses of the Dent de Jaman, and we could just make out the giant peaks of les Diablerets in the Bernese Oberland and beyond them the Eiger, the Jungfrau, the Matterhorn, all draped in purple clouds. Perched far above the toy houses of la Chapelle d'Abondance and the green scoop of valley, inhaling the smell of goat, we were in a Heidi landscape. The goat farm was perched on a precipice where a cable had been installed to take goods the suicide route from valley to hut. As we gazed with vertiginous stomachs at the near vertical steel, a rumble of thunder echoed round the mountains, followed by rectangles of orange light. I retreated to my bunk under the eaves, carefully chosen to be as far away from the skylight window as possible. An hour later the storm broke like a game of celestial skittles: rain and hail hit the roof like bullets, and thunder cracked between giant bursts of lightning. Then the wind got up, shrieking and whistling in tremendous gusts with such venom that even Richard wondered whether the hut would be picked up and hurled over the precipice. He had been disconcerted not to see any cables holding it down. I just thanked St Christopher that we were not at the top of some lonely pass with no shelter. No one slept.

The storm raged for hours, leaving wind and rain and mist in its wake. We learned that the hailstones had broken glass down in the valley and there was concern that the grapes would be damaged. At breakfast our hosts suggested that anyone who wanted to was welcome to stay for another night and, provided the stores arrived safely via the cable, we could eat as well. Shortly afterwards a cheer went up as two large dustbin bags of food were manhandled through the hut window. I went back to my bunk and dozed happily until the delicious smell of home-made soup and cheese omelette forced me downstairs. It was the best lunch of the entire walk, with enough cheese in the omelette to send Richard's cholesterol levels onto the moon.

After lunch, the weather began to clear and our host and hostess and their teenage son took us round Mont de Grange and showed us herds of chamois (a type of goat antelope) grazing on the Col de la Corne with the bouquetins and mouflons (wild sheep with curly horns). The chamois are very shy creatures, and with good reason, especially in the shooting season. The path was slippery after the rain, but we had a magnificent walk and Monsieur pointed out herbs and wild flowers including gentians and edelweiss, mostly over now. His flocks of sheep and goats were grazing on the coarse grass of scalloped plateaux which plunged vertically down to the next level of grass far below.

We were just above the tree line and I could hear a shrill whistling sound further up the mountain. I asked what bird was making such a strange sound, and was told the culprits were marmots, a cross between a rabbit and a beaver; cuddly mammals that live in burrows and come out to graze. They sit on their hind legs above their stony burrows like furry sentinels, their prehensile front paws on their chests, sniffing the air and whistling loudly when danger approaches. From a distance they look like little rocks. Along with the chamois, the bouquetins, and the eagles, they were one of the thrills of walking above the tree line.

We also learnt that our host's family live at the goat farm for three months every year and then return to the valley. They literally share their house with up to twenty-four strangers every night during the season, their only privacy being one family bedroom. Their hospitality was such that we felt more like friends than lodgers. They pointed out our route for the next day, a precipitous climb on which Monsieur had been public-spirited enough to fence in and improve the path, which eroded every winter. Madame rang our next *gîte* at Chaux-Paulin to tell them what had happened and that they were to expect us a day late.

The family was waiting for their younger son, who was just thirteen, to return in the early evening. He had been on a week's *stage de ski* and would be walking up the mountain on his own. He was no stranger to the way, but the path was slippery after the rain and it looked as though another storm was imminent. By supper time there was still no sign of him, and the rain, thunder and lightning had returned. Dusk fell early. We all looked anxiously out of the window, willing him back before darkness fell. Then, just as Madame lit the oil lamps and candles, we made out a small figure in a dark waterproof trudging up the mountainside. The general anxiety evaporated like a cloud, and the boy was given a good dressing down and told to remove his soaking clothes in the goat shed before he was allowed in the house.

Fat grey clouds hung round the mountains threatening rain, but we were more than ready to be off again having lost a precious day. We bade a fond farewell to our fellow-travellers and host family whose company we had so enjoyed during our enforced stay. One American girl and her Danish partner were walking from le Léman to Mont Blanc. Neither of them spoke French, which had caused them some problems, and as we set off we were amazed to see the girl clad in a dustbin bag. She had no waterproof, and, I reflected, if it hadn't been for those few drops of rain by the bridge, I too would be in a bag. As it was, my rapidly purchased anorak proved little better for keeping me dry.

It was a tough start up the steep path to the Col des Mattes, and the slippery conditions made us realize just how lucky we had been on the walk so far. Intermittent showers and no views meant we made good time and only stopped for a quick snack at a deserted frontier post on the Franco-Swiss border between Haute-Savoie and Valais. For the first time we had lost the feeling in our fingers so it was a short break and a quick march into Switzerland.

Immediately our familiar GR5 waymark changed to a freshly painted white-red-white which is the standard Swiss mountain footpath sign. We were plodding on through low cloud and rain when, suddenly, a large wooden hut and several flag poles loomed out of the mist. We had arrived at the Col de la Golèse, and below us lay a tarmac road and a row of parked cars. It was midday, the large hut was a restaurant, and inviting smoke was coming from the chimney. As England expects every walker to do his/her duty to help the French tourist trade, we went in and were surprised to find it filled with smart people ordering their Sunday lunch. We were shown a corner table by an attentive waiter and ordered hot chocolate and a delicious continental version of a chocolate brownie. Soon the appetizing smell of the French cuisine wafted into our nostrils, wine corks popped and it was all we could do not to stay for lunch. Instead, we reluctantly pulled on muddy boots and wet anoraks and headed out into the gloom. However, our will power was soon rewarded: the clouds parted, giving tantalizing glimpses of mountains which cheered us on our way.

Our refuge at Chaux-Paulin, a ski resort in winter, and a scarred hillside in summer, was as cold and inhospitable as our previous refuge had been warm and welcoming. The shabby lounge area looked like a run-down village hall, with a rickety bar, a few school-type tables and chairs and an old-fashioned range that was barely alight. We were at an altitude of nearly 2,000 metres and even the girl behind the bar had a fleece on and admitted it was cold. A dirty blanket had been tacked across the stepladder stairs to our dormitory under the eaves, a barn-sized room where at least fifty mattresses were spread on the bare boards or stacked in the middle of the floor. There were no windows, just holes in the wooden walls which gave us a view of the nearby mountain peaks now lightly dusted with snow. We had to go outside and into the basement to wash; the shower cubicle sat on the concrete floor looking as though it had come in on the tide, but at least the room was warm and the water hot. Back in our airy dorm we discovered life-saving duvets in a cupboard and dived inside our sleeping bags until it was time for our meagre supper: left-over vegetable soup with burnt croutons, followed by *croques monsieur* on a doorstep of bread heated up and served by the owner's sulky girlfriend. We were asked to pay the bill (a staggering 85 euros) there and then as breakfast would be a self-service meal. As we had no Swiss francs every item had been rounded up to euros. We were in no position to argue, so we paid up and went back to our draughty quarters where the wind whistled and the rain spat through the slats; crouched over our duvet, the house cat was busy peeing. Breakfast was in the cattle byre beneath and it looked as though the beasts had just left for their summer pastures. Rickety trestle tables set for thirty lined the long dark room. A basket of stale bread, some jam and a jug of milk indicated our breakfast places. There was no electric light but we managed to find a box of matches and lit a candle. Hot water for our powdered coffee came from a machine. We left soon after 8 a.m. while the owner and his girl were still sleeping.

The white tops of the Dents Blanches massif were just visible through the low cloud. It was cold and damp and we set off at a brisk pace on the easier track to Samoëns, the alpine resort where we were going to treat ourselves to a hotel for the night. A few traditional farms still survived among the twentieth-century skiscape and Richard popped his head inside one little stone hut. I followed and there in the gloom was a beaming little person in a white apron lovingly dusting a large round cheese. As our eyes grew accustomed to the dark, we saw shelf upon shelf lined with numbered round cheeses. The cheese maker kindly posed for a photo and we went happily on our way up the Col de Coux to the Franco-Swiss frontier.

While sitting on a rock beside the track, eating stale bread and a few sardines, we were hailed by two strong-looking Belgian men who were walking part of the GR5 and had been camping in Samoëns.

'How far have you come?' they enquired and sounded gratifyingly impressed when we told them. The chatty one's friend had hurt his knee and they were taking it slowly. We hadn't seen Melvin, our 'Flying Dutchman', since leaving the Jura and often wondered how he was getting on. Someone in our goat farm refuge had passed him with his girlfriend, who, our informant said, was tall, blonde and beautiful.

'Have you seen a young Dutchman, dark hair and a big pack with a tall blonde girl?' I enquired. They shook their heads, but said they would look out for him.

'Where were you the night before last?' they asked us. 'Here in Samoëns we were evacuated from the campsite and spent the night in the communal hall. It was a very bad storm and did much structural damage. Lucky no one was killed.'

Our walk down into the town was through a forest of firs and hardwoods along by the river which roared and gushed after the recent rain. Many trees were uprooted and electric cables trailed along the road in several places. It was fortunate the storm had been at night.

Samoëns was an oasis of green tucked under the sheer mountains. That evening it was bathed in sunlight and awash with tourists. I wrote in my diary that I felt exhausted in spite of our unscheduled rest day on the mountain. We found a quiet two star hotel from the twenty-five on offer, and relished a long soak in the bath followed by a delicious three course meal and the first good night's sleep for some time. The comfortable en suite room, dinner bed and breakfast cost us £68. *Vive la France* and *nulle points* to Switzerland!

Samoëns provided everything from banks and sports shops to an alpine botanic garden. We stocked up on cash and food and set off in light-hearted mood along the lush valley floor before the long climb up to the Col d'Anterne. It was 1 September and if all went well we should be in Nice by the end of the month.

In the hamlet of les Faix we passed some traditional alpine houses, long and low with a brick-built ground floor and wooden elevations with balconies running the length of the building. Great piles of neatly stacked logs stood outside the old doorways, and the only concession to gardening was the odd pot of geraniums.

THE ALPS – THONON-LES-BAINS TO TIGNES

The scenery that day varied from a dramatic limestone gorge with ladders set into the vertical rock face to alpine meadows and thick woods which clothed the rugged mountains. The magnificent Cascade de la Pleureuse wept copiously down the hillside and, as we gained height, the few remaining stunted firs lined the infant river like a natural rock garden. Once above the tree line a cacophony of shrill whistles let us know that we were in the land of the marmots; the hillside was moving as these furry mammals loped over the rock-strewn grass, grazing or standing on their hind legs watching us carefully. They would let us get quite close before they disappeared into their burrows, surprising as historically humans with guns have been a major threat. For several kilometres we found ourselves beneath the massive curtain wall of a giant's impregnable castle, the Falaises des Fiz. We were microscopic beside this great cliff face of rock. As the terrain opened out into marshy alpine pastures, we spotted a small group of isolated huts in the distance. These were the Chalets d'Anterne, our refuge for the night: a simple room with wooden tables and benches, a dormitory, and the usual basic ablutions. The hut was named Alfred Willis, a founder member of the Alpine Club who put mountaineering on the map as a sport in its own right. It was misty and damp outside and there was no heating within, but a good welcome, a hot meal and a comfortable mattress was all we needed. As a bonus we met up with Melvin, who had parted company from his girlfriend in Samoëns. He was his usual cheerful self and told us about the GR5 bush telegraph.

'Not far from the Swiss frontier we met two Belgians who asked me my name and told me they had seen you. My girlfriend couldn't understand how strangers seemed to know me,' he told us with a grin.

I left the boys to catch up while I crept into the warm womb of my sleeping bag and was drifting slowly towards sleep when my mobile phone rang. It was Ann who had put us up for three nights in Oxford. She was ringing from Canada and planned to meet us in Provence at the end of our walk. We had a wonderful chat and I couldn't help marvelling that my mobile enabled me to talk to a friend who lived thousands of miles away, while I was lying in a wooden box in a primitive hut 2,000 metres up a deserted mountain. Encouraged by this, I rang our daughters who had purchased their airline tickets to Nice for the end of the month. Our two-year-old granddaughter had a mouth full of ulcers and was running from room to room screaming. Outside the hut, damp clouds hung low over the rocky buttresses and the only sound was the occasional whistle of a marmot.

Richard had enthused so much about the views from le Brévent across the valley to the Mont Blanc massif that I refused to get my expectations up in case the weather closed in and obscured the view. The morning brought bright sunshine with a few cumulus clouds hanging round the mountain tops like white candyfloss. I felt a thrill of excitement as we set off along the yellow-ochre hillocks of the Anterne valley towards the green Lac d'Anterne and the eroded rocks of the col. For several kilometres we continued to be dwarfed by the massive bulk of the Falaises des Fiz, before we reached the rising scree of the Col d'Anterne and a simple cross that marked our first high pass (2,257 metres).

It was that unforgettable moment when the hard work pays off: we were transported to the kingdom of the mountain gods, surrounded by a rocky fortress with the Pointe d'Anterne like a giant watchtower at one end, the spiky grey peaks of the Aiguilles Rouges spread before us and, in the distance, peeping through a swathe of white cloud, the snowy peaks of the Mont Blanc massif. It was hard to leave this enchantment but we had a long way to go. As we plunged down a wide tree-covered gorge and ate our bread and cheese in warm sunshine in a sheltered spot, it all seemed too easy. We saw marmots, redstart, blue autumn gentians and a few walkers along this ancient track, which took us up a long steep pull to the Col de Brévent. By four o'clock we had been walking, mainly uphill, for over six hours and our path still threaded its way between interminable barren ridges and rocky outcrops. Then, through the V-shaped Col de Brévent, we once more saw the broad white shoulder of the Mont Blanc massif, sparkling in the afternoon sun and clear of cloud. The white fingers of the great glaciers overflowed from the icing sugar crust and dribbled between the flying buttresses of rock shoring up the sides of the mountain. It took us a further hour of hard walking over rocky paths to reach the base of le Brévent, a rocky eminence overlooking the popular resort of Chamonix which straggles along the valley floor in the shadow of the highest mountain in Europe.

Suddenly we were not alone; there were people everywhere, walkers, rock climbers, and tourists with handbags and suede shoes. Our wilderness was vanishing; before us lay the Planpraz cable car station, pylons, wheels, massive steel hawsers, cables that looped like giant skipping ropes across the Chamonix valley, and, beside a steel and glass restaurant, the gondola of the cable car itself. I don't know what Jean Jacques Rousseau would have thought, but we rapidly swallowed our scruples along with coffee and brandy. Not quite rapidly enough, however, for after only five minutes, the waiter told us the restaurant was closing as the last gondola left at 5 p.m. Not wanting to gulp my brandy down in one or, worse, leave this costly beverage on the table, I asked the waiter if I could take it with me; unable to find a little barrel to tie round my neck, he had to make do with a paper cup *pour la route*.

The refuge of Bellachat was perched on what appeared to

be an overhang of rock a kilometre or so above Chamonix. From the little wooden balcony, housing a loo with a view, we could almost touch the great glaciers of Mont Blanc, or Mount Blank as the early English tourists insisted on calling it. The setting sun turned the snowy peaks a dusky pink, deepening to purple and indigo as the light faded, leaving only ghostly shapes under the clear stars and two brilliant cat's eyes staring from the cable car station on the summit. The temperature plummeted, but inside, the refuge was heated with bodies fuelled with home-made soup, pasta and red wine.

It was a full house, for our GR5 had now joined forces with the GR Tour de Mont Blanc, and we lay like sardines on the dormitory mattresses. Snores, farts, beeping watches, zip fasteners and low moans made a nocturnal symphony of Wagnerian proportions. A pair of ear plugs had been on my wish list, and they had arrived via postman Fred. This was the moment they should have come into their own. I pushed them carefully as far into my ears as I could and immediately the rising tide of snores became a muted blur. After ten minutes I began feeling nauseous and wondered what had been in the spaghetti sauce. Then the thought that I would have to pick my way past rucksacks, boots, walking sticks and other essential detritus from twenty-four bunks, descend the ladder stairs, and go out onto the vertiginous balcony to pee or puke, increased my desire to do both. In a sudden rush of blood to the head I decided the ear plugs might be the cause of my bunk sickness, and rapidly removed them. The snorting decibels increased but the nausea quickly diminished and I spent the rest of the night trying to control my bladder. Others crashed quietly in and out. Should I go just after someone comes back? Or would it be better to wait till it's all quiet again? Did I say quiet? Perhaps I can I hang on? At 3 a.m. I couldn't, and crept out, promptly tripping over someone's water bottle, which had a chain attached to it. The stairs creaked, the door squealed and then there I was with the timeless stars above, a jewelled grid of twentieth-century lights far below, and the silent arms of Europe's biggest ice fall in front of me. It was a chilly interlude and as I emerged, the shadow of a near-naked man fell onto the frosty decking.

'Dr Livingstone I presume?' I said, recognizing the long legs and well-proportioned torso of my Alpine guide husband.

The sun was gently grilling the meringue crust of Mont Blanc when we started the long descent into the valley: two kilometres of steep rocky path that tested the resilience of the best-behaved knees. Having safely reached les Houches, we treated our wobbly legs to hot chocolate and patisserie on the sunny terrace of a *boulangerie*, near the start of the Tour de Mont Blanc. Here I was able to recharge my phone battery, running low after two nights without power. The baker's teenage son quizzed me about its many functions and looked disappointed when I came to collect it.

Waiting in Chamonix is a depressing business in bad weather and Fred had decided to fly home. There was no meeting in les Houches as originally planned. However we kept in touch by phone until we returned to the UK.

The climb to the Col de Voza was on an easy track, past ski runs and forests, and we lunched in a meadow with the last of the summer flowers, scabious, purple thistles, corn marigolds and harebells. There was a large nearly deserted hotel at the top and a station for the rack and pinion railway taking tourists from Saint-Gervais-le-Fayet to the Nid d'Aigle. We felt we must continue to do our bit for the French economy, and had a drink at the restaurant before an easy descent to the alpine hamlet of Bionnassay and a charming rustic *auberge* where Richard had planned an overnight stop. However, owing to the storm, we were a day behind schedule, and my guide reckoned we could reach the village of les Contamines-Montjoie and treat ourselves to a hotel that evening.

It was from Bionnassay, in 1784, that an amateur scientist called Dr Paccard made an abortive attempt to climb Mont Blanc. At 4,807 metres it is the highest peak in Europe and proved a formidable challenge for those intrepid early climbers. In August 1786 Jacques Balmat and Dr Paccard successfully reached the summit and in 1787 the less athletic but more scientifically respected Horace-Bénédict de Saussure also succeeded and received accolades and adulation from both the scientific and the artistic fraternities. The following year Saussure, with his son and a team of guides, spent two weeks on the Col du Géant conducting scientific experiments. At an altitude of 3,333 metres, this was a courageous exercise given the lack of the suitable clothing and equipment that we take for granted today. In this Age of Enlightenment, most attempts on the summit of Mont Blanc were scientific in nature, and the climbers were usually armed with barometers and thermometers as well as a good supply of alcohol. However, one unsuccessful eighteenth-century climber declared that the only necessary equipment for climbing a mountain was an umbrella and a bottle of smelling salts.

We were also on the ancient salt route. For hundreds of years this essential preservative was transported from the coastal areas around Nice and taken by packhorse and mule across the Alps. Today a narrow tarmac road leads down to the little hamlet where the river races and tumbles through the fir woods below the snowy peaks of Mont Blanc, and cows and goats graze in the alpine meadows. A second hay crop was being harvested and the air was filled with the fresh scent of newly cut grass.

We found a family-run hotel on the outskirts of

les Contamines-Montjoie and had the best night's sleep for months. Our young waiter at breakfast had missed his vocation in the Comédie Française. He articulated every syllable and reinforced every point with gestures to make sure we had understood. When we related some of our experiences of closed hotels he was dismissive.

'Ze French? *Mon Dieu!* Zey are lazy good-for-nazzing. Pouff!' With this he shrugged his shoulders and raised upturned palms as if offering his fellow-countrymen for sacrifice. 'Zey expect everysing' – here he clenched his fists – 'and don't work 'ard enough.'

His answer to our question of what he thought of the euro was brief.

'*C'est un désastre!*'

Les Contamines was all things bright and beautiful for the twenty-first-century tourist: food shops, ski shops, climbing shops, banks, hotels, and an elegant painted eighteenth-century church. The village has been strategically important since Gallo-Roman times as an access point for the Col du Bonhomme and Col du Joly routes. By 1500 it was abandoned but rebuilt in the eighteenth-century to cater for the new breed of tourist.

Our next three nights would be spent in mountain refuges, which thanks to the tourist industry would provide us with food. This meant lighter loads, which was just as well as we were about to start some seriously steep climbs. From the chalet du Nant-Borrant, we looked down the long fertile ribbon of the Contamines valley and up to the stony slopes of the Col du Bonhomme. Sitting on white plastic chairs among the geraniums and ice cream signs, sipping hot chocolate with the snow fields of Mont Blanc in the distance, we felt deeply contented. We had made up our lost day, the weather continued to be sunny, the last two days had been easier walking and the scenery was picture postcard. I closed my eyes to savour a moment of total relaxation and heard a voice say, 'It gets harder now but if this weather holds the rewards should make all the effort worth while. I just hope we can take the high route out of Tignes as that will mean we gain a day.'

While my vigilant guide was mapping out the route and doing risk assessments to make things as easy and pleasurable as possible, I was writing postcards and enjoying the moment in blissful ignorance of what lay ahead.

As we climbed the zig-zagging path to the col, we found ourselves in a steady stream of walking traffic which quite soon became foot-locked. If the walker above was slower than you, or halted in his/her tracks for a puff stop, the chances were that your toe would collide with his/her heel and an exchange of breathless pleasantries would follow.

'Terribly sorry.' Nonchalant gasp for air.

'Don't mention it.' Gasp, gasp. 'Do go ahead, please.'

'After you.'

Sometimes the owner of the boots above would refuse to make way and frustration would set in.

Having walked for months alone on the hills and mountains I wondered who they all were. These are our mountains, how dare you clutter them up, muttered the unreasonable side of my brain. I had forgotten that at le Brévent the GR5 had joined the Tour de Mont Blanc (GRTMB), and once inside the newly extended and refurbished Refuge de la Croix du Bonhomme, I realized why it is known as the Tour de Many Brits: at least 80 per cent of our fellow travellers were from the UK. As we sat looking out over a panorama of mountains, stuffing our faces with chocolate cake and treacle tart and drinking real tea with milk, I wondered why it was that *bonhomie* did not prevail while sharing a 'foreign field' with fellow countrymen. Here we were in a beautiful refuge perched just below the

Col du Bonhomme at 2,329 metres where the mountains that obsessed men like Balmat, Paccard and Saussure rolled away on every horizon: north to the Val Montjoie, north-east to the Tre-la-Tête massif, south to the valley of les Chapieux and the mountains of Beaufortin and south-east to the Tarentaise where we would be going, and yet we were sitting quietly in a corner and pretending not to be Brits.

Standing outside the refuge in the sunset and looking over the glowing mountain ranges we would have to cross day after day until we were nearly into Nice was both sobering and elating. The little path we would be taking next morning snaked just below the crest of the vertical sides of a staircase of rocky peaks, and eventually disappeared from sight; beyond, wave after wave of mountain passes were waiting to be crossed. It looked magnificently demanding. That night we had the luxury of a four-bunk *dortoir* all to ourselves and slept well after a solar powered shower. The French certainly knew how to look after the Brits.

We set off soon after 8.30 a.m. in sunshine, and noticed that the TMB walkers were heading up to the Col des Fours rather than taking the lower bad weather route to les Chapieux. With the exception of one man who had set off ahead of us, we once more had the mountains to ourselves. Traversing the crests, looking like ants and feeling like giants, we crept slowly south towards the High Alps and Tignes, in the Vanoise National Park, where we hoped to be in two days' time. Below us a family of chamois were grazing the course grass and the only sound was our footsteps and sticks on the tiny path; suddenly the air was filled with the black wings of a startled flock of mountain choughs who wheeled in the air overhead. At our feet we saw tiny alpine flowers somehow able to survive in such a barren wilderness. After several hours' descent, we came to the valley and the Plan de la Lai and stopped in the refuge for a cup of hot chocolate. We sat on the decking terrace above the little road and watched sullen grey clouds settling over the top of our next pass, the Col de Bresson at 2,469 metres. The young owner of the refuge told us he was now *en vacances* until the ski season started at Christmas. It was only 5 September.

Just as we were about to leave, an old Peugeot drove up and out stepped a gentleman resplendent in primrose jacket, waistcoat, neatly pressed trousers and a large black beret which jutted out above his face like corrugated iron. He strode onto the decking, shook hands with us like a long lost friend and engaged us in conversation. At least, he conversed and we listened and tried to understand some of the torrent of animated patois.

'You see me, *Monsieur, 'dame.*' Drawing himself up to his full height, which wasn't very much, he smiled mischievously. 'I am,' he said importantly, 'a true Savoyard. I am as independent as the Corsicans or the Sardinians. I am a proud man.' He stopped a moment, drew a large spotted handkerchief out of his pocket and blew his bulbous nose. '*Excusez-moi*, but two fingers to Napoleon. He had guns, but, like the Corsicans and the Sardinians, we only had pitchforks. We may be called French, but we are not. *Pas du tout*. We are Savoyards and this' – he paused dramatically and looked round at the mountains – 'this beautiful little corner, this paradise, is ours, all ours.' As his rhetoric rose in volume, his consonants whistled round a lonely tooth. He smote his plum waistcoat and grinned again.

We felt we should have clapped, but instead gave him a British good day and set off to climb 700 stony metres of one of his beautiful mountains. When we turned round, this extinct species was climbing back into his old car, which disappeared up the hill in a puff of exhaust.

Looking up at the bare mountainside, I thought it seemed impossible that any path could find its way through the obstructing rocky outcrops and formidable boulders ahead. But somehow, the white and red waymarks on the stones led us upwards to the metamorphic chaos of the col. Grey clouds, grey rocks, grey scree and a great grey monolith like the giant fin of some prehistoric monster surrounded us as we picked our way across slippery rocks for the last kilometre to a little wooden hut tucked under a cirque of mountains with a glacial lake and moraines just below it. Gusts of wind blew rain in our faces and the sight of smoke belching from our refuge chimney was a welcome one.

'Hello. Come on in and get warm.' The young woman in charge of the refuge greeted us cheerfully. A wood-burning stove heated the sparse little room, and the delicious smell of cooking emanated from a large pan on the cooker. We were the first walkers in that evening but were soon joined by Bob, the lone English walker who had set out from the Refuge de la Croix du Bonhomme ahead of us that morning. Before long a party of four arrived and soon we were drinking tea and comparing notes.

Bob told us that in 1962, when he was eighteen, he had worked on the fishing trawlers at Lowestoft. They would spend twelve days at sea and were paid £9 a week. He was currently living in Geneva and tackling the Alps in stages. He also told us that he had been caught out in our first thunderstorm: while we were experiencing the edge of the storm in the Jura, he was walking in thick cloud high above la Chapelle-d'Abondance. Every time lightning struck, the cloud turned orange, and when the storm was directly overhead the thunder was deafening and the ground shook beneath his feet. He admitted he had never been so frightened in his life.

While we were swapping horror stories, Sandra, the *gardienne*, was busy pumping a lever attached to the wall. The water, she told us, came from the lake and had to be hand pumped. She was slim but strong and capable, for not only did she have to pump water and feed up to twenty ravenous walkers every evening, but every week she trekked down the mountain to the nearest village, filled her rucksack with fresh food, and climbed up the steep path back to the refuge.

'The dry stores, bottle gas and fuel come in by helicopter at the beginning of the season,' she told us, adding modestly, 'It only takes a couple of hours to come back up the mountain and I never carry more than twenty-four kilos.'

My ablutions that night were perfunctory: a quick splash under the cold tap outside, (the hardy gentleman before me stripped off to the waist in spite of temperatures that must have been in single figures centigrade), and a quick visit to the covered hole in the ground some thirty metres from the hut, watched by a herd of mountain goats. I just hoped I wouldn't have to make the steep descent down a ladder staircase from the refuge balcony and then down the rocky mountain in the dark. Sleep eluded me, although the dormitory was warm and comfortable and the snore scale relatively low. When I couldn't sleep at night, my mind often ranged over the events of the day and our relationship. This had improved dramatically since leaving the Jura and starting our tough route across the Alps. Well, tough enough for OAPs. No one could feel anything but humbled by the beauty of these mountains, and the sheer effort of climbing the height of Everest each week from sea level, meant there was no strength left for disagreements of any kind. It was 4 September and we should be in Nice in twenty-six days' time. I was not counting the days, however, but living and savouring them one by one.

Thin cloud swirled round the refuge next morning, and the great 'fin' of the Pierra Menta stone was partially hidden. This massive pointed rock was supposedly kicked to this resting place by the Rabelasian Gargantua. The glacial lake by the refuge was, we were told, 200 metres deep and marked the boundary between Beaufortin and the Haute-Tarentaise. Its icy waters were a deep shade of bottle green that morning.

It was so dark that we breakfasted by candlelight before setting off down the mountain to Bellentre in the Isère valley and then up the other side to the Vanoise National Park.

After we had negotiated a few kilometres of the steep rocky descent, the path gradually became easier; small fields and old stone farm buildings replaced the bare rocks of the higher slopes and soon we were walking through traditional Tarentaise villages where wood and stone houses were built on the steep slope and the sound of bells clanged from the necks of cows and the elegant steeples of churches. Some of the renovated houses had geraniums frothing from balconies and shuttered windows. Others were waiting their turn, the long wooden balconies on the upper storeys, once used to dry the grain harvested from the fields just before the snow arrived, rotted quietly.

We were soon looking down on the Isère valley, now the main artery for the ever-growing skiing industry, where a busy road has replaced the old mule track to feed the ski resorts of la Plagne, les Arcs, Tignes and Val d'Isère to name but a few. Although we sat in sunshine eating our frugal lunch by the river and cooling our feet in the water, we had the familiar feeling of anti-climax which descent from spectacular mountains always brings. There was a *fin de saison* feel about Bellentre and the village of Landry on the far side of the river: a few tourists, a couple of kayakers, empty hotels, and a deserted-looking campsite. In a day or so everyone would have departed, leaving the locals to relax a little before the ski season brought another wave of tourists.

We were mentally unprepared for the long and steep climb to the hamlet of le Moulin. The GR5 took us at foothill level through a riverside forest of ash and hazel, oak, aspen and sycamore. As we gained height we found ourselves among spruce and hazel on a rough and very steep path. The air was muggy, and sweat once again streamed from face, hair and trunk. When we reached le Moulin, a few old stone houses set among alpine meadows on the hillside, we perched on a stone wall like a couple of constipated pigeons, and held a council of war. Richard had that end of day worried look.

'We could go on a few kilometres to the refuge at the Porte du Parc de Rosuel, if you could manage that, but if they're fully booked we'll be really stuck. There's nothing else in the Vanoise until we get to Tignes.' He paused, looked at the map and continued. 'On the other hand, we could walk down the main road to the nearest town where there will be hotels. It isn't that far, but it would mean walking the wrong way and giving ourselves further to go tomorrow.'

I took a few gulps from my umbilical water supply (requested from home and brought out by Fred), and felt unable to comment. At this point a fit-looking man with white hair and blue eyes asked us where we were going. He was a local who had been a mountain guide all his working life, and he suggested we use the refuge at the entrance point to the Vanoise National Park as he knew the owner.

'It is simple but good and you won't have to walk so far tomorrow,' he said.

We took his advice but it was a long hot slog up the road. After the village of Nantcroix where every window, doorway, balcony and street corner was so bright with summer blooms there was barely room for pedestrians or vehicles, the road was hot and dull. As we walked on, it appeared that there were major road works under way: great boulders were piled up beside the tarmac, which was partitioned off with very high wire netting, and JCBs and cranes littered the roadside for several kilometres. We later learned that this was because of a recent storm which had catapulted giant boulders down the steep mountainside, torn up the road, damaged an equestrian centre and dented several cars. It was a miracle that no one was killed. This sort of storm damage was not uncommon in this region. We sat on a pile of logs to eat an apple and the last of our energy bars, and I was wondering how much further my legs would carry me, when a car drew up and our guide hopped out.

'Come with me,' he invited, indicating the boot of the car where there was just room for the two of us if we concertinaed our legs (the packs took up the entire back seat of the tiny hatchback). 'I will take you to the refuge and make sure they have room for you. If there is a problem, I will drive you to a hotel further down.'

We squeezed gratefully into the boot, inhaling exhaust as it had to remain a few centimetres open to accommodate us.

When we arrived, he leapt out and returned after a few minutes with a broad grin on his face.

'*Eh bien*. You can stay. There is a fiftieth birthday party there tonight, so it may be noisy, but they can give you a bed, a shower and a meal.'

The word shower sounded too good to be true after our steep thirty-kilometre day.

'A shower, food and bed are all we need,' I said gratefully, aware that my back had not enjoyed the yoga position it had been forced into during our short car ride.

'Only a few years ago none of the refuges had showers,' our friend told me with mild disapproval.

'It's all a matter of expectations,' I replied with a smile.

There was something of a queue for this luxury as the party guests had just arrived and were busy getting themselves showered and changed. When we came downstairs, long trestle tables filled the room. They were laid with pink napkins and flowers, and a log fire blazed in the central hearth. We were given a small plastic table and chairs in an unobtrusive corner of the room. As more and more guests arrived we realized how lucky we were to have been given house room. The food – soup, sausages and potato and a gâteau, with some house wine – was all we needed. We were amazed to see that the guests were milling about for an hour and a half without glasses in their hands. It was only when the birthday girl arrived that the champagne was handed round and the party began in earnest. She was a gracious lady with shiny dark hair, brown eyes and a warm smile, and her popularity was obvious from the number of guests and their enthusiasm for her. She was kind enough to come over and speak to us, and not only apologized for the noise they would make when the dancing started, but insisted that we too had a glass of champagne. We wished her *bon anniversaire*, clinked glasses and once again applauded our much maligned continental neighbours.

The sun shone from clear skies as we left the road, just beyond our night's lodgings, and entered the Vanoise National Park. We had been told it was an easy four to five-hour walk to reach Tignes where we had the use of a friend's apartment. As we climbed the well-graded path, the sun came over the mountains and lit the natural rock garden we were walking through. The tumbling waters of a river raced through a small gorge bordered by juniper and spruce trees. Every imaginable herbaceous plant was growing through the rocks and across the bald grassy slopes: sedums, alchemilla mollis, autumn crocus, thyme, marguerites and gentians. We knew that we would have to return in June or early July to see the flowers at their best. From time to time we came across summer pastures, and a few stone huts which would have been very useful for walkers in bad weather. Not so long ago cattle herdsmen would have lived in these basic shelters where there were no windows, just an earthen floor and a fire. They would have slept on piles of grass and covered themselves with hay. All summer their only occupation would have been milking their herds and making cheese, and their sole companions would have been their fellow herdsmen and their cattle. Living by, with and in Nature, untrammelled by the luxuries which we now consider necessities, these were perfect examples of Rousseau's noble savages.

At the Col de Grassez a herd of cows was still grazing the poor grass of the pastures above the glacial waters of Entre-le-Lac. The higher we went, the more magnificent the scenery became. Far above the tree line, we were in the land of marmots, chamois, and eagles, surrounded by serrated peaks with their skirts of grey scree. The only sounds were the whistling of marmots and the clank of distant cow bells. I recalled a poem that had been pinned to the dormitory door of our refuge the previous night:

Voici l'espace. Voici l'air pur. Voici le silence.
Le royaume des aurores intactes et des bêtes naïves.
Tout ce que vous manquez dans les villes est ici préservé pour votre
joie.

(Here you have space. Here you have pure air. Here you have silence.
The kingdom of untouched dawns and unspoilt animals.
Everything you lack in the town is preserved here for your enjoyment.)

The poem then gently asked the reader to preserve these precious commodities.

From the crest of the Col du Palet, a well-marked path took us past the fissured peaks of the Aiguille Noir where we could see across to the glaciers of la Grande Motte and the Col de la Leisse. All around lay an undulating skeletal landscape, interspersed with dark peaks, sweeps of scree and small blue lakes. The gradual descent through this wildnerness was a moment of pure joy; then the ground fell away revealing an alien city far below with skyscrapers like organ pipes nestling under the great buttresses of la Grande Motte. Either I was dreaming or had just beamed down from the Starship Enterprise. Further down we saw Tignes: apartments, hotels, ski lifts and a golf course, grouped round its lake, which was gift-wrapped with a gravel path. Above our heads, steel chair lifts swung like redundant shopping trolleys and the scars of ski runs criss-crossed this dramatic amphitheatre. Only the shrill whistle of marmots broke the silence.

Tignes
Entre Deux Eaux
Plan-See
Modane
Vallée Etroite
Névache
Plampinet.
Brimeçon
Brunissard
Château-Queyras
Ceillac
Maljassek
Larche
Bousiéyas
St-Etienne-de-Tinée
Roya
Beuil
St-Sauveur-sur-Tinée
Valdeblore
Utelle
Levens
NEGRESCO
Nice
Nice
mediterranean sea.
ITALY

15. The Alps — Tignes to Nice.

0   20   40 km

Chapter Fifteen

Tignes to Nice

On 1 March 1952 the inhabitants of Tignes left their homes for good as their Alpine village disappeared under waters, held back by a dam, which would produce hydroelectric power to help the ailing post-war French economy. These 'noble savages' were given a new village and new challenges when the lust for white gold gripped the Alps several decades later. Every ten years the Chevril Lake is drained for checks in the dam wall, and the inhabitants of the new village return to the spot where their old village once stood. It must be an emotional time for those who were christened, grew up and married there, or have loved ones who were buried in a grave that is now beneath the waters of the lake.

At an altitude of over 2,000 metres and lying under the great glaciers of la Grande Motte, Tignes was the perfect place to build a ski resort which could operate for an extended season. Meanwhile a variety of water sports, and golf as well as walking and climbing, was on offer for the summer tourist. The new town, named Tignes-le-Lac, continues to grow and prosper, bringing in money for the state and employment for the locals.

We descended the steep hillside, still reeling from the shock of the new, on a path that took us round the golf course, where the marmots shared their burrows with stray balls, to the blue waters of the cut-and-paste lake. Here we sat on a comfortable bench and ate our last crust of bread, watching a group of tourists clutching poodles and cool bags moving tentatively across the mown grass in high heels. On the far side of the lake a traditional stone hut with a slate roof stood defiantly behind the faded rosebay willowherb like an old peasant. Then we walked up to our friend's apartment block and entered via an underground car park. We collected keys from the warden, and found the luxurious flat warm and welcoming; savages we might have been, but noble we were certainly not.

Tignes was sleeping between seasons; the supermarket and shopping mall opposite was closed till 31 October. However, the sumptuous tourist office was open and gave us an unsettled weather forecast. As we had caught up our enforced day's rest after the storm, we decided to make the best use of our luxurious lodgings and have a day off before tackling the Col de la Leisse, our highest pass at 2,758 metres.

Even with today's sophisticated technology, weather forecasts in the mountains are not always accurate. Our rest day was bright and sunny until the evening when it started to drizzle, and the following day clouds covered the high-rise apartment blocks and threatened rain. We threaded our way round the lake, past the deserted apartments and massage parlours of Val Claret, our Utopian city, to the steely mouth of the funicular which takes skiers through the mountain and delivers them onto the glaciers of la Grande Motte. A large notice stated that it would be reopening on 29 September.

As we started to climb, the rain turned to sleet and the sleet turned to snow; a white blanket then covered not only the path, but our precious red and white waymarks. We picked our way over slippery stones and round great rocks marbled with snow, stopping frequently to check if we were on the concealed track which had now widened out into a monochrome amphitheatre. Richard was in the lead, peering myopically into the gloom like a disorientated heron; when I caught him up and slithered to a halt, we held a council of war.

'Is this wise?' I asked cautiously. 'Why don't we return to Tignes and try again tomorrow when the weather may have improved?'

Richard didn't do going back, but he knew just how far we had to go, and we didn't want to get lost and spend a night on the mountain when we had such wonderful accommodation in the village. It was a difficult decision, but after a while he nodded sadly and we reluctantly began our slippery descent. When, on our way down, we met no fewer than three English couples on their way up, our humiliation was complete. Although we comforted ourselves that there was nowhere for these intrepid Brits to stay in Tignes, therefore turning back was not an option, it still felt like the retreat from Moscow.

Back at the apartment, Richard relieved me of my rucksack and I set off to buy some food at the only supermarket still open, which was in the next village of le Lavachet. I hurried through damp deserted streets, past hectares of plate glass, stared at by the blank windows of apartment blocks, and then disappeared into a road tunnel which made no concessions to pedestrians. I emerged, blinked the snow out of my eyes, and eventually found the supermarket. It was closed until four o'clock. I turned back, face into the wind, and discovered that I was soaked to the skin and losing the feeling in my hands and feet, which made me realize that to spend a night on a bare mountain in bad weather would be more than an endurance test.

Once inside our warm refuge, my fingers refused to undo my boot laces, and I had to use all my concentration to complete this simple task. It took less time to throw off my wet clothes and lower myself into a deliciously hot bath where

I clutched a mug of tea and thawed out. When I eventually emerged from this little paradise, I lifted my towel from the heated rail and declaimed to the four white walls: 'Thank you, Tignes. All is forgiven!'

Cloud and mist still clung to the mountains as we started our second attempt to climb the col. The warden of our apartment block was amused when we returned the key yet again and shook a warning finger at us.

'There's lots of snow up there, you know.'

Her words did nothing for morale, but this time we had to persevere whatever the weather threw at us. We set off in silence round the lake to Val Claret, past empty chalets and apartment blocks and a Heathrow-sized car park. Then we started to climb under the silent chair lifts, glancing nervously at the recent snowfalls on the tops. The temperature had risen sufficiently to melt the thin covering of snow over the path, and this time we could see our way forward. The mountain seemed steeper and climbing was harder. We had to stop frequently to regain our breath, and it seemed a long time before we reached the spot where we had turned round the day before; it was only then that we realized how near the top we had been. After an hour and a half of hard climbing, we stood triumphantly on the col and looked down a broad sweep of valley to the steely waters of glacial lakes and the frothing River Leisse curving beneath the giant buttresses of la Grande Motte. As we watched, the cloud cover lifted to reveal the snowdusted peaks of the Pointes de Pierre Brun rising above a saffron carpet, and soon patches of blue appeared between cotton wool clouds. We felt that special elation which comes after succeeding at the second attempt and fairly skipped along the mountain track, watched by a few sturdy sheep. It was lunchtime and we had no food, so it was a bonus to see the Refuge de la Leisse perched on a lump of rock far below us.

Soon we were sitting in front of a bowl of soup and a basket of bread with the sun shining overhead and hens clucking round our feet. I shared the basic privy with an inquisitive marmot.

As we left the heights, the landscape became softer and a few alpine flowers bloomed in the coarse grass of summer pastures; the valley widened out and, on a rise beside the gushing river we saw our refuge, for the night. Entre-Deux-Eaux has been run by the same family for four generations; the low slate-roofed building had been extended at one end to provide accommodation for walkers and the family still lived in the traditional farmhouse during the summer months. Madame welcomed us at the door and took us up a ladder staircase to a bedroom with two double beds covered in brightly coloured knitted squares, a sloping floor and one small window dressed with gingham curtains.

'Would you like this room or the dormitory upstairs?' she enquired.

We opted for the bedroom and enjoyed the luxury of a hot shower before supper. Just as Madame was taking orders, three tired walkers appeared and asked if they could stay the night. Madame welcomed them graciously but asked if they could delay their ablutions until after supper as the meal was ready. Soon we were all tucking into soup and sausage casserole. Our three companions were all experienced English walkers taking a short holiday to renew their acquaintance with the GR5 in the Vanoise National Park. Over dessert one of them told us of his experiences on the Great Outdoors Challenge walk in the Scottish wilderness.

'I travel light,' he told us, 'just a tent and a change of clothes. I pitch the tent, pull on all my clothes, wriggle into my rucksack, eat a few digestive biscuits and sleep like a top.'

That made us feel like real softies; the very thought of lying on the ground with only a groundsheet between you and the damp earth filled me with horror. And there I was bemoaning the loss of my inflatable mattress.

At that moment we heard the sound of hooves and shouting outside; the door burst open and three swarthy men and one woman entered, chatting and laughing. The men wore black brimmed hats above their drooping moustaches, black waistcoats and tight trousers. Their female companion had long dark hair which fell in curls down to her bare brown shoulders and wore a tight bodice, long flared skirt and boots. They were muleteers, re-enacting a journey along the old mule tracks through the Alps and enjoying themselves hugely. They ordered beers and spent an hour telling risqué stories and singing snatches of traditional songs with words that were probably not so traditional. I was just thinking we were in for a noisy night when they left as suddenly as they had come. It must have been the nearest equivalent to an alpine pub crawl, or were they the ghosts of muleteers past?

Sleep was difficult as the mattresses must have been the originals, circa 1904, with a gentle incline to match the sloping floorboards; just as well we had a bed each. Then I thought of our English friend in his rucksack. Outside the wind whistled and moaned and I wondered what the weather would be like in the morning.

It dawned windy but fair with some cloud cover which soon lifted. The refuge owner listened to the weather forecast and told us we were having a taste of '*le petit mistral*'. From the refuge door we looked over a line of washing and a few grazing goats to the undulating landscape of rock-strewn vegetation and the snow-clad massif of the Grand Paradis. We set off ahead of our English friends, and although we met up with each other from time to time, we would just exchange pleasantries and move on. There is an unwritten rule in the mountains that if you meet people en route, you may socialize with them in the evenings, but you don't walk with them. Everybody needs their own space to think their own thoughts and absorb the scenery in their own time. We zigzagged up the steep hills, picked our way across stony moraines, and crossed furious rivers (this time on well-made bridges). The mountains were harsh and wild: marmots shrilled, eagles soared overhead and from time to time we spotted herds of chamois. Then rounding a corner on a steep path we met a group of bouquetin balancing on the rocks, their great ridged horns silhouetted against the sky. The apartment blocks and skyscrapers of Tignes might have belonged to another planet.

We were still a day behind schedule, and Richard decided we could double up two short four-hour days, especially in view of the stories told by our English trio. It was a long hard walk and for the first few kilometres the wind buffeted us in exposed places, tugging at our rucksacks and threatening to throw us off balance. If this was the little mistral, I wondered what the big one was like. By midday the wind had moderated, and the scenery was so uplifting it was impossible to feel anything but humble. We walked in the shadow of the magnificent chiselled peak of la Dent Parrachée, lightly covered in snow, through summer pastures and mountain chalets in traditional stone with rounded slate roofs. Occasionally we glimpsed the valley far below, where clusters of toy houses clung to rivers of tarmac.

It was after six by the time we reached our refuge at de Plan Sec; the wind had a biting edge and dark clouds rolled round the mountains as we trudged up the final hill towards the welcome lights of the large wooden building. The reception room had a roaring log fire at one end and a bar that was doing a brisk trade. There was a delicious smell of cooking, wood smoke and beer and, even at this late season, it was full of other walkers. I guessed we must be nearing civilization. Best of all we met up with Melvin and enjoyed a wholesome five course meal with our English trio, Melvin and his friend. These mountain refuges not only provide good food, wine and shelter, they also give the long distance walker a chance to meet up with other kindred spirits and socialize. We are, after all, herd animals. When we had finished dessert, a bottle of malt whisky appeared, and we talked and laughed until the embers of the fire turned to ash, and then went outside to our dormitory block where a ragged moon lit the dark shapes of the mountains.

The morning dawned bright and sunny with a touch of frost in the air. After a good breakfast, we filled our bottles from the water trough, where a wooden spout gave a continuous fountain of ice cold water, and said goodbye to our travelling companions. Temperature inversion had formed a bank of cloud in the valleys, but the peaks were clearly visible. As we left the refuge the sun's rays had just lit a mountain called the Pointe de l'Echelle, a saffron cone whose ice cream summit filled the horizon; candyfloss clouds floated below and planes from Nice airport had left contrails which criss-crossed the blue void above. Descending from the refuge we crossed a series of dammed lakes, and then walked in warm sunshine below the great incisors of the Dent Parrachée where a glacial lake sparkled like an emerald at its base.

After five days above the tree line, our long descent into the valley of the Arc brought us shade and the intoxicating smell of resin. The sun was warm but not hot, birds were singing, and our path was strewn with pine cones; far below lay Modane, our destination for the night. We sunned ourselves on warm rocks like a couple of lizards, watched goldcrests and strange speckled birds called nutcrackers, ate a frugal lunch and felt totally content.

We were warned that Modane was a town to leave as quickly as possible; it is a staging post for tourists, being on a mainline railway and a trunk road which takes cars under the mountain to Aosta in Italy and from Lyon to Turin. It is also a service town which has everything the walker needs: hotels, banks, outdoor gear shops, supermarkets, cafés, a tourist office and even a hairdresser. My hair had reached savage proportions and badly needed taming, so I entered the smart salon and asked Madame if I could have a haircut. After a cursory glance at my unkempt locks she told me she was closing in five minutes. She wasn't even *désolée*.

Back in our modest hotel I consoled myself with a shower and hair wash and then rang the family, starting with our daughter Jo. Her usually cheerful voice was somewhat muted.

'I'm fine. Just feeling sick as a dog. It's so hard preparing food when all you want to do is throw up.'

What's the problem?' I said, feeling anxious.

'I'm nine weeks pregnant. Nobody knows so I can't get excited yet.'

Well, we could and did as we toasted this nine-week-old miracle. This addition to our two existing grandchildren was wonderful news. Living near our two daughters, we have got to know the grandchildren well and they have added a significant dimension to our lives.

Modane is where the massif of the mountains of the Vanoise meets the massif of the High Alps. 'Climbed 4,844 feet' was the entry in my diary for the day we left Modane. Feet seemed more appropriate than metres and sound so much more impressive. It was certainly a hard pull up once we had crossed under the thundering autoroute which leads to the Fréjus tunnel, and entered the quiet woods which cover the steep hillside. For a few hours the only sounds were our gasps for air and the roar of mountain streams, not dissimilar in volume. The only people we met were a young Belgian couple who were struggling even more than we were. They had just got off the train at Modane and this was their first day on their way to Menton.

At the top we came across an army blockhouse, relic of twentieth-century conflict. This was part of a system of defences rather like the Maginot Line; four great look out posts had been built to defend the frontier passes with Italy, with the forts themselves situated a hundred metres higher inside the mountain which was riddled with galleries and staircases. The forts were named after the cols they were on: Pointe Balthazar, Pointe Melchoir, and Pointe Gaspard. It was no coincidence that our next refuge was called I Re Magi. Our proximity to Italy was making itself felt; throughout the High Alps we came across massive forts improbably perched on the very tops of cols, an indication of French mistrust of their neighbours over the centuries.

Eventually we reached the top, and the path levelled off through summer pastures dotted with fir trees and surrounded by rocky buttresses and slopes of scree. It was strangely quiet, no whistling marmots, no cows, no people, no birds, just the silence of the high mountains. A simple cross marked the Col de la Vallée Etroite and from here we had an easy walk on a grassy path beside the snaking river, pock-marked with boulders. We descended the rough hillside to the Vallée Etroite, which crosses the watershed between the northern and southern Alps, to reach a natural rock garden: the mountain slopes were thinly covered in the green-gold of autumnal larches, while the rocky banks of the tumbling river were softened with horizontal junipers and alpine plants, and coloured by the faded pink of rosebay willowherb. The natural fortress of Mont Thabor towered above the scene. Here we heard the whirring hum of grasshoppers and crickets, a sure sign that we were nearing the Mediterranean.

As the little path gave way to a wide gravelled track a people carrier passed us crammed with tourists, and several families were enjoying the afternoon sunshine. One woman was pushing a buggy and her man was carrying a child on his shoulders; they were a strong handsome couple and the child, with gold curls and blue eyes, could have been a Renaissance *putto*; they were talking and gesticulating as only the Italians can.

Our refuge was also run by a cheerful Italian family. It was clean and comfortable. The family kitchen had a seating area warmed by a huge corner fireplace where several large dogs were occupying the hot spots. Upstairs we had one of a row of two-bunk rooms leading off a communal sitting area shared with only one other couple. Our tasty meal of polenta and pasta was served by a gorgeous young man, the owner's son, and was washed down with free wine; dessert was a panna cotta from heaven followed by gorgonzola to die for. The choice of Grappa or Gentiane (a liqueur made from the tall yellow gentian which grew in the Alpine meadows) came with the coffee. We slept well in spite of a thunderstorm.

Madame la propriétaire helped us find accommodation in the neighbouring valley, an easy nine-kilometre walk to a pretty village called Névache. We paid our modest bill of 76 euros and gave the Italians an appropriate gold star as we walked under the impressive bulk of a chain of summits known as the Three Kings. The air was fresh after the night's rain and the sun was shining as we climbed gently through the trees. Here we met the young couple whom we had seen struggling up the steep hillside outside Mondane. They told us it took them so long to climb to the col the previous day that it was already early evening by the time they reached it. Having found a good place to bivouac beside the river, they had barely an hour's sleep before the wind got up, followed by torrential rain, thunder and lightning. At a height of 2,434 metres, a storm can be very frightening, and they decided to pack up and go down into the valley to find shelter. The path was steep and slippery, it was dark and they only had one small torch. The girl turned her ankle on the tricky descent, but at 2 a.m. they managed to reach the valley and a deserted refuge. The door was locked, but somehow they were able to get in through an open window and spent the rest of the night in comparative safety and comfort. All things considered they looked remarkably well and cheerful. The girl was limping but they were still determined to continue and reach Menton as planned. We vacated our seat on a log for them and wished them luck.

Eventually our forest track emerged onto a saffron plateau where the Three Kings and the rugged silhouette of Mont Thabor were mirrored in the still waters of the Lac des Thures. Each day the scenery seemed better than the last, and each region had its own unique attraction. Up here we met a huge flock of sheep and saw the shepherd's hut, a small stone building with just a door on the ground floor and a window under the eaves. It stood alone in the grand emptiness of these mountain pastures with washing flapping from a line, and a horse and goat grazing round the door; an ephemeral idyll which would have warmed the heart of Jean Jacques Rousseau.

After the sparse vegetation and rocky peaks of the High Alps, the Vallée Clarée was soft and green with traditional alpine houses, cars and tourists. We ate our lunch by the babbling river, which ran through fields bordered with oak, ash and alder. A French couple were also eating by the river and, after an exchange of pleasantries, we learned that Monsieur had taken part in the Algerian war and was writing a cathartic book about it, mainly to exorcise the nightmares he had been having since watching the recent conflict in Afghanistan on television. We discussed the problems of writing, swapped addresses and were invited to stay with his family in Paris.

A few tourists were wandering round the alpine village of Névache admiring the old stone houses, where archways once used for farm vehicles are now rustic wooden doors splashed with geraniums. A little church with its one bell aloft, struck the hour with dissonant enthusiasm, and the smell of fresh baguettes floated from a tiny *boulangerie.* In this valley and others in the region, we found a wonderful variety of eighteenth-century sundials painted on the walls of houses and churches.

Our *auberge* was deserted when we arrived in the early afternoon, and the rambling garden awash with plastic bikes and balls. A large black dog barked apologetically from the balcony. The family returned at tea time and showed us to a small dormitory which we shared with two girls from the Tourist Office in Modane who were walking to Menton. Supper was served at a long trestle table and every seat was taken. After several glasses of wine my French became as fluent as it was ungrammatical. I flew effortlessly from past to present to future. I chatted happily about walking, politics and the weather with a charming gentleman to my right and an equally charming lady to my left. I empathized with a nurse opposite about poor pay and the responsibilities of a life-saving job, and by the time coffee arrived I had put the entire world to rights and was positively glowing with bonhomie. I was forced to return to the present when Richard appeared from his end of the table and rescued my table-mates from this imperfect stream of consciousness.

Our walk across the Alps was also at a watershed: not only were we beginning to smell and feel the Mediterranean, but we were going to meet Alison and Mike, our good friends who had met us on the Oxford Canal and had arranged to join us near Briançon. They had booked us into a Logis de France with them for three nights before we moved on through the regions of Ubaye and Mercantour to the Alps Maritimes and Nice. It was a window of luxury to look forward to.

The grass under the leafy trees beside the River Clarée was surreally white with frost next morning as we set off in bright sunshine to the alpine hamlet of Plampinet. Our easy path soon deteriorated as we met the first of many landslides, and we were forced to retreat and detour along the road.

Plampinet snuggles under the steeply rising hillside, the traditional wooden houses clustered round the church. Almost every house advertised itself as an *auberge* or *chambre d'hôte*, which was strange as we had been told there was no accommodation here. Perhaps, I reflected, it is better to travel hopefully. Hens and cockerels pecked the dirt along the roughly cobbled streets, and the usual pots of geraniums added splashes of colour to wooden doors and balconies. The church had a magnificent painted sundial on it and, we were told, some very old frescoes inside; we had to take their word for it as the door was locked. We zigzagged up the vertiginous but well-graded track bordered with clumps of pale grasses swaying in the breeze to reach the Col de Dormillouse where the landscape had formed a series of golden ridges, like sand at low tide, beneath smooth sweeps of scree. Two large white dogs that looked a mixture of wolf, labrador and husky were sitting above our path like police in a lay-by, watching us with interest. Later we learned that they were the guard dogs for the sheep and could be very fierce indeed. Further down we saw hundreds of sheep scattered like small woolly boulders all over the hillside, and, silhouetted against the sky, the shepherd himself surrounded by three sheepdogs. His brimmed hat was pulled well over his dark weathered face, above a red shirt, worn leather jacket, black trousers and shepherd's stick. He had long legs and an enormously powerful voice which echoed round the hills and ensured the dogs did his bidding. The coarse grass looked so dry we wondered the sheep could get any goodness from it at all, and noticed that the shepherds we saw up there kept moving their flocks on to graze another section of the mountainside.

On the far side of this Elysium we could see the grey ridge of our second col and from here we descended back into the world of the motor car at Montgenèvre. This once famous ski resort was having the late summer blues; a wide road ran between lines of empty cafés, ski shops and petrol stations, ski lifts hung limply from their cables and nothing stirred. There was little here to stir anything, although the col had once been the route used by such immortals as Caesar, Charlmagne and Napoleon I. It was Napoleon who built the first route through the town on his triumphal march across the Alps after his escape from Elba. Popular mythology relates that an eagle flew before him and an ever-increasing band of supporters followed in his wake. Whatever his faults, Old Boney left a sum of money for this region specifically to build shelters for travellers crossing the mountain passes on the mule tracks.

Richard felt we had time for a *croque monsieur* and a beer before setting off to meet Alison and Mike in a village near Briançon. We sat amongst a sea of empty tables and chairs on the decking of a bar that reluctantly served food. By the time we left it was half past three. 'It should only take an hour and a half,' Richard assured me.

It is strange how things always go wrong when you have a deadline. We had planned to meet up at 5.30 p.m. which should have given us plenty of time, but the GR5 had disappeared in a mini landslide and we had to stay on a dirt road which wound backwards and forwards for eleven long kilometres before we reached our destination only forty minutes late. Our fitness levels had enabled us to keep up a speed of four miles an hour with packs, which was not an enjoyable experience. We threw our sweaty bodies into two pairs of welcoming arms and gulped down the obligatory glass of bubbly on a bench by the river. It was so good to see them I dissolved into tears. They drove us back to their hotel, a converted farmhouse at Brunissard, a hamlet just below the Col d'Izoard, where we met up with Mike's dental partner Chris and his wife Di. Mike and Chris had trained at King's

College Hospital with Richard, so there was a lot to catch up on over the raclette cheese fondue we had for supper.

The Col d'Izoard at 2,360 metres is best known as the highest and most challenging section of the Tour de France, that institution which grips not only the heart but also the soul of every Frenchman. Standing in a lunar landscape at the top of this col, where the smooth buttresses sheer off the mountains like vertical sand dunes, we looked down on the dizzying switchbacks of the precipitous road. Instead of speed restrictions or warnings to slow down, the names of famous cyclists were painted in white across the well-maintained tarmac. The energy expended here each July was almost tangible; ironically, for the first and last time, Richard and I were whisked effortlessly up the col *en auto* as it was not on the GR5.

Mike and Alison dropped us at Briançon. We had no time to visit the famous Vauban forts of this strategically important citadel and even our attempts to find a shop failed. Lunch was half a *pain au chocolat* and some crumbly waffle, but as we were walking back to our hotel, any hungry gap would be quickly filled by delicious Queyras cuisine. It was a perfect day for walking, fresh and sunny, and the autumn tints of the bilberry bushes were throwing a red carpet across the barren mountain passes. We walked through delicate larch woods, under the unique cembro pines, home to the raucous *casse-noix* bird, and along dusty tracks accompanied by cicadas and a scent of the south. We were back at the hotel in time to have a swim in the pool before drinks and supper.

I was getting accustomed to the good life, and left Richard to tackle the next stretch of the GR5 from Brunissard to Ceillac over the Col Fromage. I sat by the pool catching up on writing, ringing home and booking accommodation along the next stage of the walk. Alison tidied up my unruly hair with a pair of scissors and years of practice, and my only exercise was half a kilometre into the village to restock our mobile larder. Our friends drove us to the village of Ceillac to meet Richard who had had a marvellous walk in perfect weather. We returned to the hotel where we had another swim, and I took childish delight in using the hairdryer in our en suite bathroom before we gathered for our final evening meal together. It had been a pleasant and restful interlude, but now, like all good nomads, we knew it was time to move on.

It was Thursday, 18 September when we left Alison and Mike at Ceillac and set off for the Col Girardin, the second highest of the walk at 2,700 metres. The approach was a steady climb through larch and pine trees beside a foaming river. Higher up, the mountains closed in on us and their scree and shale slopes had little grass to soften them. Surprisingly enough we met a dirt track, which led to the recently restored chapel of St Anne beside a lake of the same name. The lake was a vibrant emerald green watched over by a series of rocky giants rising from a base of scree. I stood gazing at the brilliant sheet of water, quite expecting a mythological creature to rise from its depths. The only creature to rise was my husband telling me it was time to go.

Fit though we were, climbing each col took a big effort. I often thought of the walker and writer John Hillaby whose erudition was such that in tedious moments he could concentrate on the life cycle of the lesser spotted newt, or hum one of the more intricate passages from a Prokofiev sonata. All I could manage was the mantra-like doggerel of 'London's Burning'. Even in the sunshine, the col was a shale desert, but, as always, at the top we were in the kingdom of the gods eyeballing an endless variety of the peaks and buttresses that make up the geological wreckage of the Alps.

Not only did we have the visual rewards, but also the feel-good factor which comes after strenuous exercise; in addition, every weary step was taking us nearer Nice.

For once we were not alone on the top; several scantily clad not-so-young men (in their seventies) were stripped to the waist sunning themselves. We left them to it, and made our way cautiously down the precipitous slope, stopping after 100 metres to look back. Where the demarcated crest of the smooth bleached col met an indigo sky, we saw the sharp silhouette of a Lilliputian frontier post and a microscopic man crawling along the crest towards it.

It was a long hard descent, hard because our feet slid on the scree and my bunion began to object. By mid-afternoon we were looking down on the stone roofs and little church of the hamlet of Maljasset. We saw our first snake basking by the path and were soon sitting on a little terrace in the steep-sided Ubaye valley, sipping beer in the warm afternoon sunshine and admiring the prayer flags that gave a Tibetan feel. A few minutes later the bare-chested gentleman and his friends from the top of the col appeared, followed by a steady stream of walkers. The refuge was so full we even had to queue for the loo.

The first five miles next day along by the river were in deep shade along the valley floor where the leaves of the silver birches and hazels were beginning to turn yellow. Richard had again joined two short days into one and we were aiming to get to Larche, an eight-and-a-half-hour day. We left the main road at a bridge slung high over the narrow gorge, a dizzying drop of ninety-seven metres to the river below. It was only then that the sun burst over the tops of the mountains and brought colour and warmth to the green and gold landscape. After a short walk along the narrow road we rejoined the GR5 and climbed steeply to the little hamlet of

Fouillouse where we had originally planned to spend the night. We called in at the little *gîte* to cancel our reservation and sat on the terrace amongst the vines and bougainvillaea downing a beer and savouring a *tarte aux pommes* which we shared with a tabby cat and her two emaciated kittens.

It was good walking, through larch woods, across the autumnal summer pastures, past roaring streams and hillsides green with azaleas and glowing with bilberry foliage. We met great flocks of sheep moving down the valleys like streams of fluffy maggots, always with a few accompanying goats. At the top of the Col de Mallemort we walked past a ruined barracks; the costly fort was perched on the summit guarding the Franco-Italian border. Even on a perfect summer's day it was a bleak place and we thought how hard it must have been for the soldiers, both those who had to build it and those who had to man it. In spite of the heat, I shivered; it must have been a terrible place in winter. Then we turned our backs on it and made the easy descent over a steep grassy hillside to the village of Larche.

The wardens of these alpine refuges are a special breed: mature, energetic, capable women, fazed by nothing and no one, who can solve any problem thrown at them while cooking and serving several courses of good food for a score or more of hungry walkers. Sometimes they have family backup, sometimes they manage solo. There were several wardens on our route that Richard would have been very happy to support. The *gardienne* at Larche was no different; the refuge was only half full and she asked us if we minded eating half an hour early as she was going out with her daughter that evening. A smartly dressed Swiss couple arrived just as we were sitting down.

'We've just arrived from Geneva,' the man boomed. 'Can we eat here?'

The *gardienne* regretted they could not as they hadn't booked and she was about to serve. 'There's a good café in the village,' she added, 'and there is room for you to stay here tonight.'

We met Madame again after breakfast and when she heard what we were doing she was kind enough to give me a banana and some Swiss chocolate.

Larche had been destroyed by the Germans in 1945, possibly as a vendetta for the active local Resistance movement. The village was burnt to the ground and the fate of the inhabitants was uncertain. When I mentioned this to the *gardienne* she was philosophical.

'It is true that this village and two others near here were destroyed by the Germans at the end of the war. That is why they are not pretty like other alpine villages.' She handed me the modest bill and added brightly, '*C'est la guerre*. Now we have moved on.'

It was Saturday, 20 September. Richard was now using the last of our Topo guides from Larche to Nice and he informed me that we had just completed 1,000 miles of our European section. By doubling our mileage on one more day we could be in Nice on 28 September, two days ahead of schedule. The walk had taken on a momentum of its own even though it wasn't exactly downhill all the way. As for our relationship, getting enough oxygen into our lungs climbing the high passes occupies the mind to the exclusion of all else. Any minor irritations were subsumed in the magnificent scenery. Each day we felt relieved that we had achieved our goal, and were thankful, as many before us must have been, for the hospitality given us in the refuges: good food, wine and a night on a comfortable mattress.

Our destination was a tiny hamlet called Bousiéyas where we had booked in at the *gîte*. The following day we would be in a town with plenty of accommodation on offer, and then more worries for Richard as the *gîte* at Roya was closed for renovation.

Meanwhile the sun shone on the River Ubayette and we watched several shepherdesses bringing their flocks down from the high summer pastures. A minor road took us up past the tree line to Lac Lauzanier, a well-known accessible beauty spot. It was here that Richard was befriended by a donkey and thought for a moment that Robert Louis Stevenson's idea of travelling with one wasn't so bad after all. We ate bread and cheese by the still blue waters and watched other people picnicking, fishing, or just sunning themselves, enjoying the mountain scenery as much as we were. It was one of the few times we shared our alpine space with tourists. Above towered the Pas de la Cavale, our third highest col. Refreshed, we struck off up and up through scree and rocks. The Topo guide warned of a local wind called the Lombarde which can blow stones at unsuspecting walkers. I was edging my way down the scree when I heard a clunk, clunk sound and several stones bounced past me. There was a shout from behind, and the three walkers who had set off this mini avalanche were telling me they would wait until I was far enough down not to be in danger. In bad weather it would have been a nightmare.

Crossing cols became like surfing waves: no sooner had we climbed one than there was another to negotiate. It was three o'clock when we left the col, and our descent took us onto a stony plateau and into a steep ravine before we puffed up the other side to the Col des Fourches at a mere 2,262 metres. Walking was always harder in the afternoons and we still had quite a way to go. Richard was busy giving me a geology lesson; he could see four geological eras from where we stood. We were right on the Italian border and once again there were gun emplacements everywhere and another massive fort perched on the highest point. Just down from the col we came across a deserted barracks where the only signs of life were a flock of sheep. The steep grassy slope soon brought us to a mountain road and we tramped down the hairpin bends Bousiéyas. The few houses were all the traditional stone farm buildings which once housed not just the family, but the livestock, the grain and the hay.

Our *gîte* only had one dormitory and, concerned that the three blokes behind us might snore, I asked for a separate room. The young warden nodded, took a large iron key off a hook and told us to follow her. We threaded our way up the steep street, past a house that sold honey, to an old building where we climbed a flight of wooden steps to a little balcony and a rustic front door. As she opened the door it took our eyes a moment to make out a simple room with cast-iron stove and floor to ceiling stack of logs, a table and four chairs, Le Creuset pans, soup ladles and a country pine dresser. Behind the kitchen range was a chopping block with a large notice above it: *Defense de fumer et de cracher* (Smoking and spitting forbidden).

Our bedroom floor was on the tilt with an antique wardrobe large enough to sleep in and a variety of colourful wall hangings. Only the shower and loo had dragged the little house into the twenty-first century. Upstairs in the grain loft were a few bunk beds and the original window with vertical wooden slats to prevent anyone's falling out.

We returned to the *gîte* for our supper, and as the expected party of six never materialized we had extra large helpings of quiche, omelette, tomatoes, bulgur wheat, cheese and fruit salad. We treated ourselves to two small jugs of wine to celebrate completing one thousand miles of GR5. While we were eating, our young warden told us that there were only four families left in the village, two shepherds, a bee keeper and a huntsman. The children had to go to school fifteen kilometres away in Saint-Etienne-de-Tinée. She also warned us that the *gîte* at Roya was undergoing refurbishment and there was only a tent and no facilities.

It was that magic twilight hour, as the French say, *entre le chien et le loup*, and Richard and I stood on our rickety balcony and looked beyond the monochrome geranium pot and the steeply pitched roof of the neighbouring house to the last few hurdles that lay between us and our destination. The darkening sky had not yet extinguished the warm glow on the western horizon and the few stars were still shy. It was one of those inviolate moments when the big questions, if not answered, are certainly listened to.

It was a relatively easy walk over the Col de la Colombière and down a dirt road to the little village of Saint-Dalmas-le-Selvage, which had belonged to Italy in the last century and dates back to the Knights Templar. Once again the church was closed. Feeling in expansive mood, we called into the little bar and restaurant opposite the stables, sat on the balcony overlooking the square and ordered a salad niçoise and a carafe of rosé wine. There's nothing like a bit of indulgence to enhance the feel-good factor.

Anyone could be forgiven for thinking that Saint-Etienne-de-Tinée was in Italy: the terracotta and yellow façades of the high terraced houses were like faded postage stamps with rust red roofs and painted shutters. That evening the narrow cobbled streets were quiet and we found a modest Logis de France, and, after a wander round the town, ate and retired to our room. It was after all 9 p.m.

In the morning, the little town was buzzing with life and vitality, and we enjoyed wandering round the market stalls and provisioning as no kind *gardienne* was going to feed us that night. Richard felt the need for a small bottle of whisky; a wise precaution. We then called in at the tourist office for a weather forecast and wished we hadn't. It had rained during the night and rain and thunderstorms were forecast. Then we headed off up the usual steep hill out of the valley and at the top found ourselves in another naked ski resort called Auron which was all tarmac, steel and plate glass. Our Topo guide billed it as 'a leading ski resort in the Alpes Maritimes and a popular summer resort'.

It was here we met up with the three French men who had showered me with stones coming off the Col de la Cavale. We had seen them again on our way to Bousiéyas and now it was quite obvious they were also on their way to Roya. They asked us anxiously if there was accommodation there and I told them it would just be a tent. They were on a walking holiday from Larche to Nice.

Roya was a genuine hamlet tucked into a cleft in the mountain. The large church with its red dunce's hat towered above half a dozen traditional stone houses. From our aerial viewpoint we spotted what looked like an army tent on a flat rectangle of grass beside the church. When we reached it and lifted the heavy flap to get in we saw what looked like a First World War dressing station: serried ranks of brown stretchers lined both sides of the large tent, and the only concession to comfort was a warped plastic table and two plastic chairs. There were no washing or toilet facilities, and no village fountain. It had begun to rain and the heavy drops thudded on the canvas and soon a trickle of water appeared near the door. A team of builders were busy renovating the *gîte* and they let me have some water from their high pressure hose.

A clatter of boots and animated conversations announced the arrival of our three French friends. They were not impressed with the accommodation and one of them delighted in telling me that *mauvais temps* was forecast. He was also anxious to practise his English.

'Storms in ze mountains are bad,' he said. 'The 'igher you are ze more dangerous iz ze lightning.'

I chewed thoughtfully on a large mouthful of cold pizza, glad we had arrived first and were at least able to sit down on the only two chairs. Meanwhile the trickle of water had turned to a stream which was busy carving a lake under our lopsided table. The rain was coming down in sheets and we were thankful we were not struggling down the mountainside.

Suddenly there was a roll of thunder, the tent flap parted and a dark figure stood in the entrance, his dripping cloak outstretched like a great bird.

'Hello again!' it greeted us. A row of white teeth grinned a welcome from the streaming face.

The Flying Dutchman had arrived. Richard gave us all a good measure of whisky and we raised our plastic cups in a toast.

There is nothing quite like the bonding you feel with a traveller who has shared the same long hard road. Melvin had become an integral part of our walk. Like us he was pushing himself to get to the finishing line and was aiming to reach Nice on 27 September, a day ahead of us.

'Cheers! Next time champagne on the Promenade des Anglais.'

I wrote my diary by torchlight in my truckle bed. Sleep was impossible. Rain hit the canvas roof like bullets, distant thunder rumbled round the mountains, and our three Frenchmen snored and farted for France. Then the dogs started, or were they wolves? They had the strangest baying bark and I guessed they were the large white dogs that had such a fierce reputation. It was also very cold and our lightweight sleeping bags provided little warmth. I told myself if I was a wounded soldier it would have been luxury, and was thankful we weren't out on the col. I wondered if it would still be raining in the morning when we would be tackling our last high pass.

It was a long night as we had turned in soon after 8 p.m., and sometime in the small hours my bladder told me to relieve it. The thought of squelching through the mud of the tent floor, undoing the heavy tent flap, and peeing in a thunderstorm was not a joyous prospect. If the lightning didn't get me, the Hound of the Baskervilles certainly would. My bladder was insistent. I started unzipping my sleeping bag and my truckle bed promptly jack-knifed. I was now caught in a hanging valley of canvas with a crow bar under my neck. Outside the dogs bayed with renewed enthusiasm. I crossed my legs and prayed for morning.

St Christopher had been working hard. When, at first light, we emerged from the damp tent, the sky was cloudless and the sun was just emerging from the bulk of mountains to the east.

Melvin spoke for us all when he said simply, 'It's a miracle.'

Richard and I left the tent soon after 8 a.m. having swallowed some water, a yogurt and a brioche. We climbed steadily in a southerly direction, watching warily as a few clouds appeared in the clear blue sky. Then, as we started the approach to the Col de Crousette at 2,480 metres the path blended into the rough mountainside and I ran out of steam. I must have been as fit as I was on our walk round Britain eight years before, but I found myself constantly out of breath, unable to walk more than a few metres without stopping. We had finished our supply of glucose and I nibbled a couple of soggy biscuits. Melvin, who had let us go on ahead, passed us while I was wilting on a rock.

'I have bad days too,' he said kindly and then strode off up the mountainside like a young goat. It was the last we saw of him as he was heading off for a *gîte* that might or might not be open, while we had booked a hotel in a village called Beuil.

Richard, who had suffered similar symptoms leaving la Chapelle-d'Abondance, was patient and encouraging. Eventually we reached the stony col only to be faced with another one a hundred metres higher. However, re-energized with the scent of victory, the second col was easily scaled and we stood on a great plateau sparsely covered with dried grass. Behind us lay a vista of peaks and memories stretching to the far horizon. It was nearly three weeks since we had stood in equal awe at the Col de la Croix du Bonhomme and gazed south at the rugged horizon filled with rocky incisors. By some miracle we had traversed them on the ancient paths and tracks once used by great men like Hannibal and Caesar as well as salt traders, Rousseau's noble savages, Alpine explorers and even the humble tourist. South lay the big valleys of the Tinée and the Var and somewhere ahead lay the sea.

'We should be able to see the Mediterranean from here.' Richard's words broke into my reverie. But there was too much cloud cover that day and that vision continued to elude us.

Later that afternoon, I lay on my comfortable hotel bed for three hours unwilling to move except to totter down to the dining room for the best meal we had yet eaten in France. The hotel gave us *demi pension* prices but allowed us to choose anything we liked from their gourmet menu: aubergines with artichoke hearts and tomatoes in vinaigrette, grilled *truite aux basilica*, dauphinoise potatoes, green salad, goat's cheese, which we lifted from a well of olive oil, garlic cloves and bay leaves. *Et pour le dessert?* Home made vanilla ice cream drowning in yellow gentian liqueur. Our bill for dinner, bed and breakfast for the two of us was only 127 euros. *Vive la France!*

We were then on the GR52A, which sounded like a London bus, taking in part of the panoramic tour of the Mercantour National Park. The sun shone, the grassy cols seemed no more than minor bumps and the walk took us through bleached limestone scenery, past olive groves and walnut trees on terraced hillsides and through ghost villages perched high on the stony hilltops. In the little village of Roubion we stopped at a café-cum-post office and shop where the owner told us there were only seventy souls left and many of the derelict houses were being renovated by incomers. Down in the valley we found ourselves in the bustling town of Saint-Sauveur-sur-Tinée where we stayed in a purpose built *gîte* in the civic recreation ground. We had to use the phone to summon the warden, who asked us to wait until she had collected her children from school. She eventually arrived, opened up, took 7 euros from us and vanished.

We were just cooking our pasta supper when an American woman arrived with a small pack and big trainers.

'Hi! Has the warden been?' she asked, and looked relieved when we told her she had. She then grumbled about the sparse facilities (which we thought were adequate) and said the charge was outrageous. Then she rummaged through her pack and produced a box of eggs and an onion.

'Say. Can you spare me any bread? Someone gave me these eggs but that's it, folks.'

When we asked how she got here, she replied: 'Hitched a lift from a delivery van. I work in Cannes and just have to get out at weekends so I hitch-hike into the mountains.'

'Do you have any problems with that?' I asked, wondering just what sort of work she did.

'Nothing I can't handle,' she replied.

'When will you go back?'

'Tomorrow, I guess.'

We wondered what this enigmatic American's circumstances were. It was obviously necessary for her to get out of Cannes at the weekends. Too polite to ask, we gave her some of our pasta and heard her crashing about in the kitchen for hours muttering darkly as she prepared her simple meal. I kept my purse and phone under my pillow that night.

It was an easy sixteen kilometres to the next village of Saint-Dalmas-Valdeblore where we had to fill in several hours before the *gîte* opened at 5.p.m. After a *pression* at the bar tabac chez Edhy, we lolled around on a bench in the shade of a walnut tree beside the locked church. A graceful lady in a long skirt and a straw hat opened the tall wrought-iron gate into the cemetery. She was holding a large bunch of chrysanthemums and might have walked out of an Impressionist painting. I lay on my back watching small chunks of blue through the fading leaves and wondered what it would be like to return to our normal world. Ahead lay so much to adjust to, finishing the walk, living in a different place (our house in Tunbridge Wells would continue to be let while we lived in our cottage on the Kent coast), and above all retirement: we would be pensioners on that finite holiday, thrown together to face whatever the future had in store for us. Adjusting after our round Britain walk in 1995 had been hard. We had taken two months off before restarting work, and stayed in a cottage in Cornwall for that period as our house in Tunbridge Wells was let. We were in limbo and didn't really know how to cope with it. Richard was worried about picking up where he had left off with resulting tension between us. As it turned out we had had no reason to worry: Richard's patients were delighted to see him back and life quickly returned to normal. When we returned home on this occasion, there would be no normal routine, just an unusual amount of time with each other.

There was a click as the cemetery gates opened, and the lady with the straw hat reappeared deep in thought, without her chrysanthemums. The wind got up and the dry leaves crackled in the breeze. The church clock tolled five times.

The wardens of our *gîte* were an Italian couple and we shared our dormitory with three builders on a local construction job. Garofalo Lorenzo was Signor Superman whose name must have been in the French equivalent of our Guinness Book of Records. Over supper he listed his physical achievements like a litany: he had walked from Barcelonnette to Nice (174 kilometres) in a record-breaking fifty-two hours in snow shoes, he was five times champion of the Tour des Alpes, he walked non-stop from Saint Dalmas to Nice in nine hours (we were planning on taking eighteen hours), and had a certificate to prove he had walked from Chamonix to Nice (461 kilometres and a vertical height of 22,000 metres) in eight days. That list came with the soup. Over the pasta course, he rolled up his trouser leg and showed us some impressive scars on his knee.

'You see,' he said excitedly, 'I had the ligament in my knee repaired and only two months later I beat the speed record for climbing the highest mountain in this region on one leg!' I was grateful when his famous leg was once more hidden under his trousers. We exchanged glances with the construction workers and Richard poured us all some more wine from the communal *pichet*. At that moment, a strident voice called Signor into the kitchen. Undeterred, Garofalo Lorenzo rose stiffly and told us proudly, 'You see I don't drink, or smoke, I eat lots of fresh fruit and vegetables and I have no problems with my joints or muscles.' He pulled a face and his hand clutched the small of his back. 'It's just that I had a disc removed from my lumbar spine when I was young.' With that he limped into the kitchen to fetch the fruit salad.

The bleached track, on the old mule route from Saint-Sauvent-sur-Tinée to Nice, was friable and wound its way through the mixture of ash, plane, Turkish oaks and fir trees which clung to the steep rocky hillsides. Occasionally the red leaves of the cotinus shrub would add a splash of colour. The cicadas were deafening and lizards would scuttle off into the dry leaves as we approached. The air smelt of broom and box and perhaps the sea. We looked down on Utelle where we were to stay in a *gîte* for our penultimate night. The village was perched on a small hill cradled below the rocky flanks of the high mountains looking over valleys in all directions. The orange pantile roofs were jammed together round the pointed tower of the stone church. We descended onto a big tarmac road where a large sign read: Nice 35 kilometres.

'Less than an hour's drive away,' Richard muttered.

It had been a long eight-hour day, and the municipal *gîte* was closed. We rang the warden who said she would be along *en quelques moments*. I sat on the concrete steps watching a group of young lads skateboarding, and hoped that the French *moment* was not like the Cornish 'directly' which meant it probably wouldn't happen. Just as we were beginning to feel cold, a lady with long blonde hair tied back with a blue spotted scarf wearing tight jeans and high heels, tottered across the cobbles. She opened up the *gîte,* and we were hardly through the door before she asked us for money between drags on her *Gauloises.* We gave her a 50-euro note and she short-changed us, making out we had given her 20 euros. When we objected, she reluctantly produced the correct change and then departed, leaving a trail of cheap perfume and cigarette smoke behind her.

The twenty-seventh of September, our penultimate day, dawned cool with high cloud. With only a three-hour walk that day, we had time to wander round the heart of this little village. The cobbled square was surrounded with old stone houses and the leaves of the plane trees rustled in the breeze. We mounted the grand flight of steps leading up to the sixteenth-century carved doors of a surprisingly large church. The stone pillars were Romanesque but the walls and ceiling had been plastered and beautifully decorated with stucco mouldings like icing on a cake. There were trompe l'oeil paintings on the walls, and the altar was flanked by classical pillars setting off a vivid sixteenth-century painting of the Annunciation. This hilltop village, guarding four valleys, and on the Alpine route between Nice and Italy, had been of strategic importance since Roman times. An information board in the church told us that the name Utelle came from *ules*, meaning eye.

Outside in the hazy sunshine, several men, armed with baguettes, chatted outside the *boulangerie*. Further down the *épicerie* was just opening. A small group of women, cradling shopping baskets, were heading in that direction. Scents of freshly baked bread, cigarette smoke and salami wafted across the square.

We entered and left the village on the ancient mule track which took us gently downhill through hardwoods whose foliage was burnt and shrivelled. We were then on the balcony of the Côte d'Azur, those limestone slopes which rise above the valley of the Var and eventually reach the sprawling conurbation of Nice itself. It was too hazy to see what our Topo guide described as 'one of the most splendid panoramas of the Alpes-Maritimes'.

For many days we had seen planes flying in and out of Nice, and now I looked anxiously up at the sky thinking of our children and grandchildren flying in that very afternoon. I felt in an emotional limbo. It was impossible to believe that we were almost at journey's end. While I was looking forward to the prospect of staying in a villa in Provence with them for two weeks, I was reluctant to give up this physically masochistic but spiritually uplifting journey.

After several kilometres on the crumbling path, we came across the Chapel of St Anthony, a tiny and very ancient building with pantile roof and mini bell tower standing beside the mule track. It was open. I entered the cool interior, which smelt of damp and incense. The large altar took up most of the space, and was elaborately decorated with faded gold statues and pillars. A fearsome picture of a muscle-bound St Anthony with a long straggling beard frowned at me from the white wall. I pressed a red button near the door and the chapel was filled with the sound of Gregorian chant. Thumbing through a visitor's book I found a simple entry from a mother who had walked the same route: *Thank you good Lord for helping me walk here. Thank you for my health, for the precious gift of children, for eyes to see and a soul to receive.*

There was a metallic click and the monks faded into oblivion. I emerged into the warm Mediterranean sunshine and saw my guide and mentor, a dot on the horizon.

Chapter Sixteen

Arrival

The Mais Fleuri was a modest hotel on the road to Nice in a village called Levens, split between the old town up the hill and a modern ribbon development on the main road below. There were some very smart houses, many with pools, olive groves and sun terraces. We saw and smelt the affluence of Nice. We arrived in the middle of the afternoon, and had a drink in the square of the old town opposite a Michael Buerk lookalike, or was it really him? The local newspaper gave a bad weather forecast for the following day. As we walked along the road to our hotel, I managed to contact Nice airport and ascertain that the family had arrived safely. Jo like me hates flying, and this journey would have been worse for her as she was now three months pregnant.

At supper we found ourselves sitting next to a table of middle-class, middle-aged English ladies. Their accents (much like our own) and their conversation about French food, prices on the Riviera and the weather grated on our frayed nerves. Pre-arrival depression was setting in. As we went through the usual routine of washing our smalls and draping them round the window shutters, it was impossible to appreciate that it was the last day of this incredible journey. In many ways we were both sorry it was over, but excited at seeing our family again and the prospect of spending time with them in the area. Then there were nagging doubts about going home to our cottage in Lydd as a retired couple and trying to settle down into some sort of routine. I had Darby and Joan visions of joint expeditions to the supermarket, lunch time entertaining, and Saga holidays.

'How do you feel about the future?' I asked.

'Just glad I don't have to fill any more teeth,' came the sleepy reply.

At 8.30 a.m. on Sunday, 28 September we set off from Levens on the last lap of the GR5 to Nice. It was a grey world where low clouds hung like giant sponges over the mountains and sagged into the Var valley. It began to rain, gently at first and then remorselessly, turning the track into a red quagmire and trickling down our backs. We realized how lucky we had been with the weather. Even a heat wave was preferable to this.

From our very last hill we looked down on a sprawling grey city beside a giant bowl of pea soup; so different from the blue sea and sparkling cliffs of Cape Wrath when we arrived on 7 June.

By midday we were on a tarmac road on the outskirts of Nice. Breakfast had been at 6.30 – bread, jam and coffee from a thermos – and we were starving. The first restaurant we passed was already busy with its Sunday clientele. The menu advertised a three course lunch for 25 euros, rather more than we had reckoned on, but we were so wet and cold and hungry that we sat outside on the veranda and persuaded the waitress to let us have just one course each for 12 euros. The sight of the citizens of Nice arriving in top of the range Renaults and Peugeots, the men in jackets and the women in linen trouser suits, made us acutely aware of our bedraggled appearance. Just as we were finishing our plate of ravioli and demi litre of rosé, a good-looking couple and their son were forced to sit at a table next to us as the inside of the restaurant was full. They exuded affluence, intelligence and charm. As we were pulling on our Gore-tex and hefting our packs, hoping for a surreptitious getaway, their curiosity got the better of them and they asked us in fluent English what we were doing. They were genuinely interested in our walk and seemed very impressed to learn how far we had come and our reasons for doing it. Their enthusiasm was a tonic to our flagging spirits.

Richard, ever conscious of our route, warned me that we still had a long way to go and that our rendezvous time was four o'clock at the Negresco Hotel. That was my idea. Richard had suggested we met the family on the Quai des Etats Unis, but I felt that was unpatriotic. It had to be the Promenade des Anglais. The thought of meeting in the rain by a litter bin – and an American one at that – filled me with horror. After all this effort we must do something to make a resounding finish. A friend had recommended the Negresco and I thought that tea there would be a good wet weather plan. Richard didn't agree, but after a long and heated discussion he let me have my way.

Now it really was downhill all the way on a tarmac road. Palm trees towered above high walls dripping with bougainvillaea. Behind them lay terracotta mansions with wrought-iron gates which opened only at their owner's behest. We scurried past and soon we found ourselves in downtown Nice, noting the very last white and red GR5 waymark on a lamp post. Our pace quickened. We were on automatic pilot. The Mediterranean was within reach.

Just keep going.

★ ★ ★

Having left the doorman wiping our mud off the marble steps of the Negresco Hotel, I peered myopically into the gloom, searching the crowded street for a familiar face. Suddenly a pink tornado hurled itself at me and clasped a small pair of arms round my neck.

'Hello, Granny!'

When I could see beyond the pink cagoule, there they all were. Katie unclasped my six-year-old granddaughter from my neck and then it was her turn for a hug. Luke, our son-in-law, was shaking Richard by the hand, while Molly, Jo's two-year-old was giving us a quizzical look from the depths of her buggy while her mum and I were reunited. Sadly, Jo's husband Tim had been unable to get away from the office. Luke, ever the gent, offered to take my pack. As I heaved it thankfully from my shoulders I said rashly, 'Thanks, Luke. I never want to carry that again.'

'I'm afraid the Negresco doesn't do dirty walkers' Richard said without a hint of regret. Maybe we should get out of here and go back to the villa. Where's the car?'

We trailed back down the road, a soggy little family, and changed our wet clothes in the cold comfort of a multi-storey car park.

We had rented a villa in the hinterland behind Nice and planned a very special holiday with all the family. The villa was in an idyllic spot, a few kilometres outside a hilltop village, with a good-sized garden and swimming pool. The house was decorated with bunting and Welcome Home signs and we celebrated our reunion in the traditional way. It may not have been the Promenade des Anglais, but it was the best homecoming ever.

The holiday slipped away too fast. We ate for England, slept like Rip Van Winkle, swam in the pool, played football on the lawn and boules on the gravel drive. On cloudy days treasure hunts were organized, and a memorable adaptation of Goldilocks was played out in the pool house with granny in the star role.

One day we went to a tiny circus in a nearby village. It was just one family: mum, dad, granny and two children under ten with an audience of a dozen or so. Dad made the best clown ever, and although the children couldn't understand a word he said they watched his every move with wide eyes. He also sawed Mum in half (as dads do), performed some Olympian gymnastics on ropes and bars, encouraged a goat to stand on a coaster-sized stool on a pile of chairs, and made a llama spit to order. Mum did some tricky juggling (as they do) and then the circus children managed a handstand on Dad's head. Ella, who was just entering the gymnastic stage, looked at these two in their glittering leotards with admiration and envy.

We made several visits to the beach, Juan-les-Pins and Cannes where the sand was golden and the sea turquoise. We played out a mock-up arrival as we had imagined it. We also had visits from friends. Our cosmopolitan friends, Ann and Rick, came over; it was hard to believe that it was over five months since we had seen them in Oxford. Then we met Simon, my godson, off a train in Nice. He was on an inter-railing holiday and sampled the good life for a couple of days before going back to Glasgow.

We were only an hour's drive away from Grasse, and I was determined to revisit the town where I had spent the most miserable three months of my life as an au pair for a recently widowed teacher called Madame Farde. Her round house had once been used for silk making and the different floors were reached by a spiral staircase. I spent the first few weeks moping in my room on the top floor. The first outing I remember was on All Saints Day when Madame Farde took me to the cemetery where her husband was buried. I still have an aversion to shiny granite, plastic flowers, plaster saints and chrysanthemums.

After that I was allowed to attend French classes at the local convent school. In return, I had to teach my class of forty teenage girls the geography of the British Isles; ten listened out of curiosity and the rest chatted happily amongst themselves. When Christmas came, with terrine instead of turkey, no tree and no carols, I decided it was time to go home. By the time I left in February, things were looking up. I was making friends of my own age, the sun began to shine, and the mimosa was in bloom.

One girl asked me to have Sunday lunch with her grandparents. Her family lived in a smart new house in Grasse, but her grandparents were in little more than a hovel in the countryside. There must have been at least ten of us round the old table in their one living room-cum-kitchen. The bird-like grandmother was dressed in black with her long white hair loosely tied up in bun, and she produced at least six courses of the most delicious pâtés, veal escalopes, salads, fresh vegetables, cheeses and deserts with wine and liqueurs. The meal lasted most of the afternoon. On any other day of the week, these hospitable people would have been outside working in the fields with oxen.

Leaving three months earlier than was planned is something I shall always regret.

'Mum, what would you like to eat?' We were sitting in a restaurant in the old town of Grasse. Jo was pushing a menu at me and raising her voice to attract my attention. Molly was already stuffing her mouth with chips. I stopped dreaming and enjoyed pasta and chips with my family in Grasse forty-four years on. After we had eaten, Richard and I walked round the old town searching for my silk house, but we failed to find it.

The cases were packed, left-over beef tomatoes, melons, biscuits and cheese were thrown into a cool bag and we all cleaned through the villa with brooms mopping up two weeks' worth of intensive usage. As we sat in the cool of the airport departure lounge, I couldn't help thinking how lucky we were. It had been a hard but rewarding journey through parts of our own country that we didn't know. The GR5 had given us a wonderful variety of landscape, people and places. We had met old friends and made new ones, come across fascinating characters and once again found nothing but kindness and hospitality. We had begun to appreciate the problems of living in countries bounded by land not sea, and the six-month walk had tested us as individuals and as a couple. Richard's head was in a newspaper which made a change from a map.

'Congratulations!' I said. 'You did it again.'

There was grunt which sounded like, 'I did what again?'

'Gave me something to write about.' I replied.

Confusingly, the plane took off in a southerly direction, flying over the cobalt blue of the Mediterranean. The pilot reassured us that he was not taking us to North Africa, but keeping the noise levels down in deference to the residents of Nice.

Soon we were heading north over the now familiar peaks and troughs of the Alps. As we climbed, the mountain ranges shrank, model villages lined the deeply gouged valleys and huts on the summer pastures were reduced to matchboxes. The flanks of the great hills were scarlet with bilberry foliage and the Mont Blanc Massif sparkled white in the sunlight. As I gazed out of the pressurized plane window it was hard to believe that Richard and I had struggled up so many of those receding cols and stumbled down so many of the precipitous slopes. Effortlessly the plane reached its cruising height and headed north-west towards Grenoble. In moments the solid grey waves had given way to a green and fertile landscape as we roared on towards Paris and the south coast of England.

I was sitting next to my granddaughter, and we spent a

happy half-hour reading stories and colouring clowns. When I next looked out we were approaching the Channel; the English and French coasts were neatly mapped out, eyeballing each other across a thin band of blue. As the white cliffs of Dover came momentarily into view, I looked at my watch; our flight had taken exactly one hour and forty-five minutes from Nice to Dover. The other way round had taken us exactly three months and six days. We were several stones lighter and one hundred per cent fitter.

'This is a message from your captain.' The taped voice brought me back to the present. Please fasten your seat belts in preparation for landing at Gatwick London Airport.'

Tunbridge Wells sprawled not so far beneath us. A small voice at my elbow enquired politely:

'Granny, what will you and Pops do now?'

www.summersdale.com